"Harris has penned the authoritative take on [...] of post-Katrina New Orleans. Combining rigorous research with a firm grasp of on-the-ground developments, he explains the educational outcomes and explores what they mean for school improvement writ large. He has delivered an invaluable resource for everyone concerned with the practice and the politics of urban school reform."

FREDERICK HESS, Director of Education Policy Studies at the American Enterprise Institute

"New Orleans has radically restructured its schools and replaced it with an essentially all-charter system. A significant number of children are better off as a result. In fact, New Orleans could be viewed as a leading example of what a 21st century School district could be. I applaud their efforts. But, one glaring problem is the impact on the Black community. The firing of school staff wiped out a significant sector of the Black middle class in the majority-Black community. They were replaced by young white people, most of them from outside of New Orleans. So many black people rightfully felt the reforms were done to them, not with them. In *Charter School City*, Harris does a great service to the ongoing efforts to reform education in this country by adeptly telling the many sides of this complex story."

HOWARD FULLER, distinguished professor of education and founder/director of the Institute for the Transformation of Learning at Marquette University

"The shift to independent charter schools in New Orleans after Hurricane Katrina has come with much hyperbole. Advocates of choice have overhyped the academic results and understated the role of school funding, while skeptics have asserted rising inequities for students and decried the firing of black teachers and their replacement with mostly white, temporary, outsiders. This book not only balances these accounts, but it explains the causes of both triumphs and shortcomings. It overturns many simple interpretations and deepens our understanding of the roles of market competition and government. Other cities considering this type of reform should read it carefully."

HENRY M. LEVIN, William Heard Kilpatrick Professor Emeritus of Economics and Education, Teacher's College, Columbia University

"Every child should have a chance to attend an excellent public school, regardless of their background or zip code. If you are committed to that goal, as I am, then this book is a must-read. Harris engages readers in the complexities of schooling and provides essential advice on how to get school reform right. The lessons here are not just about New Orleans but about American education as a whole."

GINA RAIMANDO, governor of Rhode Island

Charter School City

Charter School City

What the End of Traditional Public
Schools in New Orleans
Means for American Education

DOUGLAS N. HARRIS

THE UNIVERSITY OF CHICAGO PRESS
CHICAGO AND LONDON

The University of Chicago Press, Chicago 60637
The University of Chicago Press, Ltd., London
Published 2020
Printed in the United States of America

29 28 27 26 25 24 23 22 21 20   1 2 3 4 5

ISBN-13: 978-0-226-67178-9 (cloth)
ISBN-13: 978-0-226-69464-1 (paper)
ISBN-13: 978-0-226-69478-8 (e-book)
DOI: https://doi.org/10.7208/chicago/9780226694788.001.0001

Library of Congress Cataloging-in-Publication Data

Library of Congress Cataloging-in-Publication Data
Names: Harris, Douglas N., author.
Title: Charter school city : what the end of traditional public schools in New Orleans means for
American education / Douglas N. Harris.
Description: Chicago : The University of Chicago Press, 2020. | Includes bibliographical references
and index.
Identifiers: LCCN 2019035332 | ISBN 9780226671789 (cloth) | ISBN 9780226694641 (paperback) |
ISBN 9780226694788 (ebook)
Subjects: LCSH: Charter schools—Louisiana—New Orleans—History—21st century. | Privatization
in education—Louisiana—New Orleans—History—21st century. | Educational change—Louisiana—
New Orleans—History—21st century. | Public schools—Louisiana—New Orleans.
Classification: LCC LA297.N4 H37 2020 | DDC 371.0509763/35—dc23
LC record available at https://lccn.loc.gov/2019035332

♾ This paper meets the requirements of ANSI/NISO Z39.48-1992 (Permanence of Paper).

This book is dedicated to the more than one thousand people who perished in the aftermath of Hurricane Katrina; to countless others for whom this was another in a long line of injustices; to children everywhere who have been denied quality education and the opportunity to fulfill their potential and dreams; and to educators who work every day to give them a chance.

CONTENTS

PART 1

What Happened in New Orleans and Why It Matters

CHAPTER 1

Why New Orleans Matters

Stories have as many versions as they have characters. Nowhere is this more true than with schools. Within the same town or city, different students attend different schools. Within the same school, students have different teachers and participate in different classes and activities. Within the same classroom, students' varying needs and perspectives lead them to experience the same set of events in different ways.

The story of the New Orleans Public Schools, and where they stood in 2005, has particularly divergent versions. Many loved their public schools back then. One parent, Ashana Bigard, described to me the safe and caring atmosphere of her daughter's school:

> Dropping her off to school was like dropping her off to your auntie's house. She gonna be fine.

The schools also challenged her daughter academically and sought to meet her individual needs:

> By the time she was in second grade, she had already been tested for gifted in mathematics. [Then] her teacher called me to say, "I think she's gifted in drama," and I was like, "Well, I know she's over-dramatic. If you say it's a gift, we'll roll with that!"[1]

New Orleanians had an affinity for their schools. One of the first questions the city's natives ask when they meet someone is: "What school did you go to?" At the festive balls held during the city's Mardi Gras season, announcers introduce the members of their "krewes" by name and high school over the loudspeaker—even if they had graduated half a century earlier.

Another New Orleans native, Patrick Dobard, had a very different story. His parents had attended the city's public schools, as had his older siblings in the 1970s, and they had done well for themselves, in college and in life. In 1969,

> a young black man, without any means or anything, could graduate from a neighborhood public school, Clark [High School] . . . and then finish from Tulane [University], the Harvard of the South.

But by 1981, when he started high school, his parents had given up on public schools and sent him to a private school:

> [Clark] had deteriorated so much that they wouldn't do it. My parents wouldn't do it. Then in 2005, Clark was the lowest-performing high school, not only in New Orleans, but in the state of Louisiana.[2]

Dobard's assessment seems consistent with the broader evidence. Only 56 percent of students in New Orleans public schools graduated high school in 2005, 10 percentage points below the state average; of Louisiana's sixty-eight school districts, New Orleans ranked sixty-third on this measure.[3] With Louisiana being the second lowest-performing state in the country, this put New Orleans near the very bottom of the list of over fourteen thousand US school districts.[4] One in ten students had been picked up for truancy in the prior year.[5]

Even those who had more positive experiences, like Ashana Bigard, acknowledged that there were problems. But their accounts of the district's failures draw attention to another divide in the story. Those who tended to support the school district pointed to deteriorating social and economic conditions in the city. They were right to do so, as a nearly universal truth in education is that poverty is among the strongest predictors of student academic outcomes.[6] And in 2005, four out of five of the city's sixty-six thousand students public school students came from low-income families who relied on free or reduced-price lunches. Ashana Bigard and her children were sometimes among them.

Family incomes were low because there were few good jobs. The oil and gas industry had been in steady decline. The military, a key part of the city's storied history dating to before the American Revolution, had gradually shuttered old facilities and moved operations to other states. Naval ships sat unused on the Mississippi River, a reminder of what used to be. The city's port still brought in more cargo than almost any other in the country, but highly paid dock workers had been replaced by mechanical cranes. Instead, many parents held low-paying service-sector jobs in the tourist industry, centered on the city's famous and historic French Quarter.

Like the Rust Belt cities of the Midwest, New Orleans had seen a steady decline in almost every available social and economic measure. The population had declined from almost 630,000 in 1960 to around 455,000 in 2005.[7] This reduced the number of students in the schools, and thus reduced state funding, which contributed to the district's financial difficulties. Crime had always been high, and the city's murder rate still consistently ranked at or near the top nationally. One in fourteen adult black males from the city was behind bars.[8]

The city social and economic fabric was also stained by intense inequality. Racism remains rampant. Some of the white Mardi Gras krewes still exclude black residents like Bigard and Dobard—60 percent of the city's population. Into the 1990s, the former national head of the Ku Klux Klan was an elected member of the state legislature from the city's suburbs. Advocates of taking down monuments to the Confederacy and white supremacy have had their lives threatened. The city was diverse and integrated in the sense that races and classes mixed on a daily basis, on the streets and in restaurants. But the underlying social relationships were anything but equal. Churches and schools remained almost completely segregated, and poverty was heavily concentrated among black citizens. The city is among the worst five places in the country for raising poor, and especially black, children out of poverty.[9] The differences in social and economic conditions between the haves and have-nots carried over into schools.

But there is another side to the story of what caused school failure. It is hard to argue the school system was living up to its potential, even under these difficult circumstances. The average district superintendent over the prior decade had lasted only eleven months.[10] The federal government had recently threatened to cut off funding because of financial mismanagement. The FBI had so many investigations involving the

New Orleans Public Schools that the agency had its own office in the school district headquarters. Eleven district leaders would eventually be indicted for corruption.[11] To avoid disqualification from the use of federal funds, the state had assigned an emergency financial manager. Many schools lacked working air conditioners and even toilet paper.[12] School board meetings were known for getting out of control. When I spoke with several national education leaders, from across the political and educational spectrum, all said New Orleans was the worst school system they had ever seen.

You might not get a group of New Orleanians to agree on what ailed the schools back then, or on what was holding them back, but there is one thing they probably would agree on: New Orleans may have been the last place on earth one would have expected innovation in the schools. As one writer put it, the city was "drenched in the past."[13] The popular affinity for the schools. The centuries-old traditions of music and Mardi Gras. The historic French Quarter, with its eighteenth- and nineteenth-century architecture. Crime and corruption. Racism and segregation. In many respects, New Orleans in 2005 looked much as it had in the 1800s. It was not likely to change anytime soon.

But as students started school in the fall of 2005, things were about to change. It was hurricane season, and a storm was brewing in the Atlantic. Later that week, they would give it a name, Katrina. The city, and its schools, would never be the same.

The One Best System

New Orleans is an unusual city, and Hurricane Katrina was a very unusual event. One could be forgiven for thinking this disastrous encounter was an interesting but not especially instructive story. That would be a mistake.

This book is about one thing this distinctive city had in common with the rest of the country. It is about what the education historian David Tyack called the "one best system" of American public schooling.[14] The System, as I will call it, has been defined by several key elements: schools funded and governed by locally elected school boards, superintendents hired by those boards to manage schools, attendance zones that assign students to schools based on where they live, and state laws regarding teacher preparation, certification, and tenure to ensure that those who educate children are well prepared. Starting in the 1960s, the System also came to include a new and powerful force in school governance and management—teacher unions, which negotiate with school districts over most of what goes on in schools, especially those elements that most directly affect teachers, such as pay and job security.[15] This is just how it is done in United States. To a surprising degree, in a country known for small government, our schools have long depended heavily on government.

Though the System has been almost universally adopted, many still question it. What do we want children to learn and do? Do we want schools to prepare students more as workers, citizens, artists, or something else? What does it mean to be a good school with respect to any of these roles? Should children learn, or even practice, religion in public schools? What role do we want schools to play in shaping their communities, and vice versa? Who do we want our children to be friends with? How important is it that they mix across racial, social, religious, and economic lines? These fundamental questions have been at the heart of familiar and contentious education debates—the instruction of immigrants, prayer in schools, academic standards, racial segregation, school funding, and the qualifications of teachers, which are part and parcel to the System itself.

Yet perhaps the most important debate is this: Who gets to decide? Who should have the power to decide what our children's futures should look like and, therefore, how we should prepare them? This book is about the two main potential answers to that question. We can place responsibility in the hands of representatives elected by citizens, through *government,* or in in the hands of parents and individual school leaders, through *markets.* This question of power transcends any individual educational issue and indirectly determines how all of them get resolved. When we move toward markets or toward governments, we can expect to get schools of a different character.

Education is unlike other areas where the roles of government and markets are debated. Though the United States has a market economy, governments still directly provide some services, such as police and fire protection. In other cases, the government provides funding—for health care, roads, and other "public goods"—but leaves the day-to-day work to private organizations.[16] But few potential functions of government were deemed important enough to be taken up by the nation's Founding

Fathers. Thomas Jefferson, in particular, saw that broad access to schooling would be crucial for binding together a new nation of immigrants who had come from countries with different languages, cultures, and religions, and with almost no experience as citizens in a democracy. That schooling is a core element of a well-functioning democracy is partly why almost every state constitution mentions education as a fundamental government responsibility and why states have often required cities and towns to create schools.[17] When it comes to making decisions about the roles of government and markets, education will always require its own analysis.

Changing the One Best System of Schools

The System of American public schooling, driven by elected local boards and district management, is notable for at least three impressive successes. First, it largely achieved the Founders' goal: in building what was arguably the world's first nearly 100 percent literate population, it created a foundation for what was also arguably the first large-scale representative democracy—not to mention a highly productive workforce. Second, in a country where all aspects of life—yes, even governments—change constantly, the System has been a pillar of stability. It has survived two world wars, the Great Depression, the civil rights era, the social upheaval of the 1960s, the Cold War, and massive economic shifts from farming to manufacturing to computerization. For a century, 90 percent of the population, from large cities to small towns, relied on it. It was the *one best* system.

These successes—promoting literacy, democracy, and economic growth across the nation, and persisting through all forms of social, economic, political, and military upheaval—are remarkable. But what some see as needed stability, others see as stubborn unresponsiveness to changing needs and circumstances. Book titles like *So Much Reform, So Little Change* and *The Same Thing Over and Over* reflect the frustrations of scholars, pundits, and policymakers alike.[18] Most history books are about how things used to be different. Yet the history of schooling is often told as a story about how things have stayed the same.

The System, according to critics, has been so stable because it is politically entrenched and corrupt, placing the interests of the adults in

charge over those of the students supposedly being served, falling behind the times and outliving its usefulness. With often low voter turnout,
school boards are elected substantially by the teachers they employ, and
their families and friends, allowing educators to choose their bosses and
maintain their job security and steady pay.[19] Elected boards and unions
have little incentive to cede power to anyone else. There is no driving
force for change. This is why today's classrooms, even with better textbooks and computers, still involve teachers lecturing from the front of
classrooms to students in rows of desks, just like the ones we see in old
movies and history museums.

Supporters of the System, by contrast, argue that traditional school
districts have lasted so long because they are exceptionally well suited
to American values, cultures, and needs. Maybe public schools have not
changed because there has been no good reason to do so. Maybe local
political control has allowed each district, despite the System's apparent stasis, to change under the surface, varying students' actual classroom experience in ways that address community needs. The System is,
after all, just a way of governing and managing schools. Maybe the fact
that there are more than fourteen thousand districts has allowed public
schools to be nimble and meet local needs as the world has changed, in
ways that the general public and pundits have not recognized.[20] Schools
are "loosely coupled" organizations in which teachers work mostly behind closed doors, giving them flexibility even when school districts are
rigid.[21] Surely, the breadth and depth of content in today's textbooks, the
range of extracurricular and elective offerings, the availability and use of
computers and online resources, and the relatively relaxed approach to
dress, behavior, and discipline would all shock teachers from a century
ago. Yes, schools have changed and adapted considerably.

In other respects, schools have stayed the same, and perhaps this is a
good thing. Amid a growing sense that the nation is splintering—haves
from have-nots, whites from people of color, urban from rural, religious
from atheists—a stable schooling system and common curriculum might
help bring us together. Our nation today seems more politically polar-
ized than at any time since at least the 1970s, if not the Civil War.[22] Some
want to build walls while others want to tear down the ones we have. In
the age of the internet, social media, and cable television, we can isolate
ourselves and hear only ideas and those ways of thinking that align with
our own. Perhaps stable and similar schools are exactly what we need.

Whatever the reason for the System's persistence, its universality makes it difficult to assess potential alternatives. How are we to know if something would work better if we have nothing to compare it to? Some look to other countries, but it is hard to know whether high test scores in, say, China, Finland, or Korea, are due to their school systems or to other aspects of their extremely different societies. Education is a social activity by nature, which means that culture both creates and interacts with instruction and curricula. Do schools that seem to perform better than those in the United States do so because other countries have designed better schooling systems or, for example, because they assign greater social value to discipline and knowledge or more prestige to teaching, or because their societies are more homogenous, allowing schools to focus on a narrower range of objectives? To the degree national education policies matter, how do we reconcile concerns about the government-driven US system with the fact that many other successful countries are at least as government-driven as we are?

We can derive clearer lessons from experiences within our own borders. What we need is for an American school district to abandon the traditional approach, try something truly distinctive, and carefully study the results. This book is about just such a revolutionary shift. It is about a radical reform in an iconic American city that has demonstrated considerable measurable success—and yet, whose lessons for the future of American schooling are complex and debatable.

The New Orleans Revolution

On August 29, 2005, the eye of Hurricane Katrina made landfall just east of New Orleans. More than a thousand people died and $160 billion worth of property was lost throughout the Gulf Coast.[23] It was one of the worst disasters, more man-made than "natural," in American history, its effects exacerbated by a lack of planning and decades of questionable infrastructure decisions.

In the hurricane's wake, most cities in the region worked to rebuild their prior ways of life, including their schools, as they had been before. They cleaned out sludge-filled school buildings and rebuilt those that had been destroyed. Elected board members returned to dry off their binders of policies and procedures. Teachers came back to the same lesson plans and updated editions of their old textbooks. Everyone in these schools was changed personally by this traumatic and catastrophic event, to be sure, but the basic institutions meant to serve their needs were generally left as they had always been.

New Orleans did something different. In this city—and only this city—state leaders decided to remake the school system in a new image. Instead of restoring the System of government-based school districts, the state turned almost all of the schools over to a state agency that, over time, turned them all into privately run, nonprofit charter schools. Instead of governing schools through district rules, superintendents, and union contracts, charter school leaders took control over almost all major educational decisions. Instead of trying to ensure educational quality by training teachers, giving them job security, autonomy, and steady pay, and encouraging them to use their best judgment, charter school leaders were allowed to hire and fire teachers as they pleased, without certification or tenure rules, and to pay them as they wished. Instead of having their children assigned to schools based on where they lived, families could, in principle, choose any school they wanted; attendance zones were essentially abolished, and government funding went to the schools families chose. Instead of replacing the principal if a school faltered, the district or state could take it over, dismiss the entire staff, and either run the school itself or turn it over to another charter operator.

At least that was one way to look at it.

School Reform by Another Name:
A Market-Based Perspective

The long list of New Orleans reforms was not a random hodgehodge of ideas. Charter schools, school choice, and overhauled personnel policies collectively represent a shift from a government-driven school system toward a market-driven one. Giving parents choice turned them into consumers, forming the demand side of the market. Letting private organizations run the schools freed up the supply side to operate like businesses and mission-driven nonprofits. Reducing job security for teachers and rigid pay structures allowed school leaders to provide stronger incentives for performance. In theory, schools would have to convince enough families to choose them, so that they could earn enough revenue to at least keep their doors open. Schools would have no choice but to compete and innovate.

Looking at schooling through this market lens can be off-putting, especially to educators. Talk of markets, and related terms like privatization and competition, is so toxic that advocates of this approach avoid using these words. Reform critics sometimes decry the application of economics-based management to schools as coldhearted and ignorant of what schools do and why people decide to become educators. Staunch defenders of the System, like Diane Ravitch, point to a real and sometimes sordid history of profiteering and scandals that have plagued similar efforts in the past, not only in schooling but other areas where the government has turned over control to private organizations.[24]

These are all reasonable concerns, but the seeming allergy to the market concept does not change one basic fact: *schooling really is a market.* It is a service that has a supply side (schools) and a demand side (families). Parents pay, often dearly, for educational services for their children. School leaders have to make decisions about the use of scarce resources. This is what markets do. Trying to understand how schooling works without acknowledging its market nature is like trying to understand how a plane flies without acknowledging gravity and other elements of physics. Education is not *only* a market, of course, but the fact that it is a market has important implications.

Talking about schooling as a market is not as coldhearted and detached as it might seem. Part of the problem is the language of economics. Yes, markets are about supply and demand, but also about choice, autonomy, and freedom. Giving families choice with respect to schools can be interpreted not only as allowing them to be consumers but as giving them power and agency in providing for their children. Giving educators autonomy means unlocking market forces, but it also means allowing them to use their judgment and skills to inspire and instill a love of learning. The market for schooling can, in theory, turn control over to those who know the children best—their parents and teachers.

Critics of the market approach might still say, "no, thank you," and reiterate their many legitimate concerns. But the System, though run by governments, has always been driven by markets and consumer preferences, far more than many seem to recognize. Families choose schools, albeit indirectly, through the highly competitive *housing market*, and traditional public schools hire teachers through competitive *labor markets*.

The question, then, is not whether schooling is a market, but what *kind* of market we want it to be. The System is a hybrid, but still sits on the government side of the spectrum. At the other end, we could have a free market where the role of government is limited to providing per-student funding through school vouchers and tax credits. Schooling will remain a market either way, but some types of markets work better than others. Indeed, the market side of the System is as much responsible for its failings as anything the government has done.

The fact that I am an economist might lead critics of market-based school reforms to suppose I am naturally inclined toward the most market-driven system available. This is not the case. One of the main themes of this book is that the strongest arguments *against* a free market in schooling actually come from within economics. The idea that a market-based school system produces efficient outcomes falters when we consider the distinctive features of the schooling market. When we go beyond efficiency and add in other objectives, such as equity, the problems become worse.

The economic perspective is certainly not the only perspective required to understand school reform, but it is a critical starting point. In later sections of the book, I also use key elements of psychology (especially the role of intrinsic motivation and behaviorist approaches to classroom management) and sociology (especially the importance and formation of trust, the way in which schools function as organizations, and the roles of school and neighborhood communities). Efficiency is the objective that drives economics, while equity drives sociology, and both play important roles.

The theoretical problems with free markets in schooling are clear, but theory alone is far from enough. There was, at the time Katrina struck, some evidence about market-oriented approaches, but it was based on programs implemented on a small scale where traditional public schools were still dominant, and therefore was not very informative about what a full-fledged free market would look like. Also, even where reforms seemed to work well, based on what we could measure, there were good reasons to be skeptical of what was unmeasured.

For the leaders who held the fate of New Orleans' schools in their hands after Katrina, the theory and the evidence were inadequate to the momentous challenge before them—creating a new kind of school system. Nonetheless, the city's schools had been failing by any measure before Katrina, and some leaders demanded a change. Since the System was driven substantially by the government and unions, the reformers' natural instinct was to shift control to markets. Under the System, the government *operated* schools. These reformers wanted the government only to *govern* schools and to hire others—autonomous private organizations—to run them under contract. They wanted the government to pay for and steer the boat, but not to row it. After Katrina, they would finally get what they wanted.

The Research

My belief, before I even stepped foot in New Orleans, was that this unprecedented reform effort deserved an unprecedented effort to understand it. With substantial and generous funding from Tulane University and several national foundations, and in partnership with key local education organizations, I created a center, the Education Research Alliance for New Orleans, that I hoped might do justice to what transpired. In this book, I discuss what has become one of the largest studies of a single school district ever conducted, involving more than thirty academic reports and using almost every conceivable type of data and analysis. We have done everything from interviewing students, parents, and educators and other key actors to analyzing large data sets. We have examined everything from the effects of the reforms on student outcomes to the inner workings of school choice, the educator labor market, and the contracts that held the new charter schools accountable for student outcomes.

When I began this work, in the fall of 2012, I did not know what to expect. The city's academic trend lines were impressive, but I had seen supposed success stories end badly before. During the 1990s, Texas governor George W. Bush introduced test-based accountability reforms that produced strong gains on the state's high-stakes tests. This "Texas miracle" helped propel the governor into the White House, where his administration spearheaded the sweeping No Child Left Behind (NCLB) federal accountability law. Additional analysis, however, suggested that the Texas policy had no effect on more trusted low-stakes tests.[25]

For the other most relevant reform, charter schools, the results had been similarly unimpressive at the time Katrina made landfall. The average charter school at that time was still lower-performing than the average comparable traditional public school.[26] Some charter schools seemed to produce great results, but there were signs this was accomplished by selecting the students they wanted and pushing out students who had more challenges and pulled school scores down.

I came to New Orleans with an open mind. I did not have a strong view on these types of reforms. The positive trends in student outcomes seemed to indicate success, but it was not clear whether the trends could be attributed to the reforms. Given the national attention the reforms were already receiving, the first thing I did was to write an op-ed column in a national newspaper explaining the reasons for my uncertainty.[27] Both sides were getting ahead of themselves on the evidence, I argued.

To help ensure that we focused on the right questions and provided accurate answers and fair interpretations, I created an advisory board of local policymakers and practitioners—ranging from those who created the reforms to representatives of the teacher unions, who were among the strongest reform critics—to help develop and guide the research agenda and to provide feedback on our reports prior to publication. We hired and partnered with outstanding researchers who brought widely varying beliefs, perspectives, and methods to the work. We put all the work through rigorous internal and external peer review processes.

Years later, and with a dozen of these articles published in prominent peer-reviewed academic journals, it now appears that New Orleans is an outlier, in almost every measurable way. As I show, the reforms significantly improved a wide range of student outcomes, on average and for almost every identifiable group—rich and poor, black and white, low- and high-achieving. The positive effects also emerged without most of the negative side effects that have plagued similar reforms in other parts of the country. I have not seen other cities, or other programs, able to generate such large gains across so many metrics. Some uncertainty remains, for example, about the things we could not measure, but if evidence matters at all, what we found has to change our views about this type of reform at least a little.

"Miracle" was one word used to describe the change, though that implies that no further improvement is possible (how can you do better than a miracle?) and that we do not understand how it happened.[28] In reality, we designed our work to learn whether it worked as well as how, why, and in what sense. Did the effects flow mostly from turning schools over to nonprofit charter managers? Taking over low-performing schools? Eliminating teacher union contracts? Hiring a new kind of teacher workforce? Giving families choices? Attracting additional funding? More broadly, what exactly was driving the positive results? Perhaps it was not possible to answer this last question completely, since all the pieces were intertwined, but we could provide a sense of what probably mattered most.

The clearest contributor to improved academic outcomes was also the most controversial: taking over low-performing schools. Why did this matter so much? Prior studies had generally found no effects, or even negative effects, of school closures and takeovers. Why were the results so different in New Orleans? And why did the other mechanisms, like school choice and competition, seem to matter less, or at least less directly?

With partial answers to each of these questions, we could begin to address the larger question: what is the role of government in schools? One possibly surprising conclusion of my analysis is that economic theory and the New Orleans experience actually undercut the argument for free markets in the particular case of schooling. How can this be, given that the New Orleans reforms were both market-based and so successful? The answer is that the reforms took place in two distinct stages and forms. Early on, what was in many respects a free market yielded some improvements but also most of the problems that market theory predicts. Those problems led the state to get much more involved, and the results improved even more. The implication is that the flexibility and pressure that come with markets can be useful but still work best with government as a partner—a different sort of partner than the school district had been prior to Katrina, but an active partner nonetheless.

The New Orleans experience helps to show that the problems with schooling markets are not just theoretical. They also show that governments and markets can be combined in many different ways. Relying on one or the other, even where possible, is not as fruitful.

Why New Orleans Matters

The New Orleans experience is important. First and foremost, it is important to the children of New Orleans. With everything the city's children went through — the deaths of friends and loved ones, dispossession of homes and property, and massive disruption of daily life — they deserved a quality school system to help them put their lives back together.

It also matters because New Orleans provides a proof of concept, showing that this type of reform can produce significant, measurable academic improvement. Most education policies and programs have no measurable effect. Some have positive effects on some outcomes but not others. New Orleans is the rare case where we see large gains on a wide variety of measures, from test scores, and high school and college graduation rates, to parent satisfaction. We need to understand why this case turned out so much differently than the norm.

One common counterargument is that the New Orleans experience is so unusual that it may be hard for those in other places to draw any lessons. In terms of the *process* of reform, that is true. The New Orleans school reforms sprang from a disaster that I hope will never happen again anywhere else. The process the reformers used to put the reforms in place made matters worse, leaving lasting wounds that have made such reforms anathema in many big cities across the country. In addition to being unfair, their approach may have been unwise as it bred discontent that led many community members to ignore or distrust the measured results, threatening the long-term sustainability of the New Orleans reforms.

Perhaps more important for drawing lessons, however, is the *context*. One of the most important themes of social science research, including in education, is that the results obtained in one place often do not replicate when they are tried elsewhere. Novel education ideas work in places with similar social and economic situations. With its large population of people of color, concentrated poverty, high unemployment and crime rates, and depleted economic base, New Orleans is in many respects just like hundreds of other medium and large cities across the country, suggesting that we should see similar results in these similar places. More likely, however, the New Orleans results represent a best-case scenario. Even if other cities and states could adopt the same policies through other processes, the results probably will not be as positive in other contexts.

The evidence in this book suggests that the New Orleans reforms were effective in part because leaders responded to market failure by re-defining the appropriate roles for government. They did not rely solely on parents to "vote with their feet" and exit low-performing schools. If they had, in this unusual kind of market, they would not have seen so many metrics rise. Instead, through the closure and takeover process, the state stepped in to close large numbers of low-performing schools—imposing government accountability on top of market accountability. Economic theory and evidence also predict that schools will try to choose students as much as students choose schools. Seeing this occur during the free-market phase, reform leaders required schools to provide transportation and eventually stepped in to manage enrollment to ensure broad and fair access. New Orleans leaders did not get everything right, but it was cer-tainly better than other plausible options, and it got better over time.

This analysis, combined with evidence from across the country, also suggests some broader lessons that are the core of this book. I outline five fundamental roles for government that seem to apply under just about any conditions: accountability, access, transparency, engagement, and some form of choice. This list should be viewed as a set of minimum standards and is, in most respects, more limited than what school dis-tricts normally carry out. Conversely, it is more extensive than the list that might be submitted by advocates of free-market approaches like school vouchers.

A further implication is that something akin to traditional school dis-tricts, even after a century, is probably still one of the best options avail-able in most places. This may be the most surprising conclusion of all given how effective this market-based reform was in New Orleans. It be-comes less surprising when we consider the continued advantages that have led government school districts to be so popular for so long.

Plan for the Book

I have written this book for a broad audience of educators, parents, policymakers, and journalists with an interest in education policy. For academic readers—faculty, graduate students, and other scholars—note that I do not aim to provide a full review of the scholarly literature on any of the relevant topics. This would be impossible given the number of interconnected pieces constituting the New Orleans reforms, from teacher unions and tenure to school choice and charter schools. Attempting to cover all the research on all these topics would be a hopeless task and do a disservice to those who have addressed those topics more comprehensively. Rather, my more modest, but still challenging, goal is to be faithful to the generally accepted findings from the existing research literature. In keeping with my aim of reaching a broad audience, I leave citations of key studies and other academic debates to the endnotes.

I often refer to the public discourse about school reform in the chapters that follow, especially what "critics" and "supporters" of the System and the New Orleans reforms say. While this oversimplifies matters, it is useful for highlighting and testing the premises and lines of reasoning that dominate public debate.

Chapter 2 serves as a kind of lens through which the rest of the book can be viewed. I explain the arguments for government-driven approaches like the System versus market competition. I focus especially on the conditions under which market competition leads to efficient outcomes—good information, many options to choose from, and more—and argue that these conditions fail to hold in just about any schooling market, especially where there is limited government oversight. Schooling is simply a very unusual market.

It also turns out that the market conditions that lead to inefficiency are particularly worrisome for the pursuit of educational equity. In a free market, disadvantaged families are almost guaranteed to have the least access to quality schools. This is why transparency and accessibility are such fundamental roles for governments; they facilitate efficiency and ensure access for disadvantaged populations.

In chapter 3, I describe exactly how school reform was designed and implemented in New Orleans. This part of the story starts in the immediate aftermath of the hurricane and recounts how state and federal leaders, in direct opposition to the majority of locally elected officials, moved toward the wholesale takeover of the city's school system. Once the legal infrastructure was in place, local actors went to work, in concert with national groups, to build the new organizations necessary to implement the novel approach. It was a revolution, to be sure, but one that developed in phases. This chapter also highlights how the reforms were not just about markets versus governments; nongovernmental organizations (NGOs) were also critical.

The purpose of schooling is to serve students, and the main purpose of this book is to provide evidence about whether this happened as a result of the New Orleans reforms. Chapter 4, therefore, focuses on the effects of the New Orleans reforms on student test scores, high school graduation rates, college-going, and parent satisfaction with schools. While it was initially unclear whether we would be able to separate the effects of the reforms from the other forms of upheaval the city experienced after Katrina, I show that the effects were so large that the other factors potentially confounding the trends could not explain them. The effects of the reforms were real.

The role of school funding in the reform effort is harder to pin down. Funding increased, to be sure, and this no doubt contributed to the reform effects. However, it is extremely unlikely that funding alone could have generated these effects. In any case, increased funding was as much an outgrowth of improvement as a cause of it and would not likely have been available without the structural reforms.

The next five chapters focus on various general mechanisms that may have, collectively, generated the improved academic results. Since, ultimately, effects on students have to arise from changes in practice within schools and classrooms, chapter 5 discusses how the reforms changed the way schools used their funding, including the number and types of educators they hired and the character of the learning and work environments that resulted. School leaders were not just getting teachers to work a little harder or a little better. They were fundamentally changing the orientation of schooling and teaching.

Chapter 6 describes the intended and unintended consequences of competition between schools. School leaders felt the competition, to be sure, though their responses had little prospect of altering educational practice for the better. This chapter is where the lens of the market, described in chapter 2, starts to become useful, as it illustrates the limits of competition under the unusual conditions of the schooling market.

If the supply of schooling is the yin of the market, the yang is demand. In chapter 7, I explain how the reform leaders eliminated attendance zones and allowed families to choose any publicly funded school (and some private schools), at least in principle. To provide such access, city leaders put in place a decentralized choice process, similar to what colleges use; this evolved into a centralized, computerized enrollment system unlike almost anything seen before. In both its centralized and decentralized forms, school choice was the crux of the market model. It was what gave parents the power of consumers and gave schools, at least in theory, incentives to seek options aligned with consumer preferences. I argue here that choice was important but not in the way the simple market formulation would suggest.

The reforms gave choice and autonomy to families but also to schools. This meant that, in the event problems arose, schools would have the opportunity to work together voluntarily to solve them. Chapter 8 explains the various ways in which that cooperation could and did occur. It visually contrasts the bureaucratic structure of the school district with the loose web of relationships among schools and other nonprofits, and explains how mergers, contracting, and informal networks worked as voluntary means of solving problems. These forms of cooperation only went so far, however. I explain why voluntary cooperation, while it is a potential advantage of market systems, is unlikely to address the most pressing needs.

While it is in some ways fair to think about the New Orleans reforms as a shift toward markets, this is misleading. First, it was a state takeover—a shift from local to more centralized government control. Over time, as I explain in chapter 9, the state turned schools over to charter operators who worked under performance-based contracts. If the schools did not meet their performance metrics, then the government-appointed charter authorizer could end schools' contracts, take over the schools again, and sign contracts with other charter organizations to run them. Indeed, in a city that has roughly eighty-five schools at any given time, more than forty of the new schools created after the reforms were taken over in the first decade. This was by far the largest, most aggressive, and most systematic school takeover effort the country had ever seen. I show that this was really a new power of government that school districts typically lack. It would prove to be a key driver of the measurable improvement in student outcomes. These actions, coupled with other efforts to make the market function more smoothly, essentially redefined the role of government in schooling. Closing and taking over low-performing schools was the factor, above all others, that explains the improved student outcomes.

What happened in New Orleans meant something, especially to the students, parents, citizens, and policymakers of New Orleans. But it was bigger than that. It represented the culmination of a quarter century of national experimentation with test-based and market-based accountability. It has been the beacon that many other cities and states have looked to as they have tried to improve their own schools. As I explain in chapter 10, our findings in New Orleans align surprisingly well with the overall body of school reform research. Research on New Orleans and on cities and states across the country seems to support the theory that, while some forms of market power can be useful, some combination of markets and government is still best. The New Orleans results were better after the government intervened in the relatively free market. Similarly, in the national research, charter schools increasingly look at least as good as free-market-oriented vouchers. And neither alternative to the System—charter schools nor vouchers—is likely to yield better results than traditional public schools in most circumstances.

The discussion culminates in chapter 11, where I show that the theory about government and markets, the evidence in New Orleans, and the national evidence on charter schools and vouchers, as well as general economic theory, economic research, and basic theories of democracy, all point toward the five fundamental roles for government, which I call, collectively, Democratic Choice. While most of these individual roles have been proposed elsewhere, this list—accountability, access, transparency, engagement, and choice—is different, for what it includes and for what it excludes, and for how the specifics of the roles depend on the situation. In most cases, traditional school districts are best situated to carry out these roles, but districts sometimes fail. Reform models like that in New Orleans, what we might call quasi-markets, can be viable solutions, but, as the word "democratic" implies, they still need to be coupled with some specific roles for government.

Finally, in the concluding chapter 12, I consider the question, why does any of this matter to anyone outside New Orleans? I show, first, that the New Orleans experience lays to rest many misunderstandings about traditional school districts. Paradoxically, upending a failing version of the System highlighted some of the strengths that made it successful for so long. I also show how the New Orleans experience fits into the history and evolution of school reform, with its pendulum swings between educationally conservative and progressive approaches. The New Orleans reform effort, in this respect, was a throwback to a much earlier era.

The pieces of the reforms fit together well in New Orleans, and they fit the city's circumstances. New Orleans was ripe for this type of reform. In other cases, it probably makes sense to end the System, but this is more the exception than the rule.

The Value of Seeing Something New

Whether you support or oppose these reforms, or the roles for government implied by Democratic Choice, what happened in New Orleans after Hurricane Katrina is one of the seminal events in the history of American education. The policies adopted there represent a wish list that many reformers had been talking about for at least a quarter century, implemented suddenly and comprehensively for the first time.

Simply observing New Orleans is an eye-opening experience. Having studied school systems and reforms for more than a decade before arriving in the city, it took me several years living in New Orleans, as a parent, researcher, and community member, to rewire my own one best system mind in a way that allowed me to really understand what was happening. Observing something like a traditional school district on a daily basis for so long, its key traits can become invisible even when they are right in front of us. A century-old school system can do that to people.

It took one of the worst-ever tragedies to push New Orleans schools off the well-worn path of the System. By telling the various sides of the story, we can learn from the experience of New Orleans, honor the victims of Hurricane Katrina and the injustice they endured, and place the country on a better path toward serving all of the nation's children well.

CHAPTER 2

Schooling Markets versus Political Bureaucracy

One question, above all others, underlies most debates about public affairs. It is a fundamental question of power and authority: Who should make which decisions? This question has two main answers. Individual consumers and producers can make decisions, or decisions can be made by representatives of whole communities—cities, states, and nations—elected by voters. Markets or governments.

This was also the choice facing New Orleans in the wake of Hurricane Katrina. The problems that arose in the school district decades earlier, the ones that led Patrick Dobard's parents to send him to private schools, could be interpreted as a failure of government. Indeed, critics of the System often argue that governments are inherently inefficient and bureaucratic. New Orleans, in their view, was no aberration. Fully understanding this argument requires digging deeper into the underlying logic of both approaches. It turns out that neither governments nor markets are best in all situations. A better formulation of the above question, then, is this: Under what circumstances, and in what ways, does it make sense to employ markets and governments?

The argument for an active role for government in schooling is rooted in two ideas. The first is that some aspects of life are inherently collective or public. Education clearly fits this description. Given that education has a public nature, schooling decisions can be viewed as inherently political.[1] The second idea is that one of the most effective modes of management for large operations is bureaucracy, meaning a centralized form of organization led by an executive with clear lines of authority and ex-plicit rules for subordinates.[2] We therefore have to recognize the system of American education for what it is, a *political bureaucracy*. Given this description, it is not hard to see why school districts are under attack. Politics and bureaucracy are almost epithets in today's world, and putting the two together sounds that much worse. I will argue in this chapter that this distaste has arisen mostly because we have lost sight of what these supposedly unsavory words really mean.

The market approach is in many respects the opposite of school dis-trict political bureaucracies: instead of community members delegating their authority to board members through elections, and superinten-dents serving as executives, decisions within a market-based system are decentralized. This means the decisions are passed down, first, to school leaders who have the authority to allocate resources according to their own judgment and then to families who are ultimately responsible to, and knowledgeable about, the well-being of their children. In the market system, schools are therefore evaluated not on compliance with bureau-cratic rules, but on performance, as perceived by students and parents and reflected in their choice of schools. In short, the market approach relies on the decisions of the individual families and school leaders who are closest to the action, knowledgeable about local circumstances, and invested in the needs of their children.

To many, especially non-educators, the market theory is alluring. Markets have always been part of everyday American life and have been the main driver behind the country's long-standing economic progress. Economists like the Nobel Prize winner Milton Friedman have made this argument for free markets powerfully and eloquently.[3] When you receive a paycheck, you are a supplier operating in the labor market. When you go to the store, you are a consumer operating on the demand side of the market. Few would argue that the government should tell us what to do in these matters. The American economy, though supported by impor-tant contributions from government, has been among the world's strong-est because it has been among the freest. Friedman went a step further and argued that this principle applied to schools as well. A free market in schooling not only would be more efficient, he argued, but would align with our value for individual freedom. Indeed, the book in which he pro-posed the market-based approach, called school vouchers, was entitled *Capitalism and Freedom*.

But education is different. People, especially educators, are uncomfortable talking about education as a market because it is such an unusual one. Other scholars have criticized the market logic, focusing on philosophical concerns about neoliberalism and about the seeming folly of trying to meet public goals through private (market) means. While I come to a similar conclusion, I arrive there in a very different way, by getting underneath the surface of these arguments and being precise about why exactly the schooling market is so different. For that, we have to start at the beginning, with the assumptions behind the theory. The degree to which free markets generate efficient outcomes depends on how well markets satisfy a large of number of assumptions or conditions. While these conditions are rarely present in any market, most are "close enough" so that markets are clearly better than governments for providing goods. The schooling market is unique, however, in just how completely and thoroughly the assumptions are violated, and in the almost bizarre outcomes that they can generate, left to their own devices. Perhaps surprisingly, the most potent argument against free-market schooling therefore comes from within the intellectual home of market debates: economics.

This debate about political bureaucracy versus markets is critical to understanding what happened in New Orleans. Among other things, the discussion helps to show that the System is not, and never was, purely one or the other. Market supporters think of traditional school districts as government monopolies. Far from it. I show that many of the criticisms lodged against districts are provoked as much by hidden market forces that operate in conjunction with districts—the same market forces reformers espouse—as by political bureaucracy per se. Free markets generate many of the same problems as the System, for many of the same reasons, and through many of the same mechanisms.

This leads to a reinterpretation of the critique of the System, and to some predictions about what might go wrong with a free market in schooling—predictions that came to pass, especially in the early years of the New Orleans reform effort. My analysis also begins to suggest the wisdom of combining markets with a particular, and still active, role for government. By understanding the problems with both political bureaucracy and markets in greater depth, we can identify better solutions and see how those solutions aligned with what New Orleans' leaders eventually did.

Some will object that my discussion of the advantages and disadvantages of government and markets, and reinterpretation of the System, is incomplete and oversimplified. I agree. This is why it is important to be clear about my aim in this chapter: to capture the main tendencies and the main arguments for and against both approaches, especially those that are part of public debate. The nuances and the more academic theories will become more evident in later chapters.

Arguments in Favor of Local Government School Districts

School districts are political bureaucracies and have a surprising number of advantages when it comes to governing schools. With their formal structures and rules of authority, bureaucracies are designed to provide efficient, reliable, and uniform results. Those at the top—the executives and managers—pass directions down the ladder, and subordinates pass reports back up to communicate their progress. The expertise built up in the upper echelons of the organizational chart has more value as bureaucracies, and the number of people working within them, grow. Most organizations, including businesses, operate this way to some degree. We just avoid using the "b" word.

In the context of education, the political bureaucracy starts with school boards that hire superintendents as executives and experts to run their organizations. With years of formal training, these superintendents make recommendations to their boards about policies regarding textbooks and the hiring and firing of school principals and teachers. They use their expertise to coordinate action across district units and schools. They make sure that the System as a whole meets the needs of all students living within their jurisdictions, mostly by delivering a variety of services and resources to every school. When student needs are not being met, the superintendents can direct resources and expertise in the needed directions from the central office.

The school boards governing school districts are publicly elected. This too provides advantages. Office holders selected through a democratic process may be more likely to emphasize democratic values when making policy decisions about their schools and leadership. Since the whole community is affected by schools—businesses recognize students as future workers, and community members as future neighbors—the opportunity to vote helps ensure that these stakeholders have a voice in educational decision-making, and that voters will support funding to allow boards to govern schools effectively.

Two other important structural components, while not necessary to the above governing structure, are almost universal in the operation of school districts. First, almost all districts assign students to schools based on the neighborhoods in which they live. A key advantage of this approach is that it provides predictability to schools and families. School leaders know how many students they will have each year, and parents know which schools their children will attend when they choose where to live. Neighborhood attendance zones also reinforce social bonds and networks within local communities. Children form friendships with those down the block, and these carry over to out-of-school time and to relationships among parents.

Second, the vast majority of districts also have collective bargaining with teachers. This, along with state certification requirements and tenure protections, has the advantage of insulating personnel decisions from board members and district administrators who face pressures to hire friends and relatives for key jobs, a form of political patronage. Unions and tenure protections also increase job security and can give teachers a voice in shaping their learning and work environments, which can make the job more attractive and improve student outcomes.[4]

School districts, therefore, are able to satisfy a large number of objectives and balance philosophies that are often in conflict. Political progressives appreciate the way districts promote democratic values and good government. Political conservatives value the localness of school districts because they allow boards to cater to linguistic, religious, and cultural enclaves. Families value the predictability of schooling options and the ability to call their board members or attend public meetings to complain when they are displeased with the education their children receive. Taxpayers value many of these same things, not to mention the cost savings that can come with larger organizations.[5]

This is why school districts have become so ubiquitous and persistent. They have not been dependent on a particular political constituency, party, or philosophy. They have been well designed for the American social-political-economic context.

Arguments against Local Government School Districts

Here, again, there is another side to the story. An overarching concern is that school districts have produced stagnant and mediocre academic outcomes even as costs have risen much faster than the rate of inflation. While this criticism is exaggerated,[6] I focus here on seven specific, and interconnected, concerns that are commonly thought to undergird the System's problems: inequitable resources and outcomes, government rule proliferation, teacher unions, limited accountability, short-lived improvement efforts, constrained parental choice, and school uniformity.[7]

INEQUITABLE RESOURCES AND OUTCOMES. School districts are inequitable. On this point, there is little debate. While there has been considerable improvement in recent years, some schools still have far greater resources than others, and achievement gaps between racial, income, and other groups remain large.[8]

One simple reason is that wealthier families are willing and able to pay much more for traditional public schools through property taxes. To do so, they live in the same communities as other wealthy families, leaving the less wealthy to their own neighborhoods. This creates vast geographic disparities in income, which translate directly into spending disparities in local schools. Those with less wealth—disproportionately people of color—are less able to access these highly resourced schools, reinforcing achievement gaps. Lawsuits challenging these inequities on the basis of state constitutional provisions have helped to alleviate the problems, but segregation and funding inequalities have remained remarkably persistent.[9]

GOVERNMENT RULE PROLIFERATION. Critics of the System also charge that bureaucracy, while intended to create clear lines of authority and efficient operation, is more apt to create burdens and slow improvement and innovation. Voters (and people in general) remember bad news more than good, giving politicians an incentive to avoid scandal above all else.[10] To prevent controversy and cement their preferences into place before they leave office, elected officials create rules that prevent the worst offenses, and shift blame when things go wrong.[11] While many rules are merely "symbolic gestures,"[12] or token responses that few follow, even these can add up to real administrative burdens.[13]

Not only does this political process lead inexorably to more rules, according to critics, but it wires the thinking of educators to focus on rule compliance.[14] The only way to lose one's job is to break the rules and draw negative attention to school principals, superintendents, or school board members. Faced with these realities, the best that educators can do is to follow the rules, creating a culture of compliance, so that the first question educators ask is, Am I allowed to do this?

With rules coming from so many levels of government—local, state, and federal—they often do not fit well together. At each level, rules are the result of compromises across the spectrum of board member views, with the patchwork compilation sometimes making little practical sense. Most individual regulations were created for good reasons, but critics argue that collectively, they place a roadblock in the way of change and ingenuity. Rules are the staples of bureaucracy, and school district bureaucracies may have gotten out of hand.

TEACHER UNIONS. For critics, the problem of government rules is compounded by the growing role of unions. Negotiated salary schedules pay teachers based on qualifications—years of experience and degrees. Work rules specify class sizes, work hours, lunch breaks, formal evaluations, and professional development.[15]

Union contracts, along with state tenure policies, also provide job security. Districts must give teachers "due process" before dismissing them, which sounds innocuous enough but means placing the burden of proof on school district leaders, who must provide clear written evidence that teachers have performed poorly and show that they have been given multiple chances to improve before being fired. The potential for appeals also means that the process of dismissal takes months or even years to complete.

One implication of this is that school leaders have limited authority over their teachers. When layoffs are necessary, the least experienced have to go first (called "last in, first out"). If a teaching position opens in any school, many union contracts stipulate that the most senior teacher in the district has the first right to take it, even if the school principal wants to hire someone else (called "bumping rights"). More broadly, most school leaders have little control over recruiting, hiring, developing, evaluating, rewarding, or retaining teachers. Given that teachers are the most critical asset in any school—really, schools *are* collections of teachers and staff—it is not hard to see why the lack of school authority in this critical area could create problems.

With union rules, on top of those from all three levels of government, the principal's job is often confined to complying with rules, building community relations, enforcing student discipline, and buffering teachers from external pressures. Some research suggests that school principals spend only about 10 percent of their time on activities directly related to student instruction, such as observing and coaching teachers and reviewing curricula and lesson plans,[16] though these represent the core functions of schooling. Principals can lead, but only up to a point.

It can be difficult under these conditions for teachers and principals to create major new and distinctive educational programs. They must first gain approval from district officials and the superintendent in order to take a proposal to the board. If they get that far, they then have to convince the board to make an exception and create a program or rule only in one school, or apply it to all the schools at greater expense. If the idea conflicts with a union contract, then the contract will have to be amended or renegotiated. If a proposed rule does not also comply with all state and federal rules, it will be rejected, for fear of negative headlines and/or losing funds from those agencies. And even when a new rule or program is adopted, other rules and factors often stand in the way of effective execution and implementation.

Union contracts therefore add to an already-complex intergovernmental bureaucratic tangle—and this has had consequences for student outcomes.[17]

LIMITED ACCOUNTABILITY. A corollary to the concern about rules is the lack of accountability. Rules focus attention on process, which detracts attention from results. It is difficult to justify holding anyone accountable when rules restrict authority over the steps that might lead to success. Holding people accountable while tying their hands with rules that prevent them from meeting their benchmarks is a recipe for failure.

Consider the relationship between teachers and school principals. Union contracts often limit the ability of principals to walk into classrooms to observe teachers at work, making classroom observations seem threatening and hostile. Further, due-process provisions mean that what limited performance information is available can be used only in certain ways. The effects are predictable: principals, as we have seen, spend little time on instructional matters. Teachers, meanwhile, are frustrated by the lack of feedback they receive.[18]

While intended to protect high-performing teachers from low-performing principals, the rules also have the effect of protecting ineffective teachers from effective principals. Only 1 percent of teachers receive formal evaluations deeming their performance "unsatisfactory."[19] Yet 76 percent of teachers in one survey said that dismissing more low-performing teachers would improve teacher effectiveness.[20]

One group of sociologists has put the problem this way: "Classroom doors are closed, teachers' salaries are negotiated through third-party mechanisms, teachers are infrequently or never evaluated, and daily or periodic supervision of teachers is typically absent in most schools."[21] Another scholar has put it even more strongly, writing that teacher evaluation systems "lack attention to the very things that constitute the intellectual core of teaching: classroom discussions and learning activities."[22] It is hard to imagine harsher criticism. The issues of teacher evaluation and accountability have received national attention in recent years, but the problems remain much the same.

Accountability could also, in theory, emerge from the democratic process—from voters. The economist Albert O. Hirschman is well known for writing about accountability as an expression of voter and parent "voice." In an institution such as schooling, voice can be expressed through voting, public protests, financial donations, and volunteering for campaigns. However, the power of political voice is limited under the System. While board elections are highly localized, and this makes each vote count more, the elections are usually held separately from those for president, governor, or even state representatives, so that turnout in school board elections is some states is only around 5 percent—voter voices are not heard.[23] When we take into account not just teachers, but their families and friends, we can see that teachers may influence a substantial share of the votes in board elections, power that is reinforced, in some states, by their ability to strike. In contrast to most voters, whose interests are weaker and more diffuse, teachers have a strong interest in who serves on the boards and negotiates their contracts.[24]

Giving teachers autonomy, job security, and voice through unions and tenure, and giving voters a voice through elections, have some advantages, but also some clear disadvantages.

SHORT-LIVED IMPROVEMENT EFFORTS. Occasionally, the stars align and a board or superintendent is able to hold educators accountable and push for improvement. However, these changes are usually short-lived. The average stay for an urban school superintendent or school board member is only three years.[25] School board coalitions can also fall apart if only a single board seat changes hands, shifting coalitions and majority control.

Even if boards are able to avoid this volatility and maintain stable leadership at the top, changes in policy and practice tend to be shallow. As the sociologist Anthony Bryk and colleagues have written, schools are like Christmas trees, bejeweled with an ever-changing assortment of educational ornaments.[26] We can change the decorations relatively easily. But if we want to change the structure, we have to plant a new tree and wait patiently for it to grow. That is rare in practice.

CONSTRAINED PARENTAL CHOICE. In addition to voice, Hirschman posits a second mechanism through which organizations improve. In the case of schools, families can simply leave those that are performing poorly. They can "exit," inducing schools to either act or shut down for lack of customers.

Exit, however, is also restricted under the System. Districts generally assign students to schools based on where they live. The idea of attendance zones—neighborhood boundaries designated by the district for each school—is simple, as well as practical, since families generally prefer to have their children attend school close to home. But the zones mean that, to switch schools, families must either pay private school tuition or move their residence, at what may be substantial financial cost. Moving one's residence also imposes social and psychological costs through the loss of neighborhood friendships.

But funding does not follow students, so even if a large number of families chose to accept these costs and exercised their right to exit a school, their departure might have no effect on the teachers or the school principal. In this regard, the System is not very accountable to either voters or families.

School districts were designed to provide basic, predictable, and uniform education, by relying on the expertise of education leaders and the goodwill and professionalism of teachers. That they do. But the System's focus on process and input-oriented rules also works to prevent accountability when things go wrong. Feedback is discouraged. Low-performers are left to their own devices. High-performers are not rewarded, by either school leaders or parents. This has made it difficult, critics say, for the System to make the shift from the historical objective of basic literacy to high academic excellence.

SCHOOL UNIFORMITY. Another trait of bureaucracies, especially political ones, is uniformity. Rules apply to everyone, which means that everyone is, to some degree, doing the same thing. Democratically elected bodies, subject to constitutions requiring equal protection of all citizens, reinforce this homogenizing tendency by striving to treat all groups under their purview, including schools, equally.

This characterization is perhaps the most misleading in the list, however. While political bureaucracies do tend *toward* uniformity, this is counteracted by teachers' job security, autonomy, and loosely coupled independence within their own classrooms.[27] Education scholars David Cohen and Jim Spillane argue that "teaching and learning are more directly affected by the texts that students and teachers use," and these are mostly selected by teachers or school leaders themselves.[28] Moreover, in contrast to most other countries, where national governments make these decisions, teachers in the United States are employed by the more than fourteen thousand different school districts, each making its own decisions.[29] Under these conditions, it is hard to imagine that all schools would do the same thing. People working autonomously in complex jobs and different organizations will produce fragmentation perhaps, but not industrial-style repetition.

Rather than declare that schools are uniform, it is more apt to say that schools are incoherently similar. The thousands of decisions made by teachers average out within schools, so that schools as a whole look more similar than classrooms do. Most schools have some strict and stern teachers, some who use project-based learning, and others who use more traditional direct instruction, for example. Education scholars have long described American high schools as being like cafeterias, each with similar menus.[30] The System's political bureaucracy pulls schools toward one another, while its complexity, localness, and loose coupling allows them to drift apart.

Maybe it is time to fundamentally rethink how we govern and manage schools. Maybe the System has outlived its usefulness, at least in places like New Orleans where the district was producing abysmal outcomes on top of rampant corruption. Maybe.

The Market Alternative

Political bureaucracies represent one way to organize schools. Markets are another. Instead of relying on elected boards and the expertise of those at the top of the district hierarchy, school leaders in a free market would have flexibility to do largely as they pleased through nongovernmental enterprises—*privatization*. Instead of focusing on rule compliance, school leaders would answer to families who would have their *choice* of schools, which would compete with one another. Privatization and choice together comprise a market-driven approach, a potent combination forcing schools to compete and allowing them to innovate in response to parents' demands. Instead of relying on the received wisdom of educators prepared in university-based schools of education, entrepreneurs could create and lead schools, hire whom they please, and develop new ways of doing things that would attract more customers and revenue. Control would be back in the hands of those who know the children they are serving: the parents responsible for raising them and the educators in the schools serving them—not increasingly distant district and state government offices. Under the right conditions, these market-based incentives could provide a powerful force for improved schooling.

Market forces can lead to a wider variety of products and services as firms try to meet the varying tastes of consumers.[31] Take restaurants, for example. At each level of quality, or price point, there are different types. Cafeterias are usually at the low end of the market, with low prices and many options to choose from. Others specialize. In New Orleans, we have Creole, Cajun, French, and Vietnamese restaurants on top of the more typical Mexican and Italian. Some restaurants specialize, while others are more eclectic. In short, companies find their market niches based on consumer preferences and income levels.

All of these decisions are guided by what Adam Smith called "the invisible hand."[32] Armed with information about the price and characteristics of goods, consumers and producers make individual decisions in a way that maximizes efficiency—the greatest total well-being. There is no need for any sort of "superintendent" to coordinate it all. In markets, prices move on their own in response to market pressures and do the coordinating for us, sending signals to parents and potential school operators about what is most valued. Everyone acts selfishly, yet almost everyone is materially better off than they would have been otherwise. Greed is good, in theory.

Of course, any theory rests on assumptions. Below are the core assumptions necessary for a competitive market, one without government involvement, to produce an efficient result:[33]

1 CHOICES OF INDIVIDUALS DO NOT AFFECT OTHER PEOPLE. Since people are assumed to be making decisions based on their own preferences (and constraints), market efficiency requires that transactions between market actors do not affect anyone who is not involved in those decisions—such external effects are ignored in market transactions and yield perverse effects. (Since this assumption is about external effects, it is sometimes called the "no externalities" assumption.)

2 GOOD INFORMATION. Since markets rely on parents to choose schools, and on school leaders to make a multitude of decisions, the market is only as efficient as the information is complete and accurate.

3 MANY OPTIONS. Without many options to choose from, families cannot exit, choose alternatives, and force out low-performing firms. At the extreme, a monopolist can take advantage of the situation by charging exorbitant prices, using resources inefficiently, and producing low quality.

4 NO TRANSACTION OR SWITCHING COSTS. The costs of creating these transactions between buyers and sellers (e.g., negotiating prices and switching from one seller to another) need to be small, so that mutually beneficial transactions can occur.

5 FLEXIBLE DEMAND. While rarely stated as an assumption of market efficiency, there is an implied assumption that one can choose not to enter a given market at all, for example, to eat at home instead of entering the market as a consumer and eating at a restaurant.

6 FLEXIBLE SUPPLY. Likewise, firms must be free to enter and exit the market, and to expand and contract their production levels. This, along with flexible demand, is almost always true in markets, so it too is rarely mentioned.

7 EFFICIENCY IS THE GOAL. This is perhaps the most critical assumption of all. Markets are designed to create the greatest possible *total* well-being in society, when each individual's well-being is "added up." It does not matter who receives the greatest benefits.

When these assumptions hold, markets can be a powerful force. Consumers can gather information—about prices, quality, and product features—and search for the goods and services they prefer. When they are not satisfied, i.e., when the chosen option is not a good fit to their individual needs, they can ask for a refund and buy another brand that better matches their needs, or go without it and save the money for something else. Firms therefore have incentives to respond to consumer preferences and to innovate, creating new production methods that reduce costs and new products that consumers want. Otherwise, they will lose customers to their competitors and reduce their profits. New firms can be created at any time. Everyone does as well as possible individually, which is all that matters since no one's purchases have an effect on anyone else. This process is guided not by a centralized bureaucracy but by an invisible hand. Everyone wins, at least when the assumptions hold.

An Especially Dysfunctional Market

Not even the staunchest market advocates would argue that the above assumptions hold in practice or that the outcomes are quite as rosy as they seem. Still, the strong support for markets does depend on the assumptions being at least approximately true most of the time. Accepting a few small problems that arise with markets makes sense. A slightly dysfunctional market will still usually beat out even the best government. What happens, though, in cases where the conditions all fail to hold, and fail badly? Education happens to be just such a case. Below, I reconsider the assumptions.

SCHOOLING CHOICES DO AFFECT OTHER PEOPLE. The market logic relies on people acting in their own self-interest, which works so long as one person's self-interest does not come at someone else's direct expense. Individualism works when decisions only affect the individuals making them.

Schooling decisions involve two major types of external effects that violate this assumption. First, everyone benefits from living in a world surrounded by better-educated citizens and from a more cohesive community. Education also reduces crime and improves public health—benefits that everyone receives, not just the individual who is educated.[34] The benefits of education are also passed down to future generations, from parent to child and through broader social networks. These "positive externalities," explain why almost all economists—everyone from Adam Smith, writing in 1776, to Milton Friedman, writing in 1955—have argued for public subsidies for primary and secondary education. Without subsidies, the external effects would be ignored and markets would provide far too little education.[35]

Subsidies are insufficient, however, to address the full range of positive externalities. In private-sector markets, the service you receive from a company does not depend on the other consumers who choose the same company. When you buy a car, your choice does not affect the other people who have purchased the same make and model. This is far from true with schools. Students produce outcomes—academic knowledge, expectations, beliefs, values, and motivations—for one another. Studies consistently show, for example, that all students benefit from having peers with higher test scores and family incomes.[36]

Classmates matter to one another, and also to their teachers. Anyone who has taught for long can tell you a story about "little Johnny" who was so disruptive that he made it difficult for the teacher to focus on instruction and spend time with other students. This is why, when teachers leave the profession, the second most common reason they give is student discipline.[37] Student behavioral issues are also correlated with family income, which may explain why students' family income predicts teacher turnover; where incomes are low, it can be especially hard to attract and retain high-performing teachers.[38] The direct external effect of classmates on one another is thus compounded by an indirect effect on the supply of teachers.

A key implication of these external effects is that families choose schools based, to a substantial degree, on the types of students who attend them. This gives schools strong incentives to attract, select, and keep certain students, which in turn distorts the entire market mechanism, shifting attention in the competitive process away from the core elements of education—instruction, curriculum, and organizational culture.

IMPERFECT INFORMATION. In most markets, collecting information through word of mouth, friends and family, publications such as *Consumers Reports*, and online rating sites is relatively straightforward. With products such as cars, phones, and computers, there is plenty of information available. Most people know what they are looking for when they shop and can identify the product that is best for them.

This is not how it works with information about schools. We expect schools to do many things—to prepare children to be workers, citizens, and productive members of the community. Goals like creativity, values, social skills, and civic responsibility are hard to define and even harder to measure.[39] Moreover, the outcomes we are most interested in are not immediately apparent. Even if we clearly define what it means, say, to be a good citizen, we have to wait a long time to see if that is how our children turn out. And by the time we track children into adulthood, the information is no longer useful to assessing schools' performance. For today's kindergartners, we would have to wait thirteen years to measure any adult outcome. By that time, most of today's educators will have moved on to other jobs, and it will be far too late to hold educators responsible.

Even if we were willing to accept short-term measures, like test scores, as predictors of students' long-term outcomes, education is unique in that almost all student outcomes are driven primarily by factors outside of school control, starting years before children enter the formal schooling process (even in the womb) and continuing throughout their time in school. Outcomes in high school are driven by, among other things, the quality of elementary and middle schools students attended when they were younger. If we fail to account for the many factors other than the current school, and simply rely on, for example, the percentage of students who pass a test or graduate high school, then we will misjudge school performance. Student outcome measures, including but going beyond test scores, can be adjusted to account for outside factors, using student growth or "value-added" analysis, but this is rarely done.[40]

While families can get rough estimates of this information through word of mouth, from their social networks and online reviews, few parents directly observe what happens in schools; almost everything they see is filtered through the minds of their children. Also, as soon as any measure—objective or subjective, short-term or long-term—becomes high-stakes, there are pressures that tend to distort the data. Standardized test scores, for example, are "objective" measures, but they can be artificially inflated if schools teach to the test, that is, repeatedly drill questions like those that appear on the test.

To say, then, that families are poorly informed would be an understatement.[41] It is not their fault. While some debates on choice seem to blame families for their bad choices, my point here is different: that families are capable of making good choices for their children, and in some ways best situated to do so, but the market will not, and even cannot, provide the information they need. This information problem is far worse than in the other markets we experience in our daily lives.

LIMITED OPTIONS. Competition works best when there are many competitors. Few families, however, will ever have a large number of schools to choose from that fit their needs and preferences. The need for students to go to a brick-and-mortar school building every day means the only viable options are those fairly close to home or parents' work. Choices are geographically constrained as they are for perhaps no other product or service. Homeschooling and virtual schools ostensibly eliminate this constraint but still require an adult to facilitate learning activities and maintain focus. Few parents are in a position to do this, if for no other reason than they have to go to work. Technology alone cannot substantially alleviate the constraint of geography.

The lack of schooling options is driven partly by another assumption of free markets: the absence of *economies of scale*. To open its doors to even a single student, a school needs a principal, office, classroom, restroom, accounting system, computer system, curriculum map, library—and of course a teacher. Once all of these things are in place, adding another student comes at almost no additional cost. As classes fill up, a school will have to hire more teachers and find more space, but the other fixed costs remain. To cover these costs and be viable, research suggests, a school needs to have at least a few hundred students.[42] The pressure to create large-scale schools reduces the number of schooling options further.

HIGH SWITCHING COSTS. Suppose, despite these problems, that parents and their children can get a clear sense of a school's quality within, say, the first month or two of attendance. If they are not satisfied, then, in a free market, they could switch schools. With most products and services, this works fine. We return the unsatisfactory product to the store for a replacement or a refund, and choose another. But switching schools is much more costly, even setting aside the problem of limited options, in part because schooling is an inherently social enterprise. It can be hard for children to make new friends, and their arrival in a new school can be disruptive for students already there.[43] Increasingly, too, parents' social networks are tied to those of their children. Switching schools is difficult for everyone.

Academic costs also arise when switching schools. Even when states create uniform academic standards, schools do not always teach the same material in the same grades, or they may teach the same material using different instructional approaches. When switching schools, students have to learn and adjust to the structure of academic content, instructional philosophy, schedules, school culture, implicit norms, and rules. The higher these switching costs, the less flexibility there is in school enrollment, the less responsive schools need to be to consumer needs, and the less efficient the market will be.

FIXED DEMAND. Under typical market conditions, families can decide to purchase more or less of a good, or none at all. When prices rise, the quantity demanded drops. This assumption, too, fails in schooling. Parents are legally required to care for and educate their children, usually at least up to age sixteen—they must send their children to school somewhere. This fixed total demand means schools can persist in the market even when families are deeply dissatisfied.

RESTRICTED SUPPLY. What we hope for in a free market is that better producers expand. A company manufacturing a popular product might build a new production facility or add a night shift to increase output. Conversely, poor performers would fade away, perhaps eventually closing their doors permanently.

Again, this is not how it is likely to work with schooling. First, schools require specific kinds of buildings. It is easy to distinguish a building designed to house a school from, say, an apartment building or restaurant, and attempts to operate schools in other kinds of buildings rarely last long. The buildings must also be located in or near residential areas to address the problem of geography. Land in residential areas is usually scarce, meaning the property required for new buildings is difficult to acquire through market transactions alone. Nor is it easy to expand within an existing building. Small additions or the purchase of portable classrooms can accommodate some growth, but this can only be taken so far; just as schools are inefficient when they are too small, they become impersonal and dysfunctional when they get too large.[44] Expansion, especially within a given building, tends to reduce quality, undermining the very reason expansion might seem desirable.

The assumptions so far—about classmate effects, information, the number of options, switching costs, and flexible supply and demand—paint a grim picture of the potential of free markets to improve schooling.

When we consider one additional assumption, and how it is connected to those already discussed, we see just how bad the problem really is.

Markets and Equity

My analysis to this point has focused on what assumptions are necessary for free markets to produce *efficient* outcomes, that is, to produce the greatest total social well-being, regardless of how benefits are distributed across groups. However, any complete analysis of public affairs requires considering another widely accepted goal of education.

Equity has always played a crucial role in education debates, and this is no less true today. Inequalities in wealth and income, which correlate with race, are at or near their highest points nationally in over a century.[45] Social mobility—the likelihood that children from lower-income families will end up with higher incomes—has also slowed. Education is thought to be one of the main potential cures for these broader socioeconomic inequalities. Educating students from all backgrounds is good for everyone, but it is also the right thing to do.

Yet when we think of markets, equity is not usually the first word that comes to mind. This is for good reason. Markets are not designed to be equitable. Within any given market, some people consume the product, while others do not—based partly on what they can afford. Some get good, high-quality versions, others poor imitations. For the vast majority of goods and services, this is not a problem. In fact, it is often a good thing, accommodating differing preferences and disparate ability to pay. The efficient result essentially requires allowing people to buy different things. We do not worry that some people have fancy cell phones and others have cheap ones with fewer bells and whistles, but this is exactly what we worry about with schools.

To see why equity is especially unlikely to arise in a free market for schooling, we have to go back to the conditions required for markets to be efficient. It is not just that those conditions do not hold in the market for schooling overall, but that they are even further from the truth for comparatively disadvantaged families.

Information is important for consumers to make good decisions, but some families have much better access to information than others— greater ease of visiting schools, more extensive social networks, and friends and family who have had more experience in good schools. Low-income families often do not have cars. Their work hours are less flexible and predictable, making it difficult to visit and observe schools during business and school hours. The same factors work to limit disadvantaged students' schooling options. Transportation and job demands also make it hard for parents to get their children to school each day, participate in parent-teacher conferences, pick up their children when they are sick, or attend their sporting events and art exhibitions.

The constraints on low-income families are compounded by class-mate effects—the external effects of each family's schooling decisions on others. This gives schools incentives to select students who, for example, come from higher-income families and do not have discipline issues or disabilities. This sorting due to classmate effects is compounded by other factors, such as the fact that many families prefer being in schools with others like themselves.[46] The same forces lead to housing segregation, which, given the geography of schooling, also worsens school segregation.[47]

The "tipping point" phenomenon is also a powerful force against equity. Schools and other groups tend to tip toward segregation even when most people prefer integration.[48] When one person moves to a school with others like herself, it further isolates those in the school she left, making them more likely to move too. This creates a cascading effect, so that even though people generally want to mix with other groups, they cannot.

For these reasons, schools tend to stratify, or sort into tiers. Some schools attract the most advantaged students, which makes them attractive both to other students and to teachers. Since advantage is partly related to income, the higher-tier schools can bring in more resources through fundraisers and greater political influence over local government. This, in turn, leads other higher-income families to live near these schools. It is no surprise, then, that disadvantaged students typically end up in lower-tier schools. This is the expected result of any school system relying on market forces—and it has long-term consequences for students of color and those from low-income families.[49]

We know who gets access to the higher tiers and who gets stuck with the lower ones. Even in regular private markets, research suggests that more advantaged, highly educated adults are more satisfied with their decisions as consumers than less educated ones.[50] In this case, advantaged groups will tend to get the spots in the top-tier schools. The factors that make the education market fail, make it fail worse for disadvantaged children.

The Economics-Based Case against
Free-Market Schooling: In Summary

This analysis leads to a somewhat surprising conclusion: the strongest argument against a free market in schooling comes from the very discipline that focuses on, and even reveres, markets. Economics shows us how unusual schooling is, with its seven defining features: classmate effects, poor information, limited options, costly switching, fixed demand, restricted supply, and the importance of equity.

To the degree that schooling is subject to market forces, these defining features conspire to inhibit the potential driving forces of markets: competition, fit, and innovation. The geography of schooling means families need to choose schools nearby, and, given economies of scale, there are likely to be few options; unless you live in a place with high population density and/or an expansive mass transit system (say, New York City), your practical options will be limited. In rural areas, there is generally exactly one school building to "choose" from. This undermines competition across schools and further reduces the potential of schooling markets to produce efficiently. Note here that limited options are not due to the government but to the nature of the market.

To the degree competition nevertheless arises, it gets misdirected by classmate effects and information problems, which lead schools to compete to enroll the best students, not to provide the best instruction and curriculum. As Rick Hess has put it, schooling markets can "conflate *publicity-oriented* competitive response with *performance-oriented* competitive response."[51]

A free schooling market would provide limited incentives to innovate in the way that private firms do. The information problem makes it hard to gauge when a given innovation is useful. The lack of price mechanism means the investment — the time and energy that go into creating, say, a new curriculum — can have only a limited economic return. Also, parents usually want to expose their children to a wide range of subjects, programs, and experiences, so that they will be well-rounded.[52] This makes parents fairly conservative. Rarely do parents say, "I want something totally different for my child." On the contrary, they are mainly looking for something similar to what they experienced themselves, though perhaps of better quality. Innovation is therefore restrained.

If only one of these problems existed, the market might adapt and the result would still be more efficient and equitable than any government-driven alternative. But the reality is that none of the conditions hold and the problems from each one compound the others.

I am not the first to argue that schooling markets are dysfunctional and may not serve the public good. Education scholars like Rick Hess, David Labaree, and Henry Levin also argue that public and private goals may be incompatiable and that competition will not work as intended.[53] What I am doing is a bit different, however. First, I am providing what I believe to be a fuller accounting of the inherent problems with schooling markets, and how they compound one another. Second, I am arguing that this fuller accounting provides a stronger argument against free markets than prior analyses have suggested. Just as the strongest argument against the political nature of school districts comes from political science, the strongest case against the market approach comes from economics. Whereas most critics of free-market schooling argue that the principles of economics do not apply, I am arguing that economic principles apply perfectly, and that the nature of the market is fundamentally different in ways that have been misunderstood. Even the equity-related arguments against markets are stronger when we look at the issue from an economic perspective.

A free market in schooling will not work the way its proponents suggest because of the inherent, natural, and ingrained features of the schooling market. It is not that teachers or school leaders would behave badly in a free market. Rather, they would be doing, as they do now, what seems best for the children under their care. They would be good people making reasonable decisions in a bad system.

Trade-Offs and Decisions in New Orleans

Markets and governments each have many strengths. They are also both flawed. This chapter provides a broad outline of what each tends to do. In some situations, through wise and effective leadership, the strengths of one may outshine its weaknesses. In others, the weaknesses may overwhelm. Again, these are just tendencies, not mechanical laws.

We have been able to observe the tendencies of the System for more than a century. Many school districts still work well. Many school board members and superintendents are well prepared and dedicated to their jobs. They coordinate activities to leverage economies of scale and free up school principals to focus on the core work of instruction, without the back-office burdens of budgeting, building maintenance, transportation, and the myriad other activities that go into running schools. Many teachers, though they have no financial incentives to do so, are intrinsically motivated and well prepared to serve children, and school principals can find ways to either dismiss or "counsel out" those teachers whom they deem ineffective. In most school districts, the advantages that made school districts so popular and universal still hold today.

In other districts, however, the rules have ossified and the central office has become an albatross, stifling the benefits of professional expertise and coordinated bureaucracy that motivated the original school reformers a century ago. New Orleans was in just such a situation in the wake of Hurricane Katrina. The district had failed and led some longtime residents, like Patrick Dobard, to ask, "What happened?"

Leaders in Louisiana wanted to reduce the power of the district, but they were heading into uncharted territory with a new set of potential dangers. How much would they rely on parents and school leaders to make decisions? When would they overrule the market and close schools that had ample enrollments? How would they handle the inevitable consequences, predicted by the unusual features of the schooling market? How, for example, would they ensure that all students had fair access to quality schools, given the strong incentives that schools had to select students? More broadly, how would they rein in the worst tendencies of a free market in schooling and make the reforms work efficiently, equitably, and in the interests of the entire community?

It turns out that there are no good answers to these questions that involve either just government or just markets. In New Orleans, we will see what can go wrong both in school districts and in (nearly) free markets, and how the city eventually settled on a more successful middle way. The New Orleans experience helps us see where the role of markets should end and the role of government begin.

CHAPTER 3

Revolution

A common theme in education policy discussions is that we can change policies without having much impact on what happens in schools. Implementation is usually lacking and temporary, which means educator practices, and therefore student results, remain largely unaffected. Teachers continue to work independently, behind closed doors, and their leaders buffer them from outside forces. It is the same thing over and over, according to critics. Sometimes that is true.

If ever there were an exception, however, New Orleans is it. Here, within the span of just a few months, the state took over almost all of the city's schools, the teachers were fired, the teacher union's contract was eliminated, and schools were opened up to parental choice. Within the first five to seven years, the years I focus on in the present chapter, state and local agencies also turned over operation of the vast majority of schools to nonprofit charter school operators working under performance-based contracts, and turned over key responsibilities to a new network of nonprofit organizations. Collectively, these changes represented a shift toward market control, but it was not only that. The government and nonprofit organizations played equally important roles. They were not merely shifting prior roles across different types of institutions but redefining the roles and their underlying logic.

How did the reformers create this unusual system? And why? In the wake of Hurricane Katrina, the options were limited mainly by the imagination. Why did they choose this mix of state takeover, autonomous charter schools, and parental choice? The closely related question is, *who* chose these reforms? This is a question of political power that has long been at the heart of school reform debates. In New Orleans, unlike almost anywhere else, the answer was not a list of government bodies like school districts or unions, or abstract processes like democracy, but a few individuals who took control of their own accord, working mostly behind closed doors. Some were elected officials whom citizens had vested with this responsibility. Most were not. Some were from New Orleans. Most were not. Some decisions were made with broad public input. Most were not. That the reforms were created by a handful of individuals and some outsiders is partly what drove the radical nature of the reforms. Revolutions are not usually made by committee, and New Orleans would be no exception.

Such sudden and significant change is necessarily a product of both people and circumstances. In this case, the city had a determined, clever, and knowledgeable leader, the matriarch of what became a "reform family," ready to press for change by almost any means necessary. Many of the key policy pieces were already in place. Katrina made it possible to bring these parts together into a larger whole, sweeping out the political opposition and sweeping in some desperate circumstances. The process was ugly, but the result was unprecedented.

Before Katrina

It all started with Leslie Jacobs. Like many of the reformers who had brought the System into being a century earlier, Jacobs was a businessperson. A powerful, aggressive local insurance executive, she was often described as a "bulldog."[1] Jacobs was appalled by how the school district operated, and by its results. Beyond the corruption and dysfunction described in chapter 1, two hundred employed teachers were not assigned to classes in the year prior to the storm.[2] School buildings were deteriorating.[3] In 2003 a private investigator found that the New Orleans Public Schools inappropriately provided checks to nearly four thousand people and health insurance to two thousand. Some of those who collected checks were, according to the district's own records, retired, fired, or even dead. In a four-year period, the school district allocated more than fifteen thousand erroneous checks totaling $11 million.[4] Common control practices, such as audits, were not done on a regular basis.[5] The board also had a penchant for micromanaging the superintendent.[6]

Jacobs also liked to tell a more personal story. After getting involved in the local schools through her philanthropic work, she was elected to the Orleans Parish School Board (OPSB). Asked to select awardees for a college scholarship program, she read through applications and got to see firsthand the skills of district's best students. What she discovered was that "top students in our open admission high schools could not write complete or grammatically correct sentences." But nothing she did seemed to work. "I was trying to create a call to action and it was then that I realized that nobody would step up."[7] Just as critics of the System often describe, Jacobs ran into one rule and vested interest after another.

Change in OPSB would have to come from outside. In 1996 Jacobs was appointed by the state's Republican governor to the state Board of Elementary and Secondary Education.[8] Mirroring a national trend, she worked from the state capital in Baton Rouge to build an aggressive system for holding schools accountable, especially for their test scores. She also went a step further than most states by helping to create the Louisiana Recovery School District (RSD). From Jacobs's business perspective, what was needed was a mechanism to reconstitute schools in the same way that businesses are reconstructed through bankruptcy. Launched in 2004, just before the reforms, the RSD's job was to act like the judge in a bankruptcy court: to take over a failing school, require and oversee a turnaround plan, and eventually return it to district control.

The introduction of charter schools was the other key change in state law during this period. As independent private organizations, funded with government revenue, charter schools offered a way to take control away from both the districts and teacher unions. Passed in 1995, the state's charter law had been pushed by a second key actor, former school teacher and principal, and then-state senator, Cecil Picard. Jacobs embraced the idea and went on to recruit national charter operators, like the well-known KIPP organization, to come to New Orleans. The local OPSB fought against them, but five charter schools eventually got off the ground in the city, thanks to a state approval process that bypassed the local district. The first KIPP charter school in the city opened just days before Hurricane Katrina struck.

By reducing the power of local districts, charter schools also reduced the power of teacher unions. The union contracts were negotiated between the union and the district. In theory, unions could also obtain bargaining rights with charter schools, but this is much harder to do with individual schools, especially when the people starting charter schools, and the teachers they hire, are not especially friendly to unions.

In addition to districts and unions, the third key establishment institution that the reformers wanted to bypass or replace was university-based schools of education. Universities had been the pipeline for educators dating back more than a century. These programs shaped teacher skills and beliefs about schooling. If the reformers were going to change the way publicly funded schools worked, they had the change those skills and beliefs and, therefore, the teacher pipeline itself.

Enter Teach for America (TFA). A lynchpin of the national reform movement, TFA provided a pipeline of teachers to schools, requiring essentially no prior training in teaching. Once teaching candidates finished a summer training program, they were assigned to two-year stints as teachers, usually in high-poverty schools. The intent was that they would build on their time in the classroom to eventually become education leaders and/or advocates for school improvement. This was controversial, not only because TFA espoused other elements of school reform, but because the immediate effect was to place students in classrooms with teachers who lacked training, did not plan to stay, and did not have roots in the local communities.

New Orleans had been one of TFA's first and largest sites in 2005. The organization's South Louisiana region director, Sarah Usdin, had been born and raised in Kentucky. She joined TFA as it was first getting off the ground and taught in Baton Rouge before migrating to New Orleans. At the time Katrina made landfall, TFA's New Orleans footprint was relatively small at somewhere between 125 and 200 teachers, or 4 to 5 percent of the district total.

Usdin, like Jacobs, had seen the dysfunction of the district up close in her efforts to place TFA teachers within Orleans Parish schools. She especially lamented how the district, in the pre-reform years, held back excellent educators:

> There were some phenomenal people, actually, in the Orleans Parish HR [human resource] office who worked diligently to get good teachers in classrooms and make sure schools were fully staffed. You knew the school leaders who were really energized and engaged, knew how to do it, and others had their hands all tied [by the district].[9]

After ten years with TFA and its sister organization, the New Teacher Project, Usdin decided to move on to another venture, to build a nonprofit organization to assist the new Recovery School District (RSD) with its work turning around low-performing schools.

The foundation of the reform was therefore in place. Jacobs, working from her state board position, had led the creation of a state accountability system that could identify low-performing schools; with the creation of the RSD, the state could take over failing schools and turn them into charter schools. TFA was in place to supply a new kind of teacher. KIPP and other charter organizations had a foot in the door to create new kinds of schools. And Usdin's idea of a new reform support organization would help make all the pieces fit and work together.

Still, this was just a foundation for reform. Before Katrina, in 2005, these reform organizations had very little practical impact and served only a tiny fraction of the city's students. With limited interest and a general hostility toward reform, the city was not considered a hotbed of reform activity. One national leader in the reform movement, Greg Richmond, who founded the National Association of Charter School Authorizers, told me that before Katrina "nobody in the charter school movement nationally cared one whit about New Orleans."[10] It was a backwater—the last place we would expect anything innovative. The fact that it took Jacobs a decade even to put some of the key pieces in place demonstrated that reality. Chicago, New York, and Philadelphia were the places to be in the school reform world, not New Orleans.

That was all about to change.

The Katrina Aftermath

Radar images showed that Hurricane Katrina covered nearly the entire Gulf of Mexico, with sustained winds above 150 miles per hour. At first, it seemed the city might be spared. Once the storm pushed through, however, a different picture emerged. Jacobs, who was out of town dropping her daughter off at college, watched on television and thought: "We've lost the levees. . . . We've just lost the city of New Orleans."[11] She worried about leaving her daughter, but she had to get back. "I'm crying the whole way home."

Some 80 percent of the city flooded with up to fifteen feet of water; 70 percent of homes were heavily damaged or destroyed. The city was empty, covered in gray sludge, and smelled of chemicals. Even the birds and frogs were gone, leaving the streets, usually full of life and music, in eerie silence.

With the world watching in horror, national leaders, including the speaker of the US House of Representatives, openly questioned whether the city should be rebuilt.[12] Much of the city was, after all, below sea level, and climate change meant that the oceans were rising. To the city's leaders, this was an existential threat. They were determined, even desperate, to get the city up and running, and to do that, they would have to convince the world that it was worth saving.

Getting the schools restarted was a high priority. After food, running water, electricity, and police protection, schools are among our most basic necessities. Beyond serving as a place for learning, schools are the heart of the social lives of children and provide important social services such as counseling for traumatic events—and students and their families had just experienced one of the worst traumas imaginable. Also, without schools, parents could not work, and if they could not work, they could not return and get life back to normal.

Jacobs was also thinking about the schools, but not in the same way others were. After the initial shock of the hurricane damage, she saw an opportunity. The long-standing opposition to her ideas had been swept away. New Orleanians who were able to come back in the first few months would be spending their time putting their lives back together. Those who could not return quickly would be hundreds of miles away, building new, if temporary, lives for themselves. The city had no money. The center of gravity for rebuilding the city and schools therefore would be in the state capital, Baton Rouge, where, as a well-connected state board member, she already held ample power.

Yes, it would be important to get schools opened quickly, but Jacobs's thoughts extended far beyond just reopening the doors. Within days of the hurricane, and probably even before the last person evacuated, she was leading private discussions about a major overhaul of the school system.

The Options

Seemingly everyone had ideas about what to do, including national luminaries who had long pressed for school reform. The national reform leader Paul Hill was one of the first outside experts out of the gate. Less than three weeks after the storm, he published a commentary about the potential in New Orleans, describing the city as a "green field" opportunity, a chance to "re-create public education in New Orleans . . . from scratch."[13] Consistent with his work over the prior two decades, Hill proposed using "charters and contracts" with schools, not "rebuilding the old district structure." Rather than directly running schools, Hill viewed the district as analogous to financial portfolio managers who open and close schools the way they buy and sell stocks, based on their prospects for long-term success.[14] Here was a chance to put his portfolio idea into practice, really for the first time.

Then there was the Nobel Prize–winning economist Milton Friedman. He had put his ideas in print in 1955 and was ninety-three years old when Hurricane Katrina hit, but he was still actively engaged in policy debates. He presented his own advice in the *Wall Street Journal* a few months after the storm. What he said closely mirrored what he had written a half century earlier:

New Orleans schools were failing for the same reason that schools are failing in other large cities, because the schools are owned and operated by the government. Government decides what is to be produced and who is to consume its products, generally assigning students to schools by their residence. The only recourse of dissatisfied parents is to change their residence or give up the government subsidy and pay for their children's schooling twice, once in taxes and once in tuition. This top-down organization works no better in the U.S. than it did in the Soviet Union or East Germany.

On the above points, Hill and Friedman were largely in agreement. The difference came in what Friedman wrote next in his commentary:

Rather than simply rebuild the destroyed schools, Louisiana, which has taken over the New Orleans school system, should take this opportunity to empower the consumers, i.e., the students, by providing parents with vouchers of substantial size. . . . Parents would then be free to choose the schooling they considered best for their children. This would introduce competition, which is missing from the present system. It would be a move to a bottom-up organization, which has proved so successful in the rest of our society. To make competition effective, Louisiana should provide a favorable climate for new entrants, whether they be parochial, non-profit or for-profit. . . . Is there any doubt that the private market would provide schooling for children returning to New Orleans faster than the state?[15]

Hill wanted the government to remain actively involved by negotiating performance contracts with school operators, and taking other steps to ensure that markets served all students—a quasi-market or regulated market. In contrast, Friedman wanted the government's role to be limited mainly to funding schools with vouchers, writing a check to any school a family chose.[16]

Consistent with Friedman's advice, the Catholic Archdiocese of New Orleans floated a plan for the state to provide vouchers to roughly 10 percent of evacuated students to attend Catholic schools, at least temporarily. The idea might have seemed attractive in what has long been one of the most religious, and heavily Catholic, states in the country. While many states had constitutional bans on providing public funds to religious private schools, Louisiana was free to send public funds to private schools if they wished.

Mayoral takeover was another option. The idea had been floated by a prior New Orleans mayor many years earlier, and it had the advantage of shifting control out of the district while still maintaining local democratic control. Yet another proposal involved installing as a new district superintendent someone from the private firm that had been hired as the district's emergency financial manager. This was arguably the least radical proposal because it mostly continued governance through the same elected board and with the same union contract.

The reformers were in mostly uncharted territory. The only one of these ideas that had really been tried and studied before, for an entire district, was mayoral control, and the results were not promising.[17] But nothing seemed worse than going back to the old ways. Even some supporters of school districts and unions privately acknowledged the district's failing. The reformers were determined to go in a new direction. Jacobs called state superintendent Cecil Picard and said, "Cecil, we cannot let New Orleans [the district] reopen these schools."[18] He did not require persuading.

Initial Battles within the Reform Family

Three key factors would ultimately determine where the city went next: the experiences, ideas, and preferences of state political leaders, especially Jacobs; the state's legal framework for education, which made some paths easier than others; and the desperate situation the city found itself in after Katrina.

None of the key leaders was a fan of vouchers. The governor, state superintendent, and a majority of both branches of the state legislature were Democrats who, while accepting of many kinds of school reform, drew a line in the sand on this topic. Picard had pushed the charter school law through before Katrina, and the unions grudgingly accepted it, in part as a defense against vouchers.[19]

Another factor keeping vouchers at bay was rooted in some more distant history. After the Supreme Court's desegregation decision in *Brown v. Board of Education* in 1954, the state's leadership, almost all white, had tried to use vouchers to avoid desegregation.[20] Though few voucher supporters now held such overtly racist views, any serious consideration of the idea would dredge up that ugly history. The voucher proposal was also impractical, covering only a fraction of the students, and only on a temporary basis. Whether the Catholic schools, which in New Orleans served a mostly white and almost entirely upper-income student population, would be well-suited to serve an impoverished—and now even more traumatized—African American population was also in question.

With vouchers out of serious contention, two main options remained: mayoral takeover and a state-driven charter approach, akin to Hill's portfolio model. The conflict that ensued was, perhaps not coincidentally, between leaders linked to the mayor and those with power at the state level. The mayor was organizing committees to help rebuild and re-envision different aspects of the city, and he decided to appoint Tulane University president Scott Cowen to head up the education committee. While

Cowen did not have much prior experience with K–12 schooling policy, he was the highly respected president of one of the city's preeminent educational institutions, and a strong leader. That Tulane is a private organization helped insulate the committee from the usual local politics.

While Jacobs was also appointed to Cowen's committee, the two disagreed on both the process and the ultimate aims. She decided to go her own way, working with the state superintendent and her own group of advisors to modify the existing RSD legislation, so the state could take over almost all the schools from OPSB. She also knew that charter schools would likely play a substantial role in what was to come, though the extent of the charter role was unclear at that point.

Cowen agreed that going back to a traditional school district was a nonstarter, but he wanted to gather input from the community, with the aim of creating a new, still local, governing body and maintaining a significant supporting role for district staff.[21] He wanted a new board appointed by the mayor and perhaps other officials, more akin to the mayoral takeover. While agreeing that schools should have more autonomy, he worried that charter schools had obtained a bad reputation, which would undermine the effort. Partly for this reason, his committee suggested that the district combine site-based management with a substantial and traditional district role in running schools, including supporting school "capacity-building" and providing "professional development" and other "shared services."[22]

In some key respects—especially the support for school autonomy and diminishing the existing district's role—the committee's proposal aligned with those of Jacobs and her team. But the committee's plan had both educational and legal problems. First, Cowen's proposal, like that of making the emergency manager the superintendent, would have left many of the district's core elements intact. The idea of district-governed autonomous schools (site-based management) had been popular as an approach to district-based school improvement throughout the United States since the 1980s. The problem, as the critique in chapter 2 makes clear, is that school districts seem unable to give up control to schools. The pressure for districts to make rules, and to "do something" when there is a controversy, is simply too strong. Cowen's plan would also have left in place the district-wide union contract and state tenure provisions, which restricted school control over perhaps their most important decisions: those pertaining to personnel. These rules, and the potential continued meddling of districts in school affairs, would be substantially reduced under a charter model. If the goal was school autonomy, then chartering and contracting, or something similar, was arguably the only option.

The second problem with the committee's proposal was that it probably violated the federal Voting Rights Act, as it stood at that time, because the proposal involved replacing the elected school board with an unelected one, diminishing the voting power of African Americans. This meant that, at the very least, the idea would be tied up in the courts.[23]

As in most things, Jacobs got what she wanted. Her pre-Katrina reforms efforts had created a clear path to a state-driven charter school approach. The accountability system she helped design would provide the basis for performance-based contracts with schools; the charter law she supported ensured that schools would have autonomy to meet those benchmarks; and the RSD, the "authorizer" of the charter schools, could sidestep local politics and the district bureaucracy to ensure that failing schools would be replaced if they failed. In the short term, until charter organizations could be developed or recruited to come to the city, the RSD could also directly operate schools, making it easier for families to return to the city. There were no constitutional impediments to Jacobs's plan. Moreover, the Cowen committee's proposal, through it diverged from Jacobs's ideas in important respects, was based on many of the same broad principles and therefore provided political cover and credibility for the plans of Jacobs and Picard. The governor joined them, as would the legislature, by a narrow margin. Almost inadvertently, the foundation of policies created prior to the storm became the driving force of the rebuilding effort.

The improbability of all these pieces coming together is hard to overstate. One reason it happened is that key leaders operated like a family. In some cases, this was true literally. US senator Mary Landrieu worked to secure federal funding for the city as a whole and, particularly, for the school reform effort. (She had also worked with Jacobs to support the original RSD legislation before Katrina.) The senator's aunt, Phyllis Landrieu, was a member of the locally elected Orleans Parish School Board, and her brother, Mitch Landrieu, was lieutenant governor. This was a powerful family, and one that could marshal action at all levels of government, especially the state and federal levels, which wielded new power in the wake of Katrina.

The reformers also had a professional lineage in the national reform movement. The two men who would serve as state superintendent for most of the first fifteen years of the post-Katrina period, Paul Pastorek and John White, had both been heavily influenced by Joel Klein, the longtime New York City school superintendent. Klein had shaped their views prior to Katrina by advising Pastorek and hiring White into a district leadership role. White had also worked in Chicago under Arne Duncan, the future US Secretary of Education, who himself had been hired by the second RSD superintendent, Paul Vallas.[24] Klein and Teach for America were like the grandparents of the reform family. Most of the main leaders of the New Orleans reform efforts had been influenced by one or both of them.

Key leaders also rotated across reform organizations within New Orleans, reinforcing their mutual bonds. Sarah Usdin went from TFA to the new group she had been planning, eventually named New Schools for New Orleans (NSNO), and then went on to an elected position on the local school board. Patrick Dobard, later tapped by White to be RSD superintendent, would eventually become the CEO of NSNO.

With these close connections and shared outlook, the reformers were able to do something else common to powerful families: they kept their often-vociferous disagreements out of the public eye. There were battles over strategy and control, but few over basic principles or goals. Ultimately, they closed ranks and moved forward with a common purpose. Cowen, in particular, amended his committee's original proposal so that it did not directly conflict with Jacobs's ideas.

The roles of other leaders were marked less by what they did for the reform family than by what they decided not to do. Political scientists distinguish between the power to *create* things and the ability to *stop* things, that is, blocking power.[25] Leslie Jacobs and Mitch Landrieu emphasized this when I spoke with them about the reforms. One example was the state's governor at the time, Kathleen Blanco. A Democrat and former public school teacher, Blanco depended on the teacher unions and black leadership in New Orleans as key supporters; going along with the reformers meant going against her base. She could have blocked it all. Instead, two days after the hurricane, she told her staff, "This is going to be the end of the New Orleans school system as we know it. These families never even knew what to ask for—what a real school system looks like."[26]

The teacher unions represented another potential blocker. Several people I interviewed raised this issue and said that the unions could have done more to stop the reforms. A national union leader with inside knowledge of the New Orleans situation commented to me privately that a radical overhaul was very much justified. This soft opposition from the unions is partly what freed Blanco to sign all the reform bills that came across her desk. Other political leaders in her shoes might have blocked the reforms, but she embraced them.

In Jacobs, the reform family also had a matriarch to push past disputes and potential roadblocks. Over more than two decades, from setting the policy foundation before Katrina to leveraging the various elements for still-bigger changes afterward, Jacobs pressed forward and others generally followed her lead.

The Legal Architecture of Reform

With the broad strategy and vision in place, Jacobs turned to the ever-important details. She somehow had to revise the state's legal framework in a way that would address the immediate needs of the city, still in the midst of hurricane recovery, while also making the reforms sustainable, immune from future political and court challenges. She wanted to be aggressive but also had to maintain support for a state takeover of a school district in a state where local control was prized. But, having written most of the key sections of the state's education laws herself, she was well-situated to revise them.

STATE TAKEOVER OF SCHOOL GOVERNANCE. Carrying out the state takeover was not a simple matter, in part because state law at the time precluded it. The state had the power to take over individual schools, but only under certain conditions—persistent and extremely low levels of performance—that few schools yet met. Therefore, one of the first orders of business was to change the law to redefine the school performance thresholds. That would move 102 New Orleans schools from the control of the local district to the state board.[27] The RSD superintendent, selected by the BESE board and state superintendent, would run the schools in the short term and would have latitude to develop and implement a longer-range plan. Only thirteen high-performing schools were left under the control of the Orleans Parish School Board.

While the majority-Democrat legislature would mostly vote for the reform idea, its members did have qualms. Democrats tend to count on support from unions and, in a conservative state like Louisiana, to support local control. They also may have worried that the New Orleans takeover might be the start of a slippery slope that would eventually bring unwelcome reform to the schools in their own legislative districts. To appease enough of these reluctant legislators to pass the measure, the law was written to apply only to New Orleans, with the stated intent of returning the schools to district governance once they were no longer failing academically—again, fitting with Jacobs's notion of school turn-around as akin to business bankruptcy.

SHIFTING MANAGEMENT TO CHARTER SCHOOLS. With control turned over to the state, the state superintendent, Cecil Picard, announced publicly in early January 2006 what Jacobs had concluded privately: that he did not want the state to directly operate schools for long and planned to turn them into charter schools as soon as possible.[28] This was partly a matter of preference, partly of necessity. The RSD had only a handful of employees and had never operated a school before.

The RSD's limited capacity posed a problem because some in the reform family were worried about the potential for low-quality charters. Jacobs remembered her prior experience as a state board member before Katrina, when she had to shut down low-performing charters, an experience she did not want to repeat. She also recognized that opening bad charter schools would tarnish the whole reform idea. In contrast, if a school directly operated by the RSD failed, she could assert that this just reinforced the need for more charter schools.

KIPP came on board, expanding its role and opening more schools, but one charter management organization was far from sufficient. Jacobs traveled the country trying to recruit other existing national charter operators. Much of this task eventually fell to Matthew Candler who, at the time Katrina made landfall, was responsible for recruiting and developing charter school networks in New York City. (Like Pastorek and White, he had worked with Joel Klein.) Candler teamed up with Sarah Usdin to carry out this work through New Schools for New Orleans. The organization provided $100,000 fellowships to promising educators seeking to open schools in the city. In business language, NSNO was a like a small business incubator, in this case a charter incubator. Candler's aim was to attract or develop high-quality charter organizations to run most of the city's schools.[29]

While the shift to charter schools was arguably the most important step the reformers took, it was also the one that was never written into any law or policy. The RSD had the authority to operate schools directly and the authority to turn them over to charter school operators. That charter authority also allowed New Schools for New Orleans to have a large hand in setting the menu of schools for the state to choose from. The reforms therefore would be a partnership of government, nonprofit charter schools, and other nongovernmental organizations (NGOs).

FIRING TEACHERS AND ELIMINATING UNION CONTRACTS AND STATE TEACHER RULES. To a substantial degree, school reform is about one thing: rules. Perhaps the most important reason for turning the schools into charter schools was that school leaders wanted to remove what they saw as the yoke of rules regarding personnel. School leaders wanted autonomy over hiring so that they could create organizational coherence.

Union contracts, in the reformers' view, are a key impediment to effective and coherent organizations. United Teachers of New Orleans, an affiliate of the national American Federation of Teachers, had negotiated a contract in New Orleans before the hurricane that ran a bit under two hundred pages and stipulated compensation, transfer rules, staffing levels, and grievance and dismissal procedures. As in most such contracts, personnel decisions were based on seniority.[30]

Workloads and working conditions were clearly laid out. Teachers would work 204 days, each lasting six hours and forty minutes (for most teachers). Principals could request that teachers work additional hours for additional pay, but this required approval from the district office. Caps on class size varied by grade level, ranging from twenty to thirty-three students. The contract was focused on the inputs and processes of teaching, and made no mention of performance or quality.

While such provisions for working conditions, employment terms, and compensation are common to teacher contracts, the New Orleans' contract was unusually broad in other respects. Principals were discouraged from observing teachers in the classroom.[31] Teachers could not be reprimanded for coming to school late until they had been tardy ten times. Seven pages of the contract were devoted to student discipline procedures, including specifying when students with behavioral problems were allowed to participate in sports and other activities. The contract also required the district to maintain alternative schools for "chronically disruptive" students and detailed the types of staff who had to work in those schools.

Contract rules also established what could be taught and how. Schools were required to have a textbook selection committee, comprised of at least half teachers (the other half could be administrators or other staff), to choose textbooks with "a multi-cultural, multi-ethnic, and multi-racial perspective." Moreover, "teachers should provide the opportunity for students to do reflective thinking, to develop tolerance with conviction, and to reach their own conclusions after careful study of the facts in an impartial, open-minded classroom atmosphere." Individually, none of these ideas sounds objectionable, but it is not hard to see how putting them all in the contract would constrain any effort toward school improvement or innovation—especially as 70 percent of teachers had to vote to waive any contract provision.

Those old ways were about to end. When a school was taken over by the RSD, educators who taught there were no longer employed by the local district, and thus fell outside the existing union contract. The unions could try to reorganize teachers in RSD-controlled schools, but this would be much harder with the RSD planning to turn the schools over to many small charter organizations. Eventually, more than forty organizations were operating schools, and the unions would have to win teachers' support one school or employer at a time.

In theory, teachers might have retained some of the job protections ensured in union contracts via state tenure provisions, but Louisiana charter schools were not subject to these laws.[32] This meant that New Orleans teachers went from having considerable job security and autonomy over their work, to being at-will employees. Moreover, RSD charter schools were not subject to state rules requiring public schools to hire certified teachers and participate in the state pension system.

ELIMINATING ATTENDANCE ZONES AND EXPANDING CHOICE. One indirect effect of the shift to state control and charter operators was the near-elimination of the attendance zones that traditionally had assigned students to schools. Instead, the RSD allowed families to apply to any school they chose. This started more as a practical necessity than an ideological preference for a consumer-driven market. In the wake of the hurricane and rebuilding effort, attendance zones were untenable. Families were moving back into neighborhoods in unpredictable patterns. Many communities would not have schools nearby for years to come.

This practical necessity for choice fit well with the idea of providing families with more varied options. Charter schools generally aim to provide distinctive options, matching students to schools based on their specific needs. If that is the goal, then choice becomes all but essential. Students with particular interests in arts or science, for example, are unlikely to all live in one neighborhood. Choice allowed charter schools to create distinctive schools and allowed students with common interests to choose the ones that fit best. Neither Cowen nor Jacobs emphasized choice as a key principle of reform (e.g., it was not mentioned among the ten core principles in Cowen's committee report), but it was scarcely contested, among the reformers or the community at large. Traditional attendance zones would be out of the question for many years.

SCHOOL FUNDING. Money matters in schools, so funding formulas would turn out to play a key role. Unlike most states', Louisiana charter schools are funded almost exactly the same way as traditional public schools. While the formula is complex, the key point is that funding is based predominantly on the number of students enrolled. This meant that the vast majority of funding flowed to schools based on the number of students they could attract.[33] It also reinforced the marketlike nature of the reforms. When a customer takes her business somewhere else, the revenue goes too—and so it was with New Orleans schools.

Funding for school buildings works very differently. In traditional school districts, property tax levies approved directly by voters are used to fund specific building improvements. In contrast, charter schools nationally have no dedicated property tax base and therefore often have to cover building costs out of general operating funds meant for teacher salaries, textbooks, and other operating expenses. As part of the New Orleans reforms, however, the state took control over existing buildings and, years later, refurbished them, mostly using hurricane-related funding from the federal government.

The various schools in New Orleans also had the opportunity to raise private funds from philanthropists, and the charter schools were particularly successful in doing so. Overall, as I show in the next chapter, New Orleans charter schools would end up with a distinct funding advantage over charter schools nationally, and over the traditional public schools they replaced.

LOCAL DISTRICT REACTIONS. What may seem most surprising about how the reforms developed is just how readily the Orleans Parish School Board seemed to mimic the state-driven reforms—reforms designed to undermine the district model. The local district had successfully fought against these kinds of reforms before Katrina. Why not continue the fight? The short answer is that the local district was both pushed and pulled into changing.

Like Jacobs, many school principals were tired of the district's dysfunction, corruption, and failure. Principals were tired of the rules and of being embarrassed by the circus-like atmosphere of televised school board meetings. They thought they could do a better job themselves, if left to their own devices. This was exactly what charter schooling allowed them to do. Without a union contract or tenure or certification requirements, they could hire the teachers they wanted and fire those who did not work out. Some principals had been trying, just for this reason, to convert to charters even before the storm.

The practical realities of the rebuilding effort also mattered. Some principals were less worried about district and union rules per se and just wanted to get their schools opened as quickly as possible. The chartering process seemed like the fastest approach. The district had essentially shut down. It was also mired in debt and, with such poor accounting practices, had trouble securing a loan. With few resources to draw on, the already-dysfunctional district could not move at the pace that principals desired. Meanwhile, the federal government offered start-up funds to help new charter schools to get off the ground. For these reasons, many leaders of the thirteen remaining district schools quickly submitted applications to the district to turn them into separate charter schools, operated by nonprofit organizations. In years past, these applications would have been rejected, but the district now found itself in a much more vulnerable position.

The district was also forced to eliminate its own attendance zones. With only thirteen remaining district schools spread across 170 square miles of city land, any new zones would have been so large that the idea of the neighborhood school became a thing of the past. Also, many of the highest-performing schools in OPSB before the storms—the ones they maintained control over—had been magnet schools that already had district-wide choice before the hurricane. This history of parental choice, combined with the already-established shift to charter schools, made school choice the natural option.

Once the state law passed, turning almost all schools over to the state, it became clear that the local district would be a shell of its former self, with roughly 10 percent of its prior personnel levels. One of the local district's first post-Katrina steps was to place all teachers and staff on leave. Had it then hired back a small number on a seniority basis, as stipulated in the union contract, its entire workforce would have been comprised of near-retirees who were trying to put their homes and lives back together. Eventually the district fired all but a handful of teachers, and it decided not to renew the old union contract, which expired in the summer of 2006.

The OPSB's seeming willingness to play along with the reforms—firing teachers, creating charter schools, and eliminating attendance zones—was therefore driven mainly by dramatically altered circumstances, not a change of heart regarding the idea of school reform. The changes in direction were also consistent with what many of its own school principals had long sought and would help them compete against the RSD schools.

Once the wheels were in motion—especially the state takeover and shift to charter schools—momentum carried the decisions about union contracts, school choice, and everything else forward. Despite changes of leadership in the governor's mansion, state board, and state legislature, the reform family was able, over a continuous fifteen-year stretch, to maintain a slim majority of support for their ideas. This bought them time to complete the transition from the System to a charter-driven system and to create the expectation that this new reality was permanent.

There would be no "traditional public schools" in New Orleans anymore. The revolution was on.

The Market Makers: The RSD and the New Network of Reform Organizations

The New Orleans reforms were "market-based" in many respects, but that was too simple a term. Yes, families were allowed to act like consumers and schools like independent firms. The dismissal of teachers, combined with the provisions of state charter laws, meant that schools would have autonomy over personnel and working conditions. But it was the state government that expanded the supply of schools by approving and renewing school charters, renovating and managing buildings, and facilitating parent choice by eliminating attendance zones and requiring that schools provide transportation. As we will see, the Recovery School District (RSD) did that and much more. It was an active market-maker.

The state deliberately avoided key roles, however, and instead relied on NGOs. The two most obvious roles—recruiting educators and charter schools—were filled by the nonprofits Teach for America (TFA) and New Schools for New Orleans (NSNO), respectively.[34] By 2010, NSNO had incubated ten charter schools (about 30 percent of the RSD schools opened at the time). Its role would expand over time to include those typically in the purview of school districts: fundraising efforts, school improvement support, and strategic planning.

Even if NSNO succeeded in creating new and better schools, families would have to sort out which were the best fit for their children. Someone, therefore, would need to provide information to families about their schooling options. The RSD could have done this but, as a state agency, was distrusted by the local community. Also, the RSD already had plenty on its plate with repairing buildings, running some schools, and turning them over to charter operators. Instead, a local reporter and social activist, Ayesha Rasheed, stepped in to create and publish "The New Orleans Parents' Guide," available in print and online every year, starting in 2008. The Parents' Guide, too, was incubated within NSNO, though it became its own nonprofit organization.

The shift from just one organization governing and running schools to more than forty, not to mention these various other nonprofits like NSNO and Parents' Guide, also created a need for someone to facilitate a newly complex web of working relationships. Most of the people coming in to lead the system, though they may have shared some basic principles of schooling and reform, did not, in the beginning, know one another or how they would need to work together. Tulane University therefore created an institute soon after the reform laws passed that was intended to continue and extend the work Cowen had done as chair of the mayor's education committee in the hurricane aftermath. It was eventually named after him, and he played a key leadership role in its development.

The Cowen Institute leveraged the university's precious access to relatively undamaged office space after the storm, and the convening authority of someone of Cowen's stature, to house NSNO, TFA, and other emerging support organizations in Tulane office space, initially rent-free. This facilitated relationships among the variegated organizations. In addition, the institute published annual reports explaining the complexities of the reforms, bringing problems to light, and describing trends in student outcomes.

The importance of "intermediary organizations" such as these has been previously recognized in other aspects of education policy,[35] but the type, scope, and motivation for their roles were quite different in New Orleans. The RSD, a state agency, could have taken on many of these NGO roles, but did not for at least four reasons:

1   A NEW GOVERNING PHILOSOPHY. The organizing principle of the reforms was school autonomy, that is, taking day-to-day decisions out of the hands of government, and pushing them down to schools and other groups.

2   CAPACITY. The RSD had limited staff and was subject to many state and federal laws (open meeting laws, competitive bidding on contracts, etc.) that restricted what it could do. Nonprofits had more flexibility and could readily accept funds from the many philanthropists who wished to support the reform effort.

3   SELF-PRESERVATION. It was in the RSD's interest to avoid being seen as meddling in individual schools' management, and thus becoming a target for blame if something went wrong. Autonomy for the schools meant plausible deniability for the RSD.

4   CHECKS AND BALANCES. Assigning responsibilities to nonprofit organizations insulated the schools. Eventually, control over the schools would have to revert to the local district, which was still widely distrusted. Keeping some key activities out of the hands of elected officials provided a kind of insurance policy against the risk of future political opposition or new forms of political bureaucracy. The district would have to be careful because if it made a mistake, the nonprofits could step in to organize opposition or wrestle away key responsibilities. Given the historical micromanagement and mismanagement by the Orleans Parish School Board, the reformers were right to be worried.

Shared responsibility across the various organizations was, therefore, a key complement to the core principle of school autonomy. Government, NGOs, individual schools/charter management organizations, and parents all had key roles to play.

The Outsiders

The reform process was, by and large, a top-down one. It was also outside-in. Charter schools had developed in Minnesota more than a decade earlier. The ideas of national reformers like Paul Hill and others played a role in the initial concept and design. Many key leaders who emerged in New Orleans were influenced by Joel Klein, of New York City school reform fame, and the national organization Teach for America. John White and Sarah Usdin, along with much of the middle management of NSNO and the founders of KIPP, were all TFA alumni. The meetings that Usdin and others organized were like a who's who of the national reform community.[36]

The key roles played by the NGOs were funded largely by wealthy philanthropists, from Eli Broad (based in California) to Bill Gates (Washington state) to the Walton Foundation, of Walmart fame (Arkansas), all provided grants to support the work of the Cowen Institute, NSNO, and TFA.

The support of the foundations and national reform organizations was slow in coming, however. They did not initially realize the opportunity before them. New Orleans had a reputation as a reform backwater that seemed stubbornly resistant to change, which turned the reformers off. Walter Isaacson, a New Orleans native, best-selling author, and then president of the Aspen Institute, described to me a meeting of reform-oriented educators that his organization held:

> It was a full nine months after Katrina and [the attendees] were talking about creating big new flagship posts in certain cities. They were debating whether to do it in Delaware. [I said,] "Why the hell would you go to Delaware? Are you wimps? Delaware doesn't need you, and that's not the hardest mountain to climb. If you're going to do this, why wouldn't you go to New Orleans?"[37]

He was not the only one who had this type of experience. TFA pulled out for a time after Katrina and had to be persuaded to return. KIPP needed to be convinced to open more schools. Jacobs and Usdin had to win over the national reformers.

Eventually, they did come around. KIPP would come to have eight schools in the city—accounting for roughly 10 percent of total enrollment in publicly funded schools. Jon Schnur, cofounder of the national group New Leaders for New Schools, moved to the city for a time to help support the effort. The Gates and Walton foundations were joined by the Arnold and Bloomberg foundations in funding all the various reform NGOs.

The support the national foundations provided to TFA was especially important. Along with its sister organization, the New Teacher Project, TFA provided upward of 20 percent of the city's entire teacher workforce.[38] All sides recognized what research confirmed: no school reform would work without an ample supply of excellent educators who could provide what the charter leaders were looking for.

Even some of the groups that seemed local were seen as outsiders. The Cowen Institute, though based in one of the city's oldest educational institutions, was one of them. As Cowen put it, Tulane "was primarily viewed as a white, elitist, privileged place," detached from the city's majority-black and low-income population.[39] The vast majority of the university's students and faculty were not from the city or even from the South. (As we will see, this perception further complicated the research my team carried out at Tulane, which is the basis for the later discussion and analysis.)

The reforms were therefore both local and national. Jacobs, Picard, and Pastorek had built the state policy foundation, mostly independently of the national conversation. But there would have been little to build on top of that foundation if the national organizations had not brought in their alternative pipelines of educators. These motivated and talented reformers not only filled key roles but shaped the direction of the reforms, one classroom, school, and organization at a time—funded, of course, by the national philanthropists. It took all of these elements, working together and simultaneously, to make the New Orleans revolution a reality.

The Opposition

The reformers got what they wanted, at least in the short run. It was not, however, without fights. Teachers naturally opposed the idea of losing their jobs, especially to so many outsiders and especially given the financial distress they found themselves in. The local community had similar concerns. It was not just that national organizations and other nonlocals were playing a large role, but that Jacobs and the RSD sidestepped community engagement. The community had little say over what kinds of schools ended up in their neighborhoods. Some promises were made, but these were often broken. Cowen's committee had done the most, by far, to engage local citizens in the early years, but that input had little bearing on subsequent decisions. The firing of the teachers, broken promises, and general heavy-handedness of the reforms left a bitter taste in the mouths of many I spoke with, including some within the reform family.

This insider-outsider divide closely intersected with matters of race. The population of the city was 67 percent African American in 2005, and public school students were 93 percent African American.[40] The school workforce under the district system had been more than 70 percent African American.[41] In contrast, almost every name you have read so far belongs to someone who is white. While many school and charter management organization (CMO) leaders were black, it was not until some years later that Patrick Dobard—whose family had taken him out of New Orleans public schools to attend a private school—became the first African American to lead one of the citywide schooling organizations, as superintendent of the state RSD.[42]

The national African American reform leader Howard Fuller, who took a strong interest in what happened in New Orleans, also commented on the lack of black participation. The New Orleans reforms were "done to us, not with us," in his view.[43] Most of the state legislature's Black Caucus voted against the reforms. Several white leaders I interviewed heard criticism that they were engaged in "social engineering." This racial divide would prove to be a significant issue, on many levels, in what followed.

Having regained their footing and created new homes for themselves, citizens also regained their voices and got organized. Some picketed outside Jacobs's house, on the city's grand St. Charles Avenue. A new online, volunteer-based journalism group formed in part to keep closer watch over the vast array of new charter boards. With OPSB on the sidelines and no other citywide organization, the Orleans Parish Education Network (OPEN) was founded in 2007 to provide a forum and voice for change. The Southern Poverty Law Center, with a storied national history in the civil rights movement and a local office in New Orleans, brought its legal prowess and mission to serve low-income and underrepresented minorities. It was not just the reformers who had created a new infrastructure or brought in outside help.

Seeing both the supporters and the opponents, the storyline now begins to resemble one the historian David Tyack described in his book *The One Best System*. Tyack wrote about "a common theme" in the episodes of reform that led to the establishment of traditional school districts a century earlier:

> In each case, the proponents of reform were members of highly educated elites who believed that structural reforms were necessary to create efficient, rational, and "non-political" school bureaucracies. The opponents . . . tended to be those who had a political or occupational stake in the system or who viewed the reformers as snobbish intruders. In New York and San Francisco, in particular, the [reformers] managed to alienate a large proportion of the teachers by their publicity and tactics. In all of the cities, some lower-class or middle-class ethnic groups . . . spoke out against the "aristocratic" premises of the reformers . . . [many of whom] were not educated in the public schools and did not even live in the city.[44]

In other words, the System had been put in place by the same general logic and alliance of interests that were now trying to replace it. What had changed? Why did that alliance now want to overturn what it had created?

A key part of the answer is that in each era of reform, elite members of society have tried to gain more control over the schools. The creation of elected district boards a century earlier had accomplished that. But eventually social and demographic change caused the elite to lose their grip. Paradoxically, the only way to get that power back was to shift control again, this time to the states and NGOs. So, while it is sometimes said that we need to "get the politics out" of school reform, this is impossible. Even free markets have their own politics.[45] And with politics comes conflict.

A Revolutionary Reform

It was a remarkable confluence of events. The hurricane. The resulting weakening of political opposition. The desperation to get schools opened quickly and to deal with unpredictable neighborhood revitalization. The perception of crisis in the pre-Katrina schools. The preexisting foundation for reform—state charter, accountability, and RSD laws, plus ideas, people, and funding from national philanthropists and reform organizations. Jacobs, the determined leader who knew the laws and politics inside and out. Without any one of these things, the reforms might never have gotten off the ground. In every other city, reformers had to settle for incremental, piecemeal changes.

In the span of seven years, a new vision of public education took shape. The district rules that had driven traditional public schools were replaced by performance-based charter contracts. District-level employees were replaced by nonprofit charter school organizations. Union contracts and tenure protections were replaced by school leader discretion in personnel management. Attendance zones were eliminated and replaced by parental choice. Every school in the city was heavily affected, even the schools that continued to be operated directly by the local school district. The new system looked as little like the old one as could be imagined, and Jacobs had built in checks to keep it that way, shifting key responsibilities to the new network of NGOs. The abstract ideas of autonomy, choice, and accountability started to take a real and concrete form.

To national and local reformers, the New Orleans reform design was a dream come true, a much stronger version of the test-based and market-based accountability that had been employed nationally over the prior decade. Other districts had switched from elected school boards to mayoral control, experimented with small-scale voucher programs, and opened up a small number of charter schools. New York City certainly had more charter schools than New Orleans, but it's a much bigger city, so charters accounted for a much smaller share. No district had ever come close to replacing the One Best System with a performance-driven, market approach as New Orleans had just done.

When our research team first came together in 2014 the real question was this: Did it work? Given that the traditionalists and reformers saw the goals of schooling differently, what did it even mean to "work"? Would real competition take hold, or would the unusual features of the schooling market overwhelm the best of intentions? Would losing the advantages of bureaucratic school districts—the ability to efficiently co-ordinate resources, develop expertise, leverage economies of scale, and gain community support through local elections—prove too hard to overcome? Would the reform family and network of organizations be able to cooperate and overcome the harmful aspects of competition? Would new and varied schooling options emerge to meet divergent student needs? Would families have access to the new schools, or would schools fall prey to the incentive to choose some families and keep others out? Would the reformers be able to attract and retain the kinds of teachers and leaders necessary to reach their ambitious goals? Would the state RSD really hold charter schools accountable for performance, or would the old politics just be replaced with a new politics? Would it be the same thing over and over, or something truly new?

There were many questions. Since no one had ever tried this before, there were few answers. We sought to provide them.

PART 2

New Orleans Reform Effects and How They Emerged

CHAPTER 4

Results for Students

Leslie Jacobs and the reform family had engineered the most expansive overhaul of a school district the country had ever seen. Amid conditions of almost unfathomable despair and destruction, the reformers nearly eliminated the System. They then replaced it with autonomous, privately operated schools, built partly in the spirit of Milton Friedman's ideas, but more in the image of Paul Hill's government-market blueprint. The world wanted to know whether it worked, and the citizens and children of New Orleans deserved to know.

When we were first getting started on our research effort, I was of two minds about what to expect. On the one hand, I had studied school reform enough to be skeptical. At the time of Katrina, charter school effectiveness, nationally, was the same or slightly worse than that of traditional public schools.[1] Cases of apparent success were, under closer examination, either unconvincing correlations or contradicted by other evidence. Some charter schools were driven to boost scores, and there were many ways to do that. Teaching to the test, for example, could increase scores on high-stakes tests without really improving learning.

On the other hand, what was true nationally might not prove relevant to New Orleans. Some reformers made a plausible case that test-based and market-based accountability had not been more effective in the past because they had not been pursued aggressively enough.[2] Maybe the more intense reform effort in New Orleans—with all these reform pieces operating at once—would yield better results. Given the history of corruption, dysfunction, and some of the nation's worst student outcomes, the city's schools should have been fairly easy to improve. There were reasons to be optimistic, but also reasons to be pessimistic.

All school reform should be about serving students; therefore, we focused first on student outcomes and parent satisfaction. But drawing firm conclusions about these measures would be no easy task. The reforms had been instigated by the hurricane and the accompanying vacuum of local political control, making the two events—hurricane and reform—hard to separate. In the end, though, a persuasive picture emerged. The analysis that follows shows that the reforms were successful in improving every measurable outcome, from test scores to college graduation.

The Upward Trend in Student Outcomes

Before the storm, test scores and graduation rates in New Orleans were consistently at, or very near, the bottom of the state. Such low performance has been unfortunately common in urban schools across the country, especially those serving predominantly low-income, minority students, who start kindergarten with lower scores and have fewer home and community resources to help them catch up.[3]

After the reforms, however, the district's outcomes climbed quickly and steadily. As figure 4.1 shows, the district's ranking on elementary and middle school test score levels went from sixty-seventh to fortieth (out of sixty-eight regular Louisiana districts), leapfrogging twenty-seven districts. We see similar results when focusing on student growth or value-added measures. (I use these two terms interchangeably throughout the book.)

With ACT scores and high school graduation, the city's ranking improved from sixty-second to forty-second, and from sixty-third to fifty-sixth respectively.[4] The latter reflected an increase of almost 20 percentage points in high school graduation, 10 points more than the state's improvement. The college results were even more striking. Here, the district's ranking, on the percentage of high school graduates going directly to any college during the year just after high school, shot up from sixtieth all the way to tenth, reflecting a near doubling of the college-going rate. When we look at the absolute changes underlying these rankings (see figure caption), the results also look impressive.

Starting with simple statewide rankings like these is useful for three

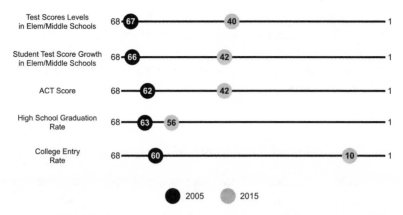

FIGURE 4.1. New Orleans's statewide rankings on student outcomes in 2005 (black circles) and 2015 (gray), before and after the reforms (based on a total of 68 districts). *Source*: Author's analysis of publicly available data; individual student anonymized files from the Louisiana Department of Education. *Notes*: Absolute increases in the underlying numbers are as follows: test scores, from 35% to 62% (basic and above, averaged across math and English language arts); ACT scores, from 17 to 18.4 points; high school graduation, from 54% to 73%; college entry, from 37% to 63%. As in other analyses, we combined results for all publicly funded schools located in New Orleans to obtain the city's results, which we compared with the other 67 traditional school districts. High school graduation is based on the state's four-year cohort graduation rate, which allows some forms of nonstandard diploma. College entry is the share of high school graduates who enroll in college immediately after high school (these results are somewhat sensitive to data source). See additional details in appendix B.

reasons. First, changes in rankings are simple to interpret. Second, rankings create comparisons with other districts that help account for statewide changes in policy and outcome measures that affect all districts. For example, students do not take exactly the same standardized test each year in elementary and middle school grades. But because the tests are standardized statewide, any changes in the tests themselves affect all students and districts—and therefore the rankings—in roughly equal ways. Third, focusing specifically on *district* rankings (i.e., all publicly funded schools in the city) is important because all schools in the district, even those left in the hands of OPSB, were heavily affected by the interconnected package of reforms (shifting to charter schools, sidelining the union, expanding school choice, and so on). For all of these reasons, the changes in district rankings provide a useful first indication of the likely effects of the reforms.

The Cowen Institute regularly chronicled results like those in figure 4.1 in its annual reports. Jacobs then funded public relations campaigns to tout the good news to the public. It was indeed an impressive start-ing point. Still, from a scientific standpoint, it was not very convincing. Though improvement had occurred on almost every available metric, correlation is not causation. We needed to dig deeper to really under-stand what caused these gains.

More Advanced Analysis and Comparison Groups

To provide more advanced and convincing analysis, and get beyond simple correlations, my colleague Matthew Larsen and I obtained data from the Louisiana Department of Education to track individual student performance (all data were anonymized; we did not have student names or any other identifying information).[5] We then applied a method called difference-in-differences, which involved comparing the trend in New Orleans to a matched sample of comparison students and districts. The intuition is that if the two groups were following the same path before the policy change, we would expect them to diverge afterward only if the New Orleans reform package had an effect. One advantage of this approach is that we can directly test the main assumption: that student outcomes in New Orleans were moving in parallel with the compari-son group before the reforms. This ensures that the comparison is truly apples-to-apples. Our analyses almost always passed this test.

Figure 4.2 provides a visualization of this method, comparing the New Orleans trends to the state as a whole. We averaged together all four main academic subjects (math, English language arts, science, and social studies) and averaged across grades 3 through 8. In our main analy-sis, we compared the average score across all subjects and grades in, say, 2005 with the average in 2015 (what we call "pooled" analysis). New Orleans (solid line) was far below the rest of the state (dashed line) be-fore Katrina, but followed a parallel path. Then, after the reforms, the city quickly started to close the gap.

In the more formal, difference-in-differences statistical analysis, we found that the reforms increased test scores by 0.39–0.45 standard de-viations, equivalent to 12–15 percentiles. (The results were similar for individual subjects.) This is a very large change by almost any standard. Usually in education research, we are pleased to find effects that are only

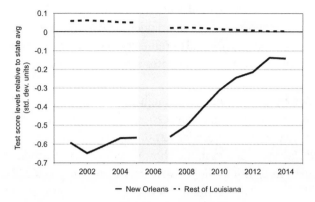

FIGURE 4.2. Positive reform effects on elementary and middle school test scores. *Source*: Douglas N. Harris and Matthew Larsen, "The Effects of the New Orleans School Reforms on Student Test Scores, High School Graduation, and College Graduation." *Notes*: As is typical in analyses of test scores, we standardized students' scale scores to a mean of zero and standard deviation of one by grade, subject, and year. The negative numbers for New Orleans, especially in the early years, therefore mean that New Orleans was far below the state average. The results for the rest of the state hover near zero mainly because of the way the tests were standardized.

one-tenth this size. These analyses are also consistent with the changes in state rankings shown in figure 4.1.

One reason we might question the results in both figures 4.1 and 4.2 is that New Orleans is quite different from the rest of the state. We can already see this in how far New Orleans was below the state on test score levels prior to Katrina (in figure 4.2). The city also had much higher poverty and lower test scores than the comparison group. We therefore carried out additional analysis limiting our comparison group just to public schools outside New Orleans that had test levels similar to those in New Orleans in the pre-Katrina period. Since New Orleans was affected by Katrina more than other districts, we also limited the comparison group to other hurricane-affected districts. This helped us create the most similar comparison group possible—again, apples-to-apples. This more rigorous matched version of the difference-in-differences method almost always yields the same pattern of positive effects shown in figure 4.2.

We also carried out a version focusing just on students who returned to New Orleans after the storm (as opposed to the above pooled approach, where we studied all students in the city's schools each year, regardless of whether they had attended New Orleans schools prior to Katrina). These alternatives also reinforce the positive impression provided by figure 4.2, and the estimates are almost always statistically significant.

Studies by other scholars, though focused on somewhat different questions, provide a similar impression of New Orleans test scores and place the city within a broader national perspective. Sean Reardon of Stanford University has examined how much students learned on average from fourth to eighth grade, by district, during the years 2009 to 2015. His results, covering essentially all districts in the United States, show New Orleans in the top twenty nationally among the two hundred largest school districts.[6] An analysis by another group at Stanford is similarly positive, placing New Orleans in the top six urban districts (of forty-one considered).[7] These analyses by other researchers did not compare the pre- and post-reform periods to see whether this was a result of school improvement, but the national comparisons do at least suggest that New Orleans students are learning relatively rapidly in the post-reform schools.

The effects for high school graduation are also large and positive. Once again, we find New Orleans and the comparison group following a parallel path prior to the reforms, and afterward see an upward break of 3–9 percentage points in the city (figure 4.3). For most of the estimates, our effects are, again, statistically significant and meaningful in size.[8]

The pattern for graduation rates is somewhat different than that for test score results, starting with an immediate spike, followed by a peak and then a plateau. The initial spike is understandable. In contrast to test scores, each graduate is the product of many years of schooling. On-time graduation for the 2007–2008 cohort of tenth graders, for example, was the spring of 2010, so the 2008 effect in the figure reflects students spending several years in post-reform schools. (The fact that we need several years of data to calculate a single high school graduation rate also explains why there is a gap in the figure from 2004 to 2007.)

Positive results also emerge for college entry. In this case, we start with cohorts of twelfth graders and calculate the percentage who enrolled in any college in the year after high school. Figure 4.4 shows an 8–15 percentage point effect for on-time college attendance. As with the

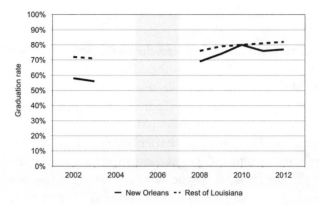

FIGURE 4.3. Positive reform effects on high school graduation. *Source*: Harris and Larsen, "Effects of the New Orleans School Reforms." *Notes*: We use the state definition of high school graduation in this figure but apply it to first-time tenth graders instead of the usual ninth graders to show the pre-reform trend. The results for other definitions are similar, though sometimes smaller and sometimes less precisely estimated. See appendix B for details.

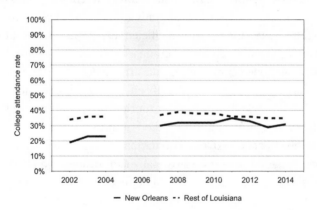

FIGURE 4.4. Positive reform effects on college entry. *Source*: Harris and Larsen, "Effects of the New Orleans School Reforms." The analysis uses data from both the Louisiana Board of Regents and the National Student Clearinghouse, provided by the Louisiana Department of Education. *Notes*: The figure shows the percentage of twelfth graders who entered college the fall following high school graduation.

high school graduation results, these seem to reflect a relatively fast initial effect.

The increases in college entry are driven almost entirely by changes in attendance of four-year colleges. The effects on two-year college enrollment are almost exactly zero, reflecting that the reforms induced some students to shift from two-year to four-year colleges and a roughly equal number to attend two-year colleges instead of no college.

One potential concern with charter schools is that, while they might help get students into college, students might not be prepared to succeed there. This has been a particular concern with "no excuses" schools (discussed in chapter 5) because students who learn in strict environments, even if well prepared academically, might not develop the skills they need to live, work, and study independently. Should they get into college but then drop out, they might be saddled with debt but still lack a degree that could help them get good jobs.

Ultimately, then, we might be most interested in the effects of the reforms on college persistence and graduation. This is harder to assess at this point because students had insufficient experience under the reforms until at least the 2010 high school graduating class, and we only have data through 2014. Given how long it takes the average entering student to graduate college, we can only identify effects for cohorts who came back to New Orleans quickly—and who experienced the reforms only in their early phases and only for a short period of time.

Still, the effects on college graduation were positive, in the range of 3–5 percentage points (and statistically significant). We also examined measures of college persistence. The effects on the percentage of students who had at least two or four years of college were 8 and 4 percentage points, respectively. While these effects might seem small, the fact that New Orleans was performing so poorly to start with means that the numbers are fairly large in relative terms. College outcomes improved by 25–36 percent over pre-Katrina levels. See appendix B for more details on all of the analysis above.

These results do suggest that some of the additional students entering college did not finish. Ashana Bigard's daughter was among them:

> She's doing okay, but she's not where she should be. She stopped college in the middle—because my mom got cancer—to help take care of

my mom. . . . She hasn't finished college yet, and she's twenty-four. She should've finished.[9]

As is often the case with college noncompletion, her daughter's situation seemed driven more by personal difficulties than poor academic preparation or college quality; many New Orleans students, with high levels of poverty, had more to overcome. The post-reform schools were apparently more effective in overcoming these challenges, but they did not always succeed either.

Overall, these results corroborate the sharp increases in New Orleans's district rankings shown in figure 4.1. The figures suggest that the reforms increased test scores by 12–15 percentiles, high school graduation by 3–9 percentage points, college entry by 8–15 percentage points, and college graduation by 3–5 percentage points. This combination of results is noteworthy, suggesting that schools were able to increase the level of academic challenge while keeping students more engaged and motivating them to continue their formal education. Past research on school choice, and other outcomes, has tended to find effects on one outcome but not others.[10] Given prior evidence on the long-term life success of high school and college graduates, these results further suggest that New Orleans students might expect somewhat higher levels of income, employment, voting, health, and happiness later in life. Observing such long-term outcomes will of course have to wait until the students get older.

Effects on Disadvantaged Groups

The reforms produced measurable improvements *on average*, but what about equity? Were some groups left behind? One prediction of the market theory, noted in chapter 2, is that schools have incentives to select students—to skim the cream—and that the requirement that all students go to school somewhere means competition will be muted and disadvantaged students will be left in low-performing schools. On the other hand, the elimination of neighborhood attendance zones gives disadvantaged students a chance to escape failing schools.

The equity story appears positive as well, though it is more complex because equity can be defined in different ways and for different student groups. Here, we focus mainly on the achievement gaps between whites and blacks, and low- and higher-income families (where income is measured by eligibility for free or reduced-price lunches). Moreover, we measure these gaps at two different levels: comparing New Orleans African American students to white students both in New Orleans and statewide.

Achievement gaps declined or remained the same on all but two of the twenty-four measures and methods we investigated. In the pooled analysis (similar to figures 4.2–4.4), we found that the gaps declined for both black and low-income students using achievement scores, high school graduation, and college entry (regardless of the comparison group). The only case where we saw an increase in the gaps was with some of the test scores. While returning African Americans and low-income students saw increases in their scores, they were not as large as for white and higher-income students within the city. Still, the large majority of the analyses suggest a reduction in achievement gaps related to race and income.

We also saw positive effects for students with disabilities, though these are more tenuous for two reasons.[11] First, whether students are labeled "special education" is determined by the schools themselves, and the reforms apparently changed how they did this: after the reforms, schools were less likely to assign students to special education. To address this, we identified students labeled as special education prior to the reforms and compared their outcomes after the reforms (regardless of whether they were labeled special education in the post-reform period). Our results suggest that the reforms also improved outcomes for students with disabilities across the various analyses.

A second challenge is that special education students sometimes take different tests than other students, and these alternative assessments changed over time. This is more difficult to address, but our various methods to account for this, again, reinforce the positive effects for this group.

Alternative Interpretations and Explanations

Though we went to great lengths in the above analyses to provide valid estimates, there were still reasons to be concerned about whether these effects were real. New Orleans student outcomes could have improved for reasons other than the school reforms: population change, problems with outcome measures due to high-stakes accountability, or the effects of evacuation schools. I summarize our analyses of these issues below and leave some additional detail to the appendices.

POPULATION CHANGE. Researchers often, and rightfully, worry that the people participating in the programs they are studying differ from those who do not participate—sometimes called self-selection. A unique version of this problem emerges in this case because the hurricane not only induced school reform but may have reshaped the city's population. Everyone left. Some returned. It was easier for wealthier families to come back to the city. While 80 percent of the city flooded, the lowest-lying neighborhoods were hit hardest, and it will come as no surprise that these areas had lower family incomes. The public housing projects for poor families—including the one Ashana Bigard grew up in—were shut down, bulldozed, and eventually replaced with a much smaller number of low-density housing units—which were not available for many years. Other families and their children came to New Orleans for the first time as part of the rebuilding effort. Given what we know about how poverty influences families and communities, and how all of this affects student outcomes, there was good reason to worry that the city's scores had gone up, not because of the reforms, but because the city's lowest-scoring students did not return.

We carried out several types of analyses to test for the influence of such demographic shifts. First, we used data from the Louisiana Department of Education on the percentage of students from families with incomes low enough to be eligible for the federal free or reduced-price lunch program, a common marker of poverty. Second, given limitations in this measure of poverty, we worked with the US Census Bureau to obtain detailed data on households with children attending publicly funded schools. Third, we considered analyses of census data by other researchers, focusing on the percentage of students in extreme poverty. In all of the above cases, we examined the data both before and after the storm and relative to the comparison groups, just as we did for student outcomes.

The fourth, and perhaps strongest evidence, came from the pre-Katrina scores of each individual student who returned versus the scores of those who did not return. If low-income and low-scoring students were less likely to return (because of heavier flooding or the closing of housing projects, for example), then the returning students should have had higher pre-Katrina scores. They did not. Since we are interested in how population change might have affected test scores, then the best evidence comes from looking not at demographics but at the scores themselves.

Fortunately, all four of the above analyses point to the same conclusion: changes in the student population had minimal influence on the changes in test scores, high school graduation, and college entry. Even in cases where it looks like population change might explain some of the changes, it is a small fraction, less than 10 percent, of the cumulative effects we report—and some of the analyses even suggest that we may be understating the reform effects on student outcomes.

After further examination, we learned more about why the public school population changed so little. Hurricane Katrina flooded 80 percent of the city and hit both the black middle-class and low-income population very hard. In the nonflooded areas, the vast majority of children attended private schools. So, yes, the number of very-low-income students dropped, but this had little impact on the average characteristics of students attending publicly funded schools. Also, while the public housing projects were shut down, they were replaced with an even larger number of federal housing vouchers.

Prior research on charter schools nationally had also raised concerns that individual charter schools select their preferred students or, for example, suspend students who are pulling down the schools' scores or disrupting their learning environments. Such practices could give a false appearance that the reforms improved student outcomes. What makes New Orleans different, however, is how comprehensive the reform was. We include all of the city's publicly funded schools in our analyses and look at the district as a whole. Any given school may select and push out students, but not a whole city.

In short, the results shown in the figures are not due to change in the population of students attending New Orleans schools. The results of these analyses are discussed further in appendix A.

PROBLEMS WITH STUDENT OUTCOME MEASURES. One of the greatest challenges to evaluating any high-stakes accountability is that the stakes themselves can distort the results. As the social scientist Donald Campbell wrote, "The more any quantitative social indicator is used for social decision-making, the more subject it will be to corruption pressures and the more apt it will be to distort and corrupt the social processes it is intended to monitor."[12] Translation: high-stakes accountability can lead to misleading numbers and counterproductive responses by educators, such as teaching to the test. In New Orleans, performance contracts based on state-determined School Performance Scores created high stakes for charter schools and therefore the potential for distorted metrics.

Practices such as teaching students how to answer particular types of questions and drilling test questions appear to be widespread in New Orleans. Every charter teacher and leader I spoke with readily acknowledged this. The debate in the city was not whether teaching to the test occurred but whether it was harmful. Teaching math, reading, science, and social studies are schools' main objectives, and the tests are designed to measure how well they have done—a message only reinforced by state education and political leaders. Those I spoke to saw teaching to the test as doing their jobs, despite the questionable educational benefits for students.[13] Education scholars such as Daniel Koretz have been especially persuasive about the problems with how schools have responded to the era of high-stakes testing.[14]

It is difficult to directly observe teaching to the test, however, because we cannot easily see what teachers do in the classroom. But we could study a much more extreme action that might result from the high-stakes measures: cheating. Some cheating scandals did emerge in a few New Orleans charter schools during 2006–2012. However, our analysis suggests the share of test scores distorted by cheating is quite small and similar to other districts. The outside company that processes the tests, and looks for patterns suggestive of cheating, threw out 684 tests from New Orleans during the 2008–2014 period, out of a total of roughly half a million. The proportion of tests thrown out by the testing company for questionable patterns was no different for New Orleans than for the rest of the state.

Test scores are not the only measures subject to accountability and distortion. For high schools, graduation rate receives almost 50 percent of the weight in overall performance measures. What David Campbell wrote about the distortion of high-stakes measures—called Campbell's Law—might apply here as well. However, we see no evidence that it did. Even when we assumed the "worst-case scenario" for data distortion, the estimated effects of the reforms on high school graduation look very much like figure 4.3.

The college results are most convincing, and least likely to be distorted, for two reasons. First, schools are not held accountable for these measures. Second, it would be very difficult for schools to distort data about each student's college enrollment—because these data are reported by the colleges, not the schools. High schools cannot "teach to college attendance" the way they can teach to the test. The 8–15 percentage point increase in college entry, and positive effects on college graduation, are therefore among the most important results of all. These effects are also especially meaningful because college attendance and graduation are perhaps the strongest predictors of a wide range of students' life outcomes.

As with the analysis of the student population, we see no evidence that distorted outcomes caused the effects we observed earlier. The test score results were likely inflated to some degree, but the fact that we saw positive effects on all of the outcomes suggests the overall improvements were real.

EVACUATION SCHOOL EFFECTS. Another theory is that the improved scores were due to the quality of schools students attended during their evacuation from the city. Students left for a minimum of four months, and for most this stretched for a year or more. If New Orleans schools were really so bad pre-Katrina, then the schools that students attended elsewhere, in their temporary homes, could have helped them catch up and raised their scores when they returned, giving the false impression that it was the New Orleans schools that had caused such growth.[15] This theory is easy to reject, however. In general, when programs improve student outcomes, the effects wear off, or fade out, over time once the program has ended.[16] Figure 4.2 shows no such fade-out in our data—the effects continued to grow for years after students returned. To be clear, the evacuation schools were better than the pre-reform New Orleans schools, but the pattern of results still suggests that this cannot explain the longer-term positive effects. This explanation, too, could be crossed off the list.

NATIONAL COMPARISONS. Even though all the above evidence suggests that what we see in the above figures reflects causal effects on meaningful academic outcomes, the results still can be interpreted differently. As I pointed out in chapter 1, New Orleans was at or near the bottom in Louisiana before Katrina, so even significant improvements do not necessarily mean that New Orleans children are now "doing well" academically.[17] Louisiana has itself long been one of the lowest-performing states in the country and has had a relatively low bar for proficiency. Once we account for this, and adjust the earlier test results for how Louisiana stands relative to other states, it appears that the reforms moved the average New Orleans student from roughly the 22nd to the 37th percentile nationally.[18] So clearly, New Orleans students have a long way to go.

Still, this argument cuts both ways. The fact that they were doing so poorly to start with only reinforces the flaws of the schools when they were under the Orleans Parish School Board. If improvement were so easy from this low baseline, the old district should have been able to accomplish it on its own.

The Role of Increased School Spending

The basic theory of the New Orleans reforms was that giving schools autonomy over personnel and other matters and giving families choice would force charter schools to compete for customers in the same way that private companies do. As we will see later, that did happen, but something else changed too. Operating spending increased 14 percent in the city compared with similar, non-reform school districts in the state.[19] The increased funding was a consequence of an increase in federal revenues, property values, and philanthropic donations (in order of size).

Even those most skeptical about the value of school spending would probably admit that a 14 percent increase in funding should have at least some impact on student outcomes. But how much of the improvement in student outcomes could be attributed to funding, as opposed to the reforms? To answer this, we began with the extreme case and examined the largest rigorously estimated effects we could find in other research. One study suggests, for example, a spending increase of this size could have an effect on high school graduation similar to what I report in figure 4.3.[20]

The effects observed in New Orleans were, however, mostly larger than we might predict from most such studies. Also, the prevalence of school district dysfunction and corruption meant that New Orleans schools were much less effective in translating resources into outcomes in the pre-reform period than were the schools in these other studies. We

measured how efficient the district was by estimating the student achievement growth of the district and comparing this to the spending difference. Like the other measures in figure 4.1, New Orleans started near the
bottom of the state (66th of 68) on student growth, even though it was
near the state average on spending—low growth with average resources.
This means New Orleans used its resources inefficiently, so simply adding
more resources, without the reforms, probably would not have helped as
much as in other districts.

Whatever the effect of these dollars, the funding itself was at least
partially an *effect* of the reforms. The reforms improved perceptions of
publicly funded schools in polling data (see below) and we see increased
electoral support for funding in post-reform school millage elections.[21]
The increase in local spending also came from rising property values,
which prior research suggests are partly driven by school quality. One of
the great strengths of school districts over the past century has been their
ability to garner enough support from citizens to contribute tax dollars,
and that appears to hold true with these reforms as well.[22]

School spending likely caused some of the increase in outcomes, but
it seems very unlikely that it was the main cause.

Other Outcomes: Parent Satisfaction

One of the arguments for giving parents more choice is that they know
more about their children's needs than anyone else and should have the
freedom to decide what is in their children's interests. Following this
logic, the focus on test scores and other academic measures may paint a
misleading picture. Research is clear that parents care about many school
attributes and outcomes beyond test scores.[23]

To address this, we considered surveys of New Orleanians about the
reforms. The Cowen Institute carried out seven surveys between 2009
and 2017. While many were of voters, most of whom did not have children in the public schools, several reports included results just for parents. Three key patterns emerge in these results.

Parents reported, first, that the reforms had improved local schools.
In 2009, 66 percent of New Orleans parents supported the state takeover,
with only 21 percent opposed.[24] Support was strongest among those who
had the most direct experience with the new kind of schools; parents of

children attending the city's charter schools reported more improvement and gave the schools higher letter grades.[25]

Support for the reforms has also largely tracked the upward trajectory in test scores. The percentage of all parents reporting that the schools were better after the reforms increased from 31 percent in 2009 to 66 percent in 2011, and remained fairly steady in later years.[26] Support was even higher when parents were asked whether the schools are "getting better" (instead of "are better"), especially among families with children attending publicly funded schools.[27] In 2011, 74 percent of all parents—and 79 percent of charter parents—reported that the schools were getting better over time.

The black community, however, remained split. This went beyond just anecdotes, like the divergent views of Ashana Bigard and Patrick Dobard. It was not until 2015, ten years after the reforms, that more black adults in the city thought the schools were better after the reforms (32%) than thought the schools were worse than before (27%).[28] Support in the black community is stronger, however, when we consider specific elements of the reforms. For example, 59 percent of black adults in New Orleans agreed that charter schools represented the best option for taking over and improving failing schools.[29]

While there is clearly a divide, a key point here is that overall parent (and voter) perceptions have tracked with student outcomes. This reinforces the conclusion that the improvement was real, and not just a misplaced emphasis on narrow and distortable academic measures. It also helps explain why the reform leaders were able to maintain much-needed political support for the controversial policy, and to continue putting more funding into it.

Proof of Concept for the Reforms

If the only goal of the reforms had been better results for typical measurable academic outcomes, then the reforms would have to be judged a great success. Effects of this size—12-15 percentiles in test scores, 3-9 percentage points on graduation rates, 8-15 percentage points for college attendance, and 3-5 percentage point effects on college graduation—are highly unusual, especially for an entire school district, over such a short period of time. Jacobs and the reformers had taken tens of thousands of impoverished students from the bottom of the state to near, or above, the state average on key metrics. Surveys suggest, too, that parents mostly believed in what educators were doing for their children.

Our analyses largely rule out alternative explanations. The cause was not the change in the population—the average scores of the returning students were actually lower than the average of the entire pre-reform population. It was not problems with the outcome measures—the improvement on such a wide range of metrics, and especially rates of college attendance, rules this out. The cream-skimming and evacuation school explanations also appear implausible. The main potential factor confounding the analysis is school spending. While this no doubt contributed to the improvement, the inefficiency of the system prior to the reforms calls into question how large an effect spending would have had on its own, and whether there would have been public support to put more funds into a failing system.

These results could even understate how much schools had improved. The experiences of New Orleans students after Hurricane Katrina were horrific. Even those who were able to flee the city in time lost their possessions and homes. It is likely that the majority of families knew someone who had died in the hurricane. Three of the most stressful things that people can experience are the death of a friend or loved one, moving residences, and loss of employment.[30] Most New Orleans families, especially the lower-income families whose children were concentrated in public schools, experienced all of these at once.

It was not just stressful, but traumatic. Psychologists who studied New Orleans evacuees reported evidence of post-traumatic stress disorder, in children as well as adults.[31] Studies of other children experiencing traumatic events have found that trauma diminishes student learning.[32] At the very least, the hurricane was disruptive. Research shows that switching schools or changing homes tends to reduce student learning, at least in the short run.[33] Perhaps for this reason, a survey of teachers who had taught in both the pre- and post-Katrina schools report that students' "home resources," broadly defined, were worse after the storm than beforehand.[34]

The reformers had gotten their first wish when New Orleans adopted and implemented this first-of-its-kind full-scale reform. They now had their second wish: their efforts had improved results for students by almost any measure. They had their proof of concept. At least in this case, replacing the system of school districts, unions, and attendance zones with choice for families, and autonomy and accountability for schools, had generated considerable measurable improvement. Given the mixed results across the country that had preceded the New Orleans revolution, this came as a pleasant surprise.

Still, the results left many questions. The reforms worked by almost any measure, but it is important to also ask why. The shift from district to autonomous charter management, the high stakes of the charter contracts, the replacement of attendance zones with parental choice, the changes in the educator workforce—which mattered most in explaining the vast improvements in measurable outcomes? How did these many factors fit together? Were schools competing, innovating, and creating variety to fit student needs? Were there unintended consequences not captured by these typically measured outcomes? Answering these questions—the focus of the next chapters—allows us to get under the surface and extract lessons about whether, when, where, and how to design and carry out reforms elsewhere.

CHAPTER 5

Structured Teaching and Businesslike Management

For educators, debates about districts, markets, and competition can be frustrating because they are so detached from what happens in schools and classrooms. Clearly, the upper reaches of school governance in New Orleans had been transformed—with school choice and school autonomy, but this fact would be irrelevant if it did not affect which educators lead classrooms, how they think, and what experiences they provide for children.

A common theme in education research, however, is that school reforms typically have little impact on classrooms. Reform efforts are usually modest, with little attention paid to sustained implementation or to the many strong forces affecting the work of teachers.[1] We should expect small policies to have small effects. Even with larger policy shifts, carried out with fidelity, each level of the system—from state departments of education down to districts and schools—buffers the ones below from undesirable changes, like umbrellas protecting each other from the rain.[2] Given that teachers under the System have considerable job security, it is no surprise when educators respond to reform by saying, "This, too, shall pass."

What happens, however, with a complete system overhaul? No one had ever seen anything quite like the New Orleans reforms. The local district had fired all the teachers and allowed the union contract to expire. With this new set of policies, the new charter management organizations (CMOs) had almost free reign to hire, fire, evaluate, compensate, develop, lead, and manage teachers as they pleased. Buffering teachers was not an option this time. The umbrellas had been removed.

Educators embody what we value in education, therefore, this chapter starts by examining how the New Orleans reforms affected *who* worked in schools before and after the reforms and what resources were available to them. Were additional resources pushed into the classroom by hiring more teachers and fewer administrators, as many reformers had argued for? What were the new teachers' backgrounds? How did the autonomy granted to schools over personnel decisions affect management? How were teachers evaluated and paid? Were teachers accountable in ways that the reformers, long critical of the job security and single salary schedules of the System, had talked about? If so, how would this affect learning and work environments? In the end, how innovative, or at least different, was the classroom experience after the reforms compared with the System that preceded it, and what were the side effects for the learning and work environments?

The answers to these questions, like everything else in New Orleans, vary across the disparate schools that emerged. Some schools went one way, some another, but even the averages changed quite a lot. The reforms changed schools and classrooms not just marginally but in a way that reflected a different educational philosophy. Teaching became more regimented and focused on basic academics. Management became more businesslike and focused on specific and measurable goals.[3] This generated the effects intended by reformers, but also effects feared by traditional public schools.

More Spending on Management, Less on Instruction

To understand most organizations, a good rule of thumb is to follow the money. If critics of traditional public schools were right, we would expect charter schools to spend less money on administration and bureaucracy and push more funding into the classroom, toward teachers. If, on the other hand, critics of charter schools were right, we would expect charter school leaders profiting from their work with higher salaries. On this count, the evidence seems to side with charter opponents.

In chapter 4, I reported results from analyses using a before-and-after comparison group approach (difference-in-differences) that showed total

New Orleans spending increased by 14 percent. If this increase had been evenly spread across spending categories, we would expect the same percentage change in administration, instruction, and other categories. But this is not at all what we see. On a per-pupil basis, *administrative spending increased by almost 66 percent*, five times more than we would have expected given the increase in total operating spending.[4]

Digging deeper, we found that half of the increase was due to a rise in total administrator salaries, and that roughly two-thirds of that was due to higher salaries per administrator. For example, school leaders saw their salaries increase by 25 percent, from just under $100,000 to $125,000 (figure 5.1a). (These and all other dollar figures in the book are adjusted for inflation, using the most recent year available.) The number of administrators also roughly doubled (figure 5.1b). Charter schools were hiring more managers and paying them higher salaries.

The increase in administrative spending is not very surprising, though, when we reconsider the peculiarities of the schooling market and some of New Orleans's specific policies. Every organization running schools needs its own accounting system, legal department, information technology system, and so on—the fixed costs of running schools. Before the reforms, a single organization, the district, carried out these activities and took advantage of economies of scale. After the reforms, more than forty different CMOs and stand-alone charters were running schools, meaning that these costs were incurred by each organization; the total cost was not quite forty times as much, but still many times more.[5] This is probably why other studies have also found higher administrative spending in charter schools.[6]

One necessary response to the economies-of-scale problem was to hire more managers. Another was to force school leaders to take on additional responsibilities. As one school leader said:

> I am the principal. I am the superintendent. I am the human resource director. I have a lot of hats. At times, it can be quite challenging.[7]

Increased responsibilities might explain the higher salaries, though, with more administrators working under them, school leaders also had more people to delegate to.

Remarkably, even with the increase in total spending, instructional spending *declined*, by almost the same dollar amount that spending on

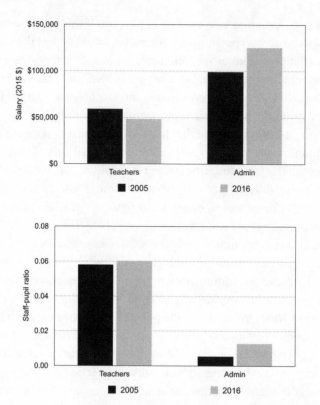

FIGURE 5.1A–B. The shift in resources to administration (changes in salary and staff-pupil ratio, by staff category). *Source*: Analysis of data from the Louisiana Department of Education with Jane Arnold Lincove. *Notes*: For the post-reform period, it was difficult to determine who the school leader was, as distinct from the CMO leader. In general, we took the highest-paid person in each school. In figure 5.1a, the post-reform numbers are only for stand-alone charter schools. This likely understates the actual average salary because our other data indicate that CMOs pay their administrators higher salaries for most positions. All salaries are in 2016 inflation-adjusted dollars and exclude fringe benefits and pension contributions. Due to some anomalies in the data, I averaged staff ratios over the years 2003–2005 to obtain the pre-reform results, and used the administrator-to-student ratio for 2015 instead of 2016.

administration increased. The story here is not the reverse of the administrator analysis, however. While the decline in instructional spending is due partly to reduced teacher salaries, schools in fact hired slightly more teachers (again, relative to the number of students).

Much of the decline in instructional spending was due to a state policy that allowed charter schools to opt out of the state pension system.[8] In addition to making contributions for current teachers, many states have struggled with the legacy costs of past generations of retirees. To cover these costs, the Louisiana state pension system charged traditional public schools 27 percent of salaries for pension costs in 2014, a large percentage of total instructional costs. Charter schools were not required to participate in the state pension system, nor to provide any other form of retirement benefits, except for payments of 6 percent into the federal Social Security system, a net savings of 21 percent.[9] Some charter schools participated in the state pension system voluntarily and others made voluntary contributions to defined contribution programs, but the overall effect was still to reduce instructional spending. Rather than shifting these saved funds into the classroom, schools moved more funds out.

The net effect, then, was that the city's charter schools were able both to hire more managers and pay them higher average salaries *and* hire more teachers. How was this possible? It was the combination of the 14 percent increase in total funding, reduced pension costs, and one other key factor yet to be considered.

Teachers: Young, Inexperienced Outsiders

Revolutions, as we saw in chapter 3, are not made by committee. Apparently, they are not made by older, more experienced educators either. Figure 5.2, based on my research with Nathan Barrett, shows that the percentage of New Orleans teachers with considerable experience declined by at least 20 percentage points in just a few years. The same drop occurred in the share of teachers with high certification levels.

Given that teaching experience is, according to research, virtually the only measurable factor associated with teacher performance, hiring young and experienced teachers seems like a strange way to improve schools. Experience matters—in all jobs, not just teaching—because people learn by doing. In their first attempt, teachers have to figure out how to keep their classrooms orderly, create or adapt lesson plans, choose and find the necessary instructional materials and equipment, learn school rules, develop relationships with colleagues, and learn everything that cannot easily be taught in the classroom and university textbooks. The job gets easier, and teacher performance improves considerably in the second year, and more gradually thereafter, for ten years or more.[10] At that point, more experienced teachers are, on average more effective

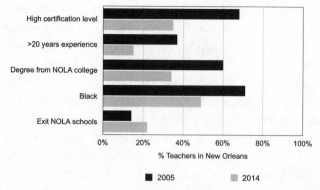

FIGURE 5.2. Significant changes in the teacher workforce. *Source*: Nathan Barrett and Douglas N. Harris, "Significant Changes in the New Orleans Teacher Workforce" (Education Research Alliance for New Orleans, Tulane University, 2015). *Notes*: This analysis is based on teacher-level data for New Orleans from the Louisiana Department of Education. "High certification level" refers to the A and B certification levels used by the state; C-level, temporary, other, and no certification are counted as low certification. "Exit NOLA Schools" reflects the annual percentage of New Orleans teachers who stopped teaching in New Orleans publicly funded schools, some of whom continued teaching in a public school in other districts, in private schools, or out of state.

and can also pass on their hard-earned wisdom to the next generation of younger teachers and play leadership roles as department chairs and mentors.

The reduction in instructional spending, and hiring of younger teachers, did, however, fit with the increase in administrative spending. With younger temporary teachers, schools would need to spend more time and money on, for example, teacher recruiting, feedback, and professional development. All of these additional efforts required more administrator time. School leaders would have more responsibility over a wider range of tasks, so schools spent accordingly—on administration.

The spending shift from instruction to management was therefore logical in some respects, but combined with other changes, it rankled reform critics. It was bad enough teachers lost their jobs for reasons unrelated to individual performance and at a time when many were in a state of personal crisis due to hurricane damage, but then to spend less on teachers made it seem like reform leaders were profiting on the backs of a local community that was struggling to rebound.

Post-reform New Orleans teachers were not just younger, but differed from the pre-Katrina workforce in almost every measurable way.

After Katrina, New Orleans became an attractive destination for young people looking to change the world and its schools. It had always been a magnet for young people, especially musicians, artists, and restaurateurs. Now, it was also cool to be in New Orleans as a national hub—the Silicon Valley—of school reform.

Once the city started to get back on its feet and it was safe for people to return, applications for teaching positions poured in, not just from pre-Katrina teachers trying to get their jobs back, but people from all over the country.[11] The result, also shown in figure 5.2, is that the percentage of teachers who were black or had degrees from one of the many New Orleans–area universities dropped by more than 25 percentage points. Black teachers, once a strong majority in the city's public schools, were now a slight minority.

Given these changes, it is unsurprising, as the bottom comparison in figure 5.2 shows, that teacher turnover nearly doubled after the reforms. Basic labor economics teaches us that turnover is highest among adults who are young, have little training, and do not live near family.[12] Young people are not well informed about the world of work, least of all in the first job they try. This combination of low experience and higher turnover is common in charter schools nationally.[13]

The New Orleans reform-oriented leaders reduced teacher experience, certification, and local roots, all at the same time. This allowed schools to reduce teacher salaries and instructional costs. More importantly, it transformed the community of educators.

A New and Younger Generation of Business-Minded Leaders

To see why the teacher workforce changed so dramatically, we need to look at who did the hiring. At least half of school leaders, and many others leading the network of nonprofits, had worked their way up as teachers through Teach for America. In addition to the higher salaries, the titles given to those in key leadership positions were not those long associated with education, like principal and superintendent, but rather the titles of business leaders. They were "CEOs." New Schools for New Orleans (NSNO), a key cog in the new model, was seen as a charter school "incubator," a term normally used for organizations facilitating business start-ups. These leaders read not educational philosophers like John Dewey or Michel Foucault but, more often, business books like *Good to Great*, which describes the characteristics of companies that succeed or fail.[14] This new breed of education leader followed in the business footsteps of the reform architects.[15] Jacobs had first gotten involved as a volunteer through her business and had also modeled the RSD on private-sector bankruptcy courts. "I am fundamentally a businessperson,"[16] she commented, readily acknowledging that her expertise was in law and finance (and, we might add, politics), not teaching and learning. The same can be said of Cowen, who had risen through the ranks as a business professor.

In the pre-reform system, few teachers became school principals before their own children were twenty years of age or older—being a principal was simply too time-consuming for those with school-age children to care for. After the reforms, this reversed in the RSD schools. After a few years in the classroom, amid such high turnover, teachers still in their twenties became veterans, relatively speaking. The leaders of the reforms were younger than the average teacher had been before the reforms, and sometimes even younger than the children of the pre-reform school principals. (This is also true of the leaders of key local nonprofits and schools for whom we could find background information.) They hired teachers accordingly. As one school leader put it:

> We have a unique opportunity right now in New Orleans. We have attracted talent here like never before. This is talent that has no legacy ties to a Catholic or private school, with no opinions or long-standing associations positive or negative for OPSB.[17]

Another leader put it this way:

> If you're from New Orleans, then [the reformers think] you probably don't know what's going on. This is their thinking: we want to get someone from outside.[18]

In many schools, the decline in local roots was therefore a deliberate strategy.

As with everything else, these changes were neither immediate nor universal. In the immediate aftermath of the hurricane, most teachers and leaders, some of whom had both considerable experience and de-grees from university schools of education, simply returned to their old jobs. But over time, as schools were handed over to charter operators, the shift to less-experienced, alternatively certified teachers was pro-nounced. The new educators would be unlike the old.

The Right People for the Job?

It was not at all obvious how these changes in educator background could produce such improvements in student outcomes. In addition to the widespread research agreement on the value of educator experience, a growing body of evidence suggests that black students are more success-ful when they have black teachers.[19] There was a real question whether inexperienced white teachers, often from the suburbs and from other states, who would likely only be there for a few years, would be able to connect with New Orleans students.

Still, it was more plausible than it might seem that the changes in the workforce would be a positive contributor to the reform effects on stu-dent test scores, high school graduation, and college attendance. While inexperience and turnover usually seem to reduce student outcomes in traditional school districts, they do little to explain the overall variation in teacher performance.[20] Many experienced teachers are ineffective, and many inexperienced ones are excellent. Studies of teacher certification, moreover, usually do not find an association between these credentials and teacher performance.

Teach for America (TFA), with its partner TeachNOLA, came to typify this shift in the educator workforce.[21] Local educators and commu-nity members were not enthused about these organizations or the types of teachers they brought in because, for all of the above reasons, it ran against the grain of traditional understandings of school improvement. With little experience or training, and no plan to stay in teaching, the new teachers had little reason to invest in honing their educational craft or developing collaborative professional communities, in ways that would ultimately improve schools. In this view, the workforce change seemed to sacrifice today's students for other purposes. Giving jobs to TFA teachers and others who had taken alternative routes seemed like the corporate equivalent of giving local jobs to unskilled workers overseas.

But the reality is, again, more complex. Several national randomized trials showed that TFA teachers were at least on par with teachers who graduated from university-based schools of education and, in some cases, those who had more experience. The reasons are not entirely clear, though the conventional wisdom is that TFA teachers, being among the top recent college graduates in the country, are highly capable people, hard-working strivers, likely to be successful in almost any job as complex as teaching. In addition to the book smarts and work ethic demonstrated by their high GPAs from elite colleges, they needed at least some knack for teaching and a spirit of public service to make it through TFA's competitive application process.[22] This may be why the positive findings from the experiments were reinforced by a state-commissioned analysis of TFA teachers in Louisiana, in which alternatively prepared teachers— the majority of teachers in New Orleans—actually outperformed those with traditional preparation on student achievement growth.[23]

These hallmarks of good teachers—experience, certification, low turnover—might also play a different role in a radical reform effort such as this. CMOs did not hire young and untrained teachers just because they were cheaper, but because they were more pliable and energetic. As one New Orleans school leader put it, "I think you can find talented teachers but it's more difficult to find people who are willing to work hard enough. ... People who come early and stay late."[24] Few of the young teachers had their own children, so they had more time to devote to the job. They also came with few strong preconceived notions of what schools should look like or what teachers should do. This was important to school leaders who were under pressure to perform and wanted things done their way.

Having more seasoned professionals, as in traditional public schools, might have backfired under the circumstances. The educational approaches espoused by charter leaders would not have fit. This could be, in part, why even those charter schools that sought out more experienced teachers had trouble finding them. New Orleans post-reform schools had a well-earned reputation for being demanding places to work, with long hours and, now, less autonomy, little job security, and often no pensions. Once the new teachers began to have their own families to care for, such employment was no longer an attractive proposition.

As much as it runs against the grain of traditional educational thinking, the shift in the educator workforce was predictable and largely reflected what charter leaders seemed to be looking for.

The Market for Teachers: Unions, Tenure, and Teacher Accountability

With their business mindsets, autonomy, and pressure to succeed, we would expect school and CMO leaders to push out straggling low-performers and to compete hard for the best teachers. That they did. We surveyed pre-Katrina teachers who had returned to teach in the city post-Katrina—the only group of teachers who could make a direct comparison between the former school district and the post-reform schools.[25] Among these returning teachers, 76 percent reported that, after the reforms, low-performing teachers were much more likely to be fired than they had been before the reforms. Of all the potential changes in the learning and work environments we asked about, this was easily the largest shift.[26]

These findings are corroborated by additional analysis where we calculated the likelihood of continuing to teach in New Orleans for teachers with different levels of performance, as measured by the achievement growth of their students. We also did this separately for a group of neighboring districts that operated under traditional school district governance to get a sense of whether New Orleans was different.[27] As figure 5.3

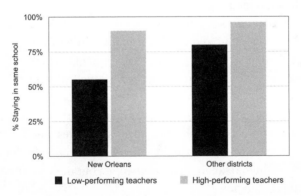

FIGURE 5.3. High-performing New Orleans teachers stayed at higher rates than low-performing teachers. *Source*: Nathan Barrett et al., "When the Walls Come Down: Evidence from New Orleans on Teacher Labor Markets in the Absence of Unions, Tenure, and Certification Rules" (National Center for Research on Education Access and Choice, Tulane University, forthcoming). *Notes*: Low-performing teachers in the figure comprise the bottom decile in value-added; high-performing teachers, the top decile. Percentages are unadjusted (i.e., they do not control for experience or other differences in teacher characteristics) because the objective is to understand the net effect of the reforms on teacher workforce dynamics.

shows, low-performing teachers were less likely to return the following year than high-performers in both New Orleans and neighboring districts, but the pattern was much more pronounced in New Orleans, where low-performing teachers were much less likely to stay.

The competition for teachers is also evident in the way they were compensated. When high-performing teachers switched charter schools, they received small raises on average, in contrast to low-performing teachers, who did not. However, beyond that, and in contrast to research on charter schools in other states,[28] we see mixed evidence on whether New Orleans charter schools paid teachers based on performance.

Even if the competition for the best teachers was not always reflected in compensation, I heard numerous stories of schools recruiting top teachers away from other schools. Some school leaders asked their existing teachers to recommend friends who worked at other schools (many of whom they had met through Teach for America and TeachNOLA), and then called to recruit them. As with other aspects of competition, this can be healthy. When employers must compete for workers, they have incentives to reward their best people and treat them well. The stories were not all positive—some principals poached teachers in the middle of the school year, which is arguably harmful to students—but the pressure to keep the best educators was likely an important antidote to the lack of job security.

School leaders also had to contend with some basic key features of personnel management and the labor market in education. Measuring teacher performance is difficult, and salary equity within schools matters—these same factors are partly what have made district salary schedules so common. The charter schools were also competing with neighboring traditional public school districts that rewarded these credentials. CMOs therefore created their own salary schedules, and teacher compensation seemed to track experience and certification. School leaders desperately wanted to keep their best people, but there were constraints on what they could do.

The desire for greater control over personnel has been one of the driving forces behind national school reform efforts for more than a decade. In New Orleans, school leaders got their wish. On personnel matters, schools could operate as private, nonunionized organizations, push out low-performing teachers, and compete for the high performers. Under the System, principals had to rely on teachers' intrinsic motivation; after the reforms, the relationship became more transactional—if teachers did what was asked, they would be rewarded. If they made the cut, they got to keep their jobs, receive a slightly higher salary, and get placed on the fast-track to management.

An Improved Learning Environment

The value of any education reform has to be measured by its impact on what happens in schools and classrooms. Such changes rarely occur, however, because rules that come from on high are usually too narrow and weakly enforced to break through the bureaucratic tangle and the buffers erected by school administrators.

Once again, however, New Orleans would be an exception, as schools and classrooms changed in fundamental ways. To measure changes in the learning and work environments, we again turned to our surveys of returning teachers. These teachers indicated, for example, that their post-reform schools focused on multiple goals more so than had pre-reform schools, including academics but also socio-emotional learning and perhaps vocational outcomes.[29] This broader focus was surprising considering the reputation of charter schools for focusing narrowly on raising test scores. One potential explanation is that business leaders are more apt to set measurable targets, especially when they have the autonomy to pursue them aggressively. School leaders in New Orleans therefore probably talked about goals more often, and this may be why teachers reported an increase in all the different potential targets, academic and otherwise.

The notion that New Orleans charter schools had a broad goal orientation is reinforced by two other factors. First, since a basic precept of goal-setting is that goals should be measurable, we would expect organizations that are more goal-oriented to also be more data-driven. This is what we found in New Orleans.[30] Across all the changes in the learning and work environments we examined, returning teachers agreed most strongly with the idea that administrators in the post-reform schools used data much more actively to guide decisions. One way to see this is through the network of nonprofits that emerged to assist the city's schools. New Schools for New Orleans carried out regular, data-driven evaluations of the schools it helped incubate. A national group, Achievement Network, had contracts with about a quarter of the schools in the city to provide schools with professional development and standardized tests (interim assessments) to ensure that students were on track to succeed on high-stakes state tests.

This data-driven, goal orientation is also consistent with what sociologists of education have observed about differences between public and private schools. As Valerie Lee and colleagues stated in a national school analysis, "Coherent goals, characteristic of schools with integrated cultural linkages, may be found more often in private than in public schools. . . . Schools with a strong central purpose work to coordinate the technical core operations with this purpose."[31] Charter schools are not private schools in quite the same sense, but they are privately run and have similar school-level autonomies that apparently lead to this same result.

Teacher support and professional community also seemed to improve after the reforms. Returning teachers reported that their school leaders observed teachers in the classroom and received feedback more often. How far did New Orleans charter schools go to create a coherent professional community? Some even trained their bus drivers, so that they would apply the same behavior and discipline rules to students on the way to and from school.[32] While these processes may have driven up management costs, it is not hard to see how they might be useful in promoting organizational coherence.

Overall, it would appear that the reforms improved the learning environment.[33] Who could argue with setting clear goals, measuring progress toward them, and providing more support within a stronger professional community? These were not the ideas of out-of-touch businesspeople or public school skeptics but of mainstream scholars from university schools of education.

Unintended Consequences: Lower Teacher Satisfaction

As always, however, there is another side to the story. Though the learning environment improved, teachers who taught in New Orleans prior to Katrina and returned to teach after, reported being less satisfied with their jobs after the reforms. This was not surprising when we consider the full range of changes in school environments. Most highly educated workers prefer jobs that are high on job security, compensation, and autonomy, and have reasonable work hours. Under tenure and union contracts, that is what they got. This is partly why, contrary to the conventional wisdom, research suggests that teachers nationally (i.e., those that work almost entirely in traditional public schools) have lower turnover relative to comparable professions.[34]

Under the New Orleans reforms, CMO leaders talked about the elimination of tenure and the union contract as key to their success — but this also meant less job security. Perhaps less security was acceptable for the young and temporary teachers coming out of programs like TFA, but the returning teachers in our survey more likely saw their job more as a career. In other research, we found that the removal of tenure protections increased the chance of exit similarly for low- and high-performing teachers.[35] Other survey research suggests that even the teachers with the highest performance measures worry about their jobs.[36] In other words, the loss of job security has meant losing both low- and high-performing teachers.

Teachers also value their autonomy.[37] One of the intents of market-based reform is to give *schools* autonomy over their work, to free them from the strictures of multilayered regulations and administrative rules. But autonomy for teachers and autonomy for schools are not the same. With the possibility that their schools could be closed down, either by market forces or by the state, school leaders passed the pressures on to their teachers, who were no longer free to choose whether they followed the leader. Not surprisingly, then, returning teachers reported in our surveys that they worked longer hours and perhaps had less autonomy than they had had under the System.[38]

These patterns show how hard it is to improve schools. Enhancements in the learning environment — increased support, professional community, and goal orientation — were not enough to offset the loss of job security, diminished autonomy, and longer hours. In some respects, there seems to have been a trade-off. The longer hours may have given teachers time to collaborate with one another and build professional community. The reduced job security may have made it easier for school leaders to set goals and guide the whole school toward them.[39] The ability to fire teachers was part and parcel of a goal-oriented, data-driven system.

This is not to suggest it is impossible to improve the learning environment and simultaneously make it more attractive to teachers. But it appears there is a trade-off when it comes to accountability.

No Excuses and School Culture

School culture is another important element of the student and educator experience. As a social enterprise, schooling involves norms, expectations, and relationships that affect not only whether educators are satisfied but how effective organizations are in fulfilling their missions.

Paul Pastorek, another of the New Orleans reform architects, and the second post-Katrina state superintendent, told me that his thinking on this has been heavily influenced by a 2003 book claiming to show that some schools around the country were achieving high success with students in poverty and arguing that all schools should be able to do so. The conclusion that poverty is no excuse for poor performance is right in the title of the book, *No Excuses*.[40] The phrase stuck and gained traction. A no-excuses school became one where expectations are high for all students, regardless of their background, where the learning environment is strict and orderly, and where test data are used actively to gauge progress. Advocates for this approach believed that too much blame had been shifted to families and that educators were the ones truly responsible for poor performance. While it can be difficult to determine which schools should receive the label, our best estimates indicate that 25–40 percent of New Orleans schools were probably in this amorphous no-excuses category.[41]

The evidence on no-excuses is similar to that for TFA. Research on charter schools in Massachusetts had found that schools identifying themselves as no-excuses were especially effective in raising student achievement (see chapter 10). The sociologists Adam Gamoran and Cristina Fernandez have also noted that the list of traits characterizing no-excuses schools mirrored those of "effective schools" research in the 1970s.[42] No-excuses is also similar to what private schools have often provided for more many middle-class families—think of the stereotypical Catholic schoolteacher rapping students' knuckles with a ruler.

The data-driven aspect of no-excuses can be seen in another way in New Orleans. Almost half of the city's schools had their teachers keep close track of student behavior using apps installed on teachers' phones and tablet computers, which they carried with them during the school day. In what some would consider an example of positive behavior response interventions (PBIS), the software, produced by the educational technology firm Kickboard, allowed for fine-grained descriptions of student behavior, and teachers could customize the software to measure what they felt was important. School leaders, too, could see how students were doing, in real-time, tracking the data that teachers entered. We found that the introduction of such software packages helped reduce the number of suspensions in many New Orleans charter schools.[43]

The concern, however, is that the entire philosophy represented by these approaches might be counterproductive in the long term. When the rewards and punishments are withdrawn—that is, when children become adults—they may revert to more negative behavior. Or, worse, the reliance on extrinsic incentives might actually undermine students' intrinsic motivation for positive behavior.[44] This approach also seems to send the wrong message—that people should act because of the rewards they will receive rather than because it is the right thing to do.

Not all New Orleans schools adopted the no-excuses approach or the behavior management software, but many adopted at least key elements of it. In addition to State Superintendent Pastorek's interest, the city's second RSD superintendent, Paul Vallas, tried to launch a separate organization to help take over low-performing New Orleans schools. Though this never came to fruition, the name he proposed for the organization is noteworthy. He wanted to call it "No Excuses."[45]

Teaching (like a Champion?)

Ultimately, the purpose of education policy is to improve student outcomes, and that requires improving what happens in the classroom. Based on what we have seen so far—changes in the teacher workforce, learning and work environments, and school culture—it seems almost certain that instruction and curriculum would also have changed. But how? What did these young, inexperienced, highly accountable teachers actually do? What did their students experience in the classroom?

Teaching is complex, and as such is notoriously difficult to observe, describe, and categorize. First, there is the "what" of teaching—the content. State standards provide general guideposts, but strong teaching also requires a curriculum, textbooks, and instructional materials, which teachers are generally on their own to find or create. Then, there is the "how" of teaching: different instructional approaches (e.g., phonics versus whole language in reading), teaching methods (lecture, discussion, inquiry, projects, experiential learning, personalized learning), and approaches to classroom management. These can be put together in an almost infinite combination of ways, representing a given teacher's style.

The many teaching options are often organized into two basic categories of educational philosophy. The progressive approach, associated with John Dewey and others, focuses on students' personal and social development, and embraces student-centered learning, a love of learning, and creativity. This philosophy is more closely aligned with supporters of traditional public schools, as it highlights the less tangible, harder-to-measure aspects of student learning. In contrast, the conservative educational philosophy focuses on academic learning, instilled through teacher-centered approaches, such as direct instruction and student discipline. While many conservative thinkers also value creativity, they believe it originates in academic knowledge, which provides the building blocks for creating new ideas. The job of the teachers, then, is to deliver content, and their effectiveness in doing so can be measured through standardized testing. No-excuses schools are undeniably in this conservative camp.

New Orleans parent Ashana Bigard's declaration that her daughter's pre-reform school was like "auntie's house" highlights this philosophical division. She also described the New Orleans public school she had herself attended in the 1990s:

> [The principal's] like, "What are you interested in learning?" [If] five or more students wanted to learn something, they would co-create [a class] as a sign-up. If none of the teachers could teach it, they would ask somebody from the community to come teach it.

This is practically the definition of a school with a progressive philosophy. In contrast, her daughter's experiences, after the reforms, fell much more on the conservative side:

> I started her at pre-K. [The school] was giving her work that was second-grade work. They would send her home with sixty [homework] problems.[46]

These might be extreme cases, and most educators fall somewhere in between, but there are clear differences in goals and assumptions about children's needs built into these stories.[47]

Unfortunately, there is less hard evidence on curriculum and instruction in New Orleans than for other topics we studied. But it is fair to say that the charter schools maximized time on task, especially on core academic subjects—math, reading, science, and social studies. This conclusion is based, indirectly, on the data-driven, no-excuses approach that many schools adopted, the strong pressure schools were under to raise test scores, and what educators told us informally. Also, each time we tried to field a survey of students in New Orleans schools, school leaders were adamant that it not take time away from academic instruction. Naturally, students learn more when they spend more time being instructed, and this focus on time on task may be partly why test scores increased so much.[48]

We also saw some evidence of a narrow academic focus in interviews with art teachers and school leaders. Student transcripts indicated that only about half of students were enrolled in at least one art class each year. Also, many school leaders sent a clear message that these classes were secondary, a way to motivate students to perform in *core* academic classes. If students had disciplinary issues or did not perform well in math, for example, some schools even gave students "enrichment detentions" designed to keep them out of art and other non-core classes as a punishment.[49] The schools varied quite a lot in their arts focus (more on this in chapter 7), but the tendency, even in this city known for the arts, was to make it a low priority or a tool for raising test scores.

Reinforcing these findings further, I noticed that New Orleans education leaders, especially those who went through TFA and TeachNOLA, relied on one particular book to guide their thinking about teaching: Doug Lemov's *Teach Like a Champion*. The book focuses on setting high expectations and creating structured classrooms.[50] "Ideology-driven guidance represents the most common form of advice teachers receive," Lemov writes. "A teacher might be told that a classroom should be democratic, for example . . . but such a classroom is not assessed for whether student achievement rose but whether the teacher did what the democratizing guidance described."[51] Lemov therefore emphasizes the importance of skills that can be directly assessed, for example, with standardized tests. This book, too, is clearly in the more conservative camp.

Teach Like a Champion also misses the idea of culturally relevant peda-gogy. Education scholar, Gloria Ladson-Billings, describes this as "an ability to develop students academically, a willingness to nurture and sup-port cultural competence, and the development of a sociopolitical or criti-cal consciousness."[52] This means teachers should use what students bring with them to the classroom as a foundation on which to build other forms of knowledge. In contrast, more conservative approaches tend to empha-size expectations for knowledge about the culture of dominant groups in society and focus on the aspects of this canon that students are missing—their deficits—which can downplay or demean their own cultures.

Lemov's critics, however, also had a problem. They could argue that he was selling students (and teachers) short, setting modest and narrow educational goals, but they could not dispute that too few students in tra-ditional public schools receive even the basics of academic content, and that this keeps them from reaching more advanced levels. What Lemov proposes may not seem especially ambitious, but if learning is a ladder, an uncomfortably large share of American students, including those in New Orleans schools in the pre-Katrina period, were stuck on the first step. As reform matriarch Leslie Jacobs put it, "If we can't teach the kids to read in thirteen, fourteen years . . . how are we going to teach them [other things like] character education?"[53] This was partly why the stan-dards and accountability movement started and continues today. You can criticize Lemov, but not without recognizing how the quality of instruc-tion is lacking, especially in schools serving disadvantaged populations. He also has good reason to focus specifically on classroom management, which is one of the strongest predictors of teacher effectiveness, and to concentrate on the skills measured by standardized tests, which have be-come important to student's life outcomes.[54]

The pendulum has always swung back and forth between different educational philosophies and approaches.[55] With the New Orleans re-forms, it swung sharply from the progressive toward the conservative side.

Conclusion: What Changed in Schools

History tells us that we have to move mountains, not just adopt new poli-cies, to change what happens in classrooms. While that rarely happens, it did in New Orleans. It appears that hiring business-minded, results-oriented education leaders, holding them accountable for results, and giving them autonomy—the recipe of the reforms—led to a profound change in who ended up working in the schools, in the environment and culture they created, and in what they did in the classroom.

Hiring inexperienced, untrained teachers may have bolstered, or at least did not inhibit, the reform package's large and positive contribution to students' measurable outcomes. This is not as surprising as it might seem. The traditional hallmarks of good schools—teachers with experience, certification, preparation, and low turnover rates—do matter to some extent. But whether and how they matter depends on the broader educational model within which they are situated. Schools are complex systems that work well only when the pieces are in tune with one another. The hallmarks of good teachers and schools probably are partial signals of the quality in traditional public schools, whose internal logic depends heavily on teacher expertise, judgment, autonomy, and intrinsic motivation—what some would call professionalism. If traditional public school teachers are exiting at high rates from those schools, it is most likely because the learning environment and poor leadership are driving them out.

In contrast, under market-based school reforms that give autonomy more to school leaders than to teachers, and where accountability is strict, high turnover could just mean that the leaders are, as intended, pushing out low-performers. Younger, less extensively trained teachers are less skilled in many ways, but also more open to doing things in new ways and working longer hours, as charter leaders expected. The old rules of school success, to the degree they were ever useful, do not seem to apply under this new model.

The management side of the New Orleans reforms also fits well with the instructional approach. Schools with inexperienced teachers and high turnover require active and intensive management—active hiring processes, regular professional development, and more frequent observation and feedback for teachers. Schools with strict discipline need more administrators to enforce those policies. With this management-driven approach, schools spend their funds accordingly. This, too, is quite different from traditional public schools.

These changes in management and educator background created entirely new school cultures and learning environments. New Orleans charter schools, especially those serving the most disadvantaged populations, were instructionally conservative. The intent was that teachers would use strict discipline to maintain order in their classrooms, deliver standardized content effectively, and spend as much time on task as possible.

The schools were also, not coincidentally, transactional. Teachers in many charter schools kept close track of students, rewarded good behavior, and punished bad behavior with suspensions and expulsions (especially in the early years). Likewise, effective teachers were lured away with higher salaries, while low-performers—those that generated too little measurable achievement—were shown the door.

The wisdom of this transactional approach is up for debate. On the one hand, the results in the prior chapters suggest that it can yield measurable results in the short term. Given what research says about how extrinsic incentives can undermine intrinsic motivation, however, it is not clear what this will mean for students in the long run.[56] Critics of market-based reforms have also raised concerns that the transactional approach "de-professionalizes" teaching, attracting and retaining educators with less experience, fewer skills, and limited knowledge, and giving them too little autonomy in the classroom—thus reducing the likelihood of their staying in the profession to develop their talents. The analysis here does little to allay those concerns. The transactional approach takes for granted that we can measure teacher performance fairly well, but this is a tenuous assumption. Even in the best-case scenario, the transactional approach can create some real problems.

Good or bad, much of what we saw in the New Orleans schools is the norm in the business world: high pay and CEO titles for managers; the power to hire, fire, and otherwise manage personnel as they please; the focus on data and measurable goals; the transactional nature of relationships and the antipathy toward unions. Some advocates of the reforms get defensive when I use the term "businesslike." They worry that this plays into the hands of their critics. The New Orleans reformers have preferred to describe their schools as "mission-driven." That is a reasonable description, too. The issue is that this term does not clearly distinguish charter schools from the alternatives. Traditional public schools are also mission-driven, but the missions are driven more by individual teachers working in loosely connected classrooms than by powerful school leaders. But no one would say the System is businesslike, in the way charter schools are.

The point here is not to defend or criticize any particular system but to accurately characterize the various options and determine how the new approach may have contributed to the measurable improvements documented in the last chapter. New Orleans's publicly funded schools after the reforms were very different from those that preceded them. Being conservative, transactional, and businesslike very likely helped generate the better measurable outcomes. If we set specific goals focused on academic content and measures like high school graduation, and provide incentives or educators to reach them, then those measurable goals are likely to be achieved. Though the reformers were not aware of the decades-old "effective schools" research, they nevertheless followed closely in its footsteps.

None of this, therefore, was really innovative. The reforms had pushed schools back to the conservative ways of generations past—they went retro. The next question is, why? Markets are supposed to generate innovation, so why, in this case, did they go back to older ways? The following chapters help us answer this question.

CHAPTER 6

Competition's Unintended Consequences

The New Orleans school reforms were built, first and foremost, around charter schools that are individually autonomous and collectively competitive. In theory, opening up school management to nongovernmental organizations—that is, privatization—without district rules and union contracts, could produce innovation and a variety of options to serve diverse student needs and interests. Such beneficial market responses might be even more likely when families can choose schools. Consumer decisions to enroll in and exit schools would provide school leaders with valuable information about student needs and school performance and, simultaneously, create incentives for schools to improve. If schools failed to respond, they would close, new ones would enter to replace them, and more successful ones would expand. Compared with political bureaucracy, the market would provide school leaders greater flexibility and motivation to make good decisions and produce better results. If the large positive effects on student outcomes are any indication, then this theory seems to have some validity.

But the reality is, again, messier. Though the results did indeed look strong on average, the evidence I present in this chapter suggests that this was not due to competition, at least not directly or in the conventional way it is usually described. School leaders spoke about competition and their reactions to it, but the specific steps they took in response were too superficial to generate the student outcomes we observed. The reform leaders themselves even rejected the idea that competition could explain the results.

Some predictable unintended consequences also emerged. I show, in particular, that school leaders responded to competition in ways that were sometimes unhelpful or even counterproductive. Perhaps as a result of these responses, as well as the nature of markets discussed in chapter 2, the reforms generated a range of school performance levels that was as wide as it had been before. Schools also shifted away from some community-oriented roles that they were well situated to fulfill but that competition largely precluded.

There was a lot of good news in New Orleans, to be sure, but competition was not at the root of it.

Unhealthy Competition

One thing for certain is that school leaders felt competition. Huriya Jabbar, one of our research partners, interviewed leaders in thirty schools. "When asked if their school competed with other schools for students, responses included emphatic statements [such as] 'Yes, Lord!' and 'Absolutely!'"[1] Moreover, all but one of the thirty interviewed could quickly name the specific schools they competed with and the strategies they employed. As the market theory would predict, principals tended to compete more with schools that were located nearby, recruited away more of their students, and had similar educational orientations.[2]

Increased marketing and improved relationships with parents through school office personnel were some of school leaders' most common competitive responses—sometimes called the "glossification" of schooling. There is probably no harm in these relatively inexpensive activities. But other responses would probably make even the most reform-minded person bristle. "Every kid is money" is the way one school leader described competition. While the statement is true in the sense that each school's funding level is determined by the number of students, parents and community leaders do not want school leaders to think of their children as dollar signs any more than they want them to focus on complying with the fragmented rules of government agencies and unions. The fact that charter leaders were willing to share these unfortunate views suggests these ideas were accepted and noncontroversial.

Just as interesting was what school leaders did not say. They rarely mentioned in the interviews any steps that would improve their educational offerings in a substantive way. This is not to say that the schools were not increasing educational quality—the student outcomes in chapter 4 demonstrate otherwise. The question is, how did they do it? According to the reform leaders, it was not "markets," "competition," and "incentives"—words they disliked almost as much as the skeptics of the reforms. It may be that school leaders saw competition more as the game they had to play, alongside their real work. In that case, when asked about how they compete, it would make sense for them to talk about the superficial, likely harmless, steps they took as school leaders to get by in the market system. But this was not a game. There were apparently substantive efforts at educational improvement being made, but competition was not the driving force behind them.

Tools of Inclusion and Exclusion

Other unhealthy competitive responses are rooted in the schooling market's unusual feature of classmate effects. Parents recognize the importance of their children's friends and peers, and this gives school incentives to select their preferred students. Even without such incentives, it is easier for schools if they get to choose their students and avoid those who might create problems or be a poor fit.

These incentives are reinforced by another factor: state accountability systems, and charter contracts, fail to reflect the full array of factors influencing student outcomes. In focusing on student achievement *levels* at the end of the school year, these official performance metrics capture partly the successes of students' current schools, as intended, but also the substantial contributions of students' home environments (e.g., parents reading to their children and helping with homework) and the quality of students' prior schools.[3] This is why, throughout this book, when I analyze "performance," I measure it using student growth, which accounts for these factors that are outside of school control. The state unfortunately did not take these same steps with its performance metrics and this, combined with classmate effects, pressured schools to select more advantaged students.

How did schools respond to these incentives and shape their enrollments? The answers fall into four general categories. These are, in chronological order: school design, recruiting, admissions, and post-admission decisions. First, if families have distinct views about the needs of their children, and school leaders are responsive to them, then we can expect schools to design options that vary based on academic and extra-curricular programs, location, school culture, and more. Once the school design is in place, school leaders can recruit students through marketing; if they want to attract middle-class families, they can advertise in middle-class neighborhoods. Likewise, admission requirements keep out low-performing students and those with disciplinary records. These criteria, often deemed acceptable, especially in private schools, also provide cover for discrimination on the basis of race, income, and other factors. Finally, even for students who do get admitted, schools can readily push out certain students if they subsequently seem to be poor fits.

Student selection using the first three of these broad categories—school design, recruitment, and admission—is often referred to as cream-skimming. When we add in the post-admission tools, we get the phrase "creaming and cropping." Within these four categories, at least twenty specific steps have been documented as tools of exclusion in charter schools nationally.[4] In the list below, I have identified with an asterisk (*) those where the practice has been documented in New Orleans.[5]

Ways charter schools select their students

- School design
  - Offering programs that are attractive to a particular group*
  - Choosing to locate in a certain neighborhood
  - Charging fees for basic activities or school uniforms*
  - Requiring families to do volunteer work (especially during school and work hours and/or allowing wealthier parents to pay a fee to avoid this requirement)
  - Requiring families to provide their own transportation from home to school
  - Offering buses, but with few convenient bus stops*
- Recruitment
  - Marketing in particular publications or locations near the homes of the preferred demographic

- ○ Sending sometimes subtle signals in marketing materials about what kind of students will be a good fit*
- ○ Holding invitation-only open-house events*
- ○ Suggesting to prospective families that their schools cannot meet certain needs or that families should consider other schools*
- Admission
  - ○ Having academic or behavioral admission requirements*
  - ○ Creating long and complicated admission forms*
  - ○ Requiring that applications be submitted in person during business hours or placing questions on application forms that suggest some families are unwelcome (on the basis of, e.g., race, immigration status, disabilities)*
  - ○ Admitting students based on recommendations from other parents, teachers, and board members*
  - ○ Interviewing families as part of the application process*
  - ○ Requiring parents' attendance at an open house (possibly during business hours) as a condition of admission
  - ○ Accepting more applications than desired, or underreporting available seats, to prevent the authorizer/district from assigning challenging students midyear[6]*
- Post-admission
  - ○ Expelling students*
  - ○ Not filling empty seats when students leave (i.e., not backfilling)*
  - ○ Making life difficult for students (e.g., with regular suspensions or making parents come to school to pick up their children), so they want to leave[7]

Clearly, we are not just talking about theory anymore. While it is difficult to know how frequently schools select students—directly or indirectly, intentionally or otherwise—we have good evidence that each practice on the list does occur. School leaders acknowledge using many of them, while other methods of exclusion have been discovered in other ways.

In New Orleans, roughly 10 percent of elementary schools and more than 20 percent of high schools had performance-related admission requirements a decade after the reforms. This had the effect of making those schools look better than they really were on accountability measures. If you only accept students who have high test scores, then your schools will have high scores almost no matter what happens in the classroom. Importantly, almost all of these selective schools had been opened prior to the reforms and remained under local district control because of their "high performance," reflecting the fact that the pressure to select students arises in all types of school systems.

The state-governed RSD schools, though they were barred from explicitly using selective admissions, still took advantage of the many opportunities to select indirectly. In interviews with roughly half of the city's school leaders in 2013, many acknowledged questionable selection practices.[8] One school leader explained that "the more we advertise and push the fact that we have openings, the more less-capable students we get"—so the school avoided advertising.[9] Another CMO leader admitted to me privately that at least one of the schools in his network had gone through a list of applicants with someone who knew the students, crossing many of the names off the list as troublemakers. In a public presentation, a teacher acknowledged secretly providing lists of high-performing students to another school that wanted to recruit them. In still other cases, schools would identify parents whose children fit their preferred profile and ask them to recommend the schools to others. Reducing the number of officially available open seats also occurred. In eight of the twenty-eight participating schools that did not have explicit admission requirements, school leaders acknowledged engaging in these more subtle forms of selectivity.

Whether these modes of exclusion were inappropriate or illegal can be hard to judge. If schools are allowed, even encouraged, to specialize in serving specific student needs and to achieve organizational coherence, then the practical implication is that some schools will be successful only with the students they are designed to serve. Was the school leader who told potential students, "this isn't the right fit," being helpful to those students?[10] Perhaps, but these results still raise questions about "nonselective" schools.

Evidence of creaming and cropping practices also emerged in a lawsuit led by the Southern Poverty Law Center (SPLC). Students with disabilities and their families, the plaintiffs in the case, presented their experiences of being turned away by state RSD schools that claimed they could not serve the students' special needs. The schools were probably correct, as serving students with disabilities well does require teachers who are specially trained and have access to the necessary educational materials and facilities, and small class sizes.[11] Many of these actions by school leaders were probably intended to be in the interests of students, though in other cases, school leaders may have thought that accepting the students would diminish their competitive position in the market. Ideally, the interests of schools and students would align, but the unusual features of schooling mean that this often not the case. Moreover, it is difficult for even well-intentioned educators to distinguish the two. Schools cannot know what other opportunities any given family might have. When families are turned or nudged away, they may end up in schools that are a better fit or an even worse fit. Educators hoped for the best — they wanted to help students — but they were also taking this decision out of the hands of families.

These results are not surprising. Other cities with large numbers of charter schools have had the same experiences with creaming and cropping their student enrollments.[12] Equally unsurprising is that many of these exclusion tools disproportionately affect disadvantaged students. Even when schools are otherwise welcoming, low-income families often cannot easily afford fees, do volunteer work, provide transportation, attend invitation-only events and open houses, or meet admission requirements. Achieving equitable access would prove much more difficult than simply ending attendance zones and creating competition.

Discipline

Some of the most vocal opposition to the reforms came from people concerned about strict discipline, an element of the no-excuses approach that many schools, but far from all, embraced. Indeed, in the immediate aftermath of the reforms, there was a sharp spike in the number of suspensions and expulsions.[13] Newspaper articles depicted schools that had as many security and police officers as other support staff.[14] Part of this increase may have been due to the hurricane aftermath itself. Students' homes and communities were chaotic, and this carried over to their school behavior. Crime rates in the city spiked as youth gangs sought to reassert control over their territories. Concern that this violence would spill over to the schools was understandable. School leaders also talked about having to use harsher punishments to create school cultures that were more conducive to learning.

Whatever the explanation, the initial spikes in disciplinary incidents mostly went away over time. A decade later, our analyses suggested that suspensions and expulsions were nearly identical to what they had been prior to the reforms, although suspensions for serious offenses remained more common in each of the post-reform years we studied.

Why the subsequent drop and stabilization in discipline incidents? Prompted by the SPLC lawsuit and media reports about the initially strict discipline, public pressure began to build for schools to ease up. Also, the RSD instituted a centralized expulsion system and restricted the range of behaviors that could be considered for expulsion. While the number of suspensions and expulsions had already declined by the time the system was centralized, it did help alleviate public concerns and keep exclusions down. The school district also agreed to join forces with the state RSD, so that all expulsions in all the city's publicly funded schools were handled under common rules. The education leaders we talked with agreed that the lawsuit, and associated public attention, helped drive these changes.

Well after the SPLC lawsuit and centralized expulsion system, I asked Ashana Bigard whether she thought discipline practices had begun to relax. She gave a different impression:

> Not at all. Just got a call from a parent with a kindergartner who has been suspended for the day several times.

Bigard, and many others, including school leaders, questioned whether the data we had access to were fully accurate.[15] Schools report their data, which are difficult to verify, and they are not required to track one apparently common form of discipline: in-school suspensions. Even system leaders question the accuracy of the discipline data. "What the schools are better at," Bigard told me, "is not documenting it." Suspensions, she said, were still often mostly for minor offenses:

> Oh, mostly it's for disruption in class, like talking too much, wandering outta their seats. We had a little boy, six. . . . He wandered off campus, and they wanted to expel him. We're fightin' it because, we're like, "He's six. Was the teacher disciplined for not keeping an eye on him?" She suspended my child when she was in second grade for bringing a doll to school.

Schools also continued to use discipline to push out disruptive students, often calling parents in the middle of the school day—and the parents' workday—to come pick up their children for misbehavior:

> We had a parent who was just fired from her job because the school was calling her so much at her job to come pick up her son.

The centralized expulsion system may have prevented schools from directly kicking out students, but schools could make students' and parents' lives difficult enough that they would be forced to leave anyway.

These disciplinary actions by schools reflect a different element of their more conservative natures. Had a child brought a doll to a school where educators had a more progressive outlook, the response might have been to use it as a way of getting to know the child better: Who gave you the doll? Who did you name it after? Her connection to the doll might have served as a bridge to learning. But the more conservative approach prioritizes orderly school cultures, following rules, and focusing instructional time on schools' chief responsibility: measurable academic success. It is certainly easier for teachers to do their jobs when students are following the rules, not talking in class, not wandering around, and not playing with toys they brought from home. Seemingly minor offenses do affect the learning environment.

Though strictness is hard to measure, a combination of hard statistical evidence and frequent anecdotes suggests that schools remain somewhat more aggressive in punishing students, compared with traditional public schools before the reforms, and still use discipline as a way of both maintaining order and inducing more disruptive students to leave. No-excuses was more than just catchy phrase. It reflected the day-to-day reality for a large share of educators and students.

Transportation and Distance to School

One key reason the schooling market is unusual is that students need to get to school every day. Louisiana state law requires publicly funded schools, with a few exceptions, to provide transportation to students who live more than a mile from school.[16] With 30 percent of families in the

most impoverished neighborhoods lacking any form of personal transportation, this mandate is motivated partly by a desire to ensure broad
access to schooling and increase daily attendance. One education leader,
talking about what would happen without bus transportation, said:

> You can get high absenteeism just because they [parents] don't want
> their little one walking ten blocks in the cold or in the rain, or the car
> breaks down and you may not see a student for three days while it's get-
> ting fixed.[17]

The introduction of school choice greatly increased the travel times required for students to get to school.[18] According to our research by Jane
Arnold Lincove and Jon Valant, three-quarters of bus stops from a sample
of New Orleans publicly funded schools had pickup times between 6:00
and 7:00 a.m., and another 5 percent were picked up before 6:00 a.m.[19]
This was a particular problem for families with multiple young children.
Again, Ashana Bigard:

> I'll never forget. We had a parent who—she could barely talk with the
> amount of crying she was doing, because she had a six-year-old son and
> seven-year-old daughter, and they were at two separate schools. The
> buses picked them up eight blocks apart. She had to take turns standing
> with her children at five something in the morning. She put rape whistles
> around their neck and be like, "If somebody comes up to you and I'm not
> with you . . . blow this whistle real loud."[20]

Even when safety was not an issue, the median bus commuting time was
thirty-five minutes; five round trips would add up to more than six hours
on the bus every week. The students picked up at the earliest bus stops
had daily rides of ninety minutes or more, each way. In the post-Katrina
era, students were traveling an average of two miles further to get to
school—no surprise given the end of neighborhood attendance zones.[21]
These long commute times meant less time with family and early
wake-up times, which have been shown to reduce student learning.[22]
Moreover, many students could not participate in after-school extracurricular activities—the buses left right after school, so if students stayed
later they would be stranded. One school leader expressed concern

that bus transportation created inequitable access to important school activities.

Even when students could participate in after-school activities, it was often difficult for parents, especially those without cars, to attend artistic performances or sporting events, much as it was difficult for them to pick up children who were sick or in trouble. This led to a larger disconnect between schools and parents, who rarely visited the now more-distant schools their children attended. Distance and bus transit were "causing a disruption in the relationship with parents," according to one school leader.[23]

Transportation became a gatekeeper of sorts. Since the selective-admission schools governed by the local district did not have to follow the transportation requirement, students who managed to gain admission also had to find a way to get there. While it is difficult to determine how many families were affected, this likely reduced the number of low-income students who applied to selective schools and increased the chances that those who got in would choose not to attend or transfer to schools closer to home. Another nonselective school tried to skirt the transportation rules, apparently in order to draw more students from the local neighborhood and save money, though it was eventually forced to come in line and follow the rules.

The financial and administrative burden of all of this was nontrivial. Transportation costs roughly doubled after the reforms to about $700 per student. But there were less obvious and more indirect costs as well. Bus transportation not only weakened schools' relationships with parents and diminished extracurricular opportunities for students, but prompted continual requests from families for changes in bus times and routes, creating new work for school staff.[24]

There is no getting around the geography of schooling. Requiring that schools provide transportation helped, but it created problems of its own.

New Market Tiers, Much Like the Old

Market theory suggests that, under the usual conditions, schools will be forced to compete with one another. If government funds are allocated on a per-pupil basis then, when low-quality schools lose students, they also lose money and eventually close. The remaining schools would receive the same per-pupil funding level and compete on an even, competitive playing field. Under this theory, the differences in quality across schools should be small.

But we have now seen many signs that this is not how the schooling market works in practice. The incentives for schools to exclude students are simply too great. Some schools attract more privileged students and work to keep others out, whether directly, with admission requirements, or indirectly, with discipline, transportation, and other tools. The schooling market, therefore, seems likely to produce the same kinds of tiers that we see in regular markets.

We put the theory to the test with our data. First, we measured school performance in terms of student achievement growth. Next, we measured how much these school quality measures varied across schools and compared the quality variation in New Orleans to other districts.[25] Before Katrina, we found that the school performance variation in New Orleans was slightly higher than in the rest of the state's traditional public school districts. This reinforces the argument I heard often from reformers that some of the pre-reform schools worked well while others were deplorably poor. This wide variation in performance was apparently worse in New Orleans than elsewhere in Louisiana.

After the reforms, the variation actually worsened, moving in the opposite direction of what the market theory would predict. Over time, however, market forces seemed to kick in, and by 2016, the variation in school performance was similar, or slightly lower, compared with before the reforms. If the goal was to give everyone access to the same level of quality, the reforms had failed.

Why do we see such continued variation in quality? Some examples may help to illustrate.

The View from the Top Tier

One school highlights all of the above tendencies toward tiers especially well. Prior to the reforms, Saenger Elementary School had been located near Tulane University, serving many of its faculty and staff.[26] With these socioeconomic advantages, students entered with high scores and the school was considered high-performing. For this reason, in the post-Katrina takeover process, it was left under the control of the local district.

After Katrina, keeping Saenger School strong was also important to the university. The city's colleges were desperate to attract faculty, staff, and administrators back to the battered city. Having good schools nearby was critical for working parents. However, Saenger only covered the elementary grades. The university's employees would need all grades, K–12.

The situation was ripe for a partnership. Tulane needed to promise its employees good schools, and therefore reached out to the Saenger leadership. With the support and lobbying of the university, Saenger was able to gain control of a local high school building so that it could expand to cover grades K–12 on these two separate campuses. Crucially, the district allowed Saenger elementary to keep its old attendance zone, one of only a handful of schools in the city allowed to do so.[27] The school's leaders also pushed successfully to make the new middle and high school campus selective-admission.

The partnership went still further. The school and university signed a contract that, among other things, required the middle/high school part of Saenger to hold roughly one-quarter of its student slots open for the children of university faculty and staff. The university also agreed to compensate Saenger for its efforts, on top of the per-pupil allocation that all schools received from various levels of government. The school's students could take college courses at Tulane free of charge, and the swim team used the university's pool. In its marketing, the school cobranded itself with the university's logo. A local celebrity adopted the school, providing additional funding and prestige.

The partnership was clearly a good move for both the university and school, but was it is a win for the city? It certainly was in the short run. The city needed the colleges to open and to bring its citizens back. The school also turned out to be very popular. In 2013 Saenger had four to nine times as many applicants as slots available.[28] In 2018 it was designated a National Blue Ribbon School by the US Department of Education and *US News and World Report* had it ranked as the fourth best high school in the state. Moreover, it accomplished all this while bringing more resources into the school system and being one of the most racially diverse schools in the city, with a roughly even split between white and minority students; 20 percent came from low-income families.

On the one hand, Saenger was a publicly funded school that had the look and feel of a private school. It was run by a private organization, used admissions criteria like private schools, and gave guaranteed seats to another private organization, Tulane. The school's leaders also went to great lengths to prevent teachers from unionizing, and to maintain a school funding formula that advantaged schools like Saenger, which had fewer students with disabilities or low family incomes. The CEO of the combined school was paid more than $300,000 per year, the highest school leader salary in the city. Saenger would eventually accumulate a reserve fund of over $15 million.

The fact that Saenger had many times as many applicants as seats meant that recruiting and marketing were unnecessary. But this also meant that the vast majority of applicants were turned away, not to mention those who did not bother to apply with such thin odds. The school's diversity also came with some qualification; given that the city's population was 60 percent black, the fact that the school was only one-third black meant that white students were twice as likely to gain access. Low-income students enrolled at even lower rates.[29]

Clearly, even in this market-oriented system, where per-pupil government funding was equalized, some schools could carve out significant advantages.

The View from the Lower Tier

At the other end of the spectrum, we have Armstrong Elementary, a school located just a few miles from Saenger. Like the other schools governed by the state RSD, it had open admissions. More than 95 percent of the school's population was eligible for free or reduced-price lunches, and 40 percent were English language learners or had disabilities qualifying them for special education services. Students came to the school with considerable trauma, and the school took all comers, no matter their needs.

The school also had fewer resources than Saenger to meet this higher level of need. There was no $15 million reserve fund, no endorsements from local celebrities, no partnership with a prestigious local institution. The school relied almost completely on government funding—and for this it had to scramble. Teachers and leaders spent their spring and summer months knocking on doors to recruit families. When they briefly reduced these efforts one year, they paid for it with a sharp drop in enrollments and revenue. The building that the charter had been assigned was ill-designed for classroom instruction, and its aging heating and cooling systems often broke down.

Nonetheless, by almost all accounts the school served its students well and used its limited resources wisely. Armstrong School had one of the highest achievement growth scores in the city. It had the same school leader for almost a decade straight and a lower-than-average teacher turnover rate. To supplement its resources, the school applied for small competitive grants. It hired four counselors to deal with trauma, bilingual paraprofessionals to help with English language learners, and special education teachers, all while avoiding budget deficits. As the unsuitable building lacked interior walls, teachers had to get by using partitions to hide the sights and sounds overflowing between classes.

By any reasonable measure, the educators in Armstrong were as successful as any in the city, but schools are not judged based on reasonable measures. In a market setting, they are judged, to a considerable extent, on the types of students who attend them. With government accountability, they are judged by test score levels, not how much students learn. After several years, and despite all these accomplishments, Armstrong School earned a middling grade of C from the state, just enough to maintain its contract, but not what it deserved.

That Armstrong had such high growth was impressive, given its limited resources and disadvantaged student population. But if you asked the average parent which of the two schools was in the top tier, Saenger was much more likely to be mentioned. The state affirmed this by giving Saenger a higher grade of A.

We therefore have to distinguish between the real tiers—based on who provided the best curriculum, instruction, and leadership—and the misperceived ones. Schools like Saenger would inevitably rise to the top by attracting or selecting students with high prior academic performance, which attracts even more such students in subsequent years, which generates positive effects among classmates, which helps attract and retain the best teachers. It is a self-reinforcing cycle, cementing schools' preexisting advantages. It can be a virtuous circle for schools like Saenger, but it works in reverse for schools like Armstrong. It also virtually guarantees us a wide variety of quality and tiers.

Schools as Community Anchors and Service Providers

The incentives created by the reforms were problematic in other ways as well. One of the arguments for school districts had always been that schools would serve as community anchors, providing not only the core services expected of them—the basic academics of math, reading, science, and social studies—but what we might call public or community services.

When I was young, my district elementary school hosted meetings of various neighborhood clubs I belonged to. In New Orleans, schools had similarly opened their doors to organizations providing adult education and some health-related services. As one local educator leader put it, many pre-Katrina public schools "had shifts all the way through the evening," including literacy and health programs after regular school hours.[30] Though not required as part of the schools' core functions, the district saw these services as part of their broader mission. This was part of what the local leader termed the "holding power" of neighborhood schools, "those things that . . . made that connection with the community."[31]

Pre-kindergarten is another optional service often provided in K–12 schools. That early education is important is not in question. Reformers and traditionalists alike wanted New Orleans children to have access to early learning opportunities. But this was precisely the type of service that charter schools were unlikely to provide on their own. Part of the problem was that state funding for early childhood education only covered about half the cost of high-quality pre-K. However, this was clearly not the only issue; pre-K had been similarly underfunded before the reforms. The difference was that the district had found ways to make up for inadequate pre-K funding with general operating funds.

Once schools began the shift to charter operators, research led by Lindsay Bell Weixler showed that the number of pre-K slots schools offered dropped by 34 percent.[32] In our interviews with school leaders and local pre-K experts, three interconnected reasons emerged. First, charter schools were held accountable only for the results of older students because standardized testing did not begin until third grade. It would therefore be at least five years before a child staring pre-K might take a test that would affect the state School Performance Scores—and thus, the school's chances for contract renewal.

Charter schools could conceivably have gained by providing pre-K instruction if students had come for pre-K and stayed for later grades. But this led to a second problem. Our analysis showed that the student mobility rate was too high; pre-K students did not stay in specific schools long enough to benefit schools in terms of later enrollment, revenue, or higher scores. Given how the reforms were designed, there was little incentive for charter schools to provide pre-K.

Third, the schools (and some entire CMOs) were often too small to leverage the economies of scale required to provide early education at a reasonable cost. School districts often have pre-K coordinators who can manage all the pre-K programs in a given city. Each school or CMO wishing to offer pre-K would have to hire its own coordinator.

Some charter schools provided pre-K anyway. In interviews, their leaders reported that, while they understood how pre-K provision sacrificed resources and test scores, they still felt it was the right thing to do. Other schools also used pre-K as one of the many ways they indirectly selected their students. As in most states, schools in Louisiana could provide a mix of subsidized pre-K seats (without tuition) and tuition-based seats. Schools that wanted to bring in more advantaged students could do so by offering tuition-based seats that were affordable only for middle-class students. The state allowed students who entered a school in pre-K to automatically enroll in the school's kindergarten. But none of this, apparently, was enough to keep the number of pre-K seats in publicly funded schools from significant decline. While most students ended up being served instead by other forms of pre-K or child care, some research suggests that these other options are of lower quality.[33]

Again, the decline in pre-K slots was a predictable result with schools facing short-term pressures to raise enrollment and the test scores of older students.[34] But the broader point is that charter schools are unlikely to provide the kinds of optional community services—pre-K, adult education, and otherwise—that district supporters and community members often saw as part of schools' public or civic responsibility.

The shift toward autonomous, privately operated schools detached schools from their communities, and this had consequences.

Conclusion

Decentralized market-based systems have many potential advantages over centralized political bureaucracies. Giving schools autonomy and forcing them to compete can produce greater organizational coherence and measurable increases in student outcomes. As predicted in chapter 2, however, school leaders responded to competition in ways that were often superficial or counterproductive.

It was a battle for survival. School leaders thought differently about schooling ("every kid is money") and acted differently, cutting out pre-K programs, creaming and cropping students, and generally focusing less on the hard-to-measure pursuits of education, such as the arts. In maintaining the low and high tiers, they also reproduced the problem of uneven quality they were trying to solve.

It would be difficult to find another market where the sellers work so hard to keep certain customers away. In this respect, the market for education is like that of a private club.[35] Such groups aim to bring together people who have common goals or interests. Building on shared values and perspectives, they can create cohesive communities. But this comes at a cost, as it reinforces existing inequalities based on race, income, and other factors. Country clubs, for example, sell their nice facilities and activities, and accept new members based on the recommendations of long-standing members. They rely on prestige and exclusivity. So do top-tier schools competing in the marketplace. Of course, the vast majority of educators want all students to have access to *a* great school, just not necessarily *their* great school. This is not only inequitable, but also inefficient because it means schools, especially those in the top tier like Saenger, compete not on the quality of instruction, curricula, and programs, but on the types of students they can attract.

Regardless of how we interpret these results, as unintended consequences or harmless side effects, it still seems clear that competition was not a primary or direct driver of the fast rise in student outcomes. School leaders did not respond to competition with the kinds of instructional and management changes that we would expect to generate better student outcomes. This conclusion is reinforced in the next chapter, where I explore the other side of the competitive equation. The responses of educators, after all, cannot be understood without the responses by parents.

CHAPTER 7

The Difficulty of Making Choice Real for Families

In 2010, about five years after the New Orleans reforms started, a pro-reform group outside of New Orleans funded a documentary about the problems with traditional public schools and the potential of charter schools as solutions. In *Waiting for Superman*, a story unfolds of families fretting about the futures that await their children and pinning their hopes on winning lotteries to get into a local charter school. The school auditorium is packed as parents and children wait to hear whose numbers will be called. When the lottery numbers are announced, the winners cheer as if they had won a million-dollar lottery instead of a school lottery—as if Superman himself had arrived to save them. Everyone else, meanwhile, cries and buries their heads in their hands.

The implication is that allowing families to choose schools, particularly charter schools, could change students' lives forever. When parents are allowed to "vote with their feet" for the schools that best meet their preferences and needs, and schools are given both autonomy and incentives to respond to parent demands, students have a chance to escape failing schools. The documentary is heartbreaking to watch, but does it paint an accurate portrait?

Chapter 6 suggested that this logic can be misleading, with the many unhelpful and unhealthy responses to competition and the continued wide range of school performance. As we will see, the early version of school choice in New Orleans did little to help matters. When the reforms first started, and attendance zones were abandoned, schools were on their own to manage admissions and enrollment. Families applied to individual schools, and school leaders chose which students to let in. It was "school choice," but not what had been promised to parents.

Partly in response to these well-publicized problems, John White, Leslie Jacobs, and the other reformers centralized enrollment within the RSD, using a computer-based lottery, so that families could do the choosing instead of schools. While this centralized process was technically sophisticated, it did not, in the end, succeed in making most families feel that the process was fair or that they had real choices. The inordinate demand for certain upper-tier schools made the odds of acceptance very low. Families' choices were also constrained by personal circumstances and geography, and schools, in finding market niches, restricted the options families saw as viable.

Overall, choice played a crucial role in the city's academic gains, albeit not in the simple way that the theory, and the documentary, suggested. Providing real choice is a real challenge.

From Attendance Zones to Decentralized Choice

In the aftermath of Katrina, with only a small number of schools open in the least flooded areas and families returning in unpredictable patterns, local leaders had been forced to all but abolish attendance zones. Default neighborhood schools were no longer available, so parents, if they wanted their children to attend a publicly funded school in the city, became responsible for filling out and submitting applications to each school they were considering. In this respect, it was like applying to college.

Schools were allowed to give preference to applicants who had a sibling attending the school or a parent working in the school and, in some cases, to those who lived nearby. Selective admissions schools could consider the relevant eligibility criteria. Beyond that, every student applying for a slot in a given school and grade was supposed to have an equal chance. If schools had more applications than available slots, they were supposed to select the winners at random. These rules were not enforced, however. As we saw in chapter 6, many schools took advantage of their autonomy to exclude students and improve their competitive positions. John White described the situation when he first arrived in New Orleans:

> You had a set of schools that were almost designated to be schools of last resort [and] there were some schools where mysteriously [students] could sort of never get in.[1]

Some families also found it challenging to navigate the various deadlines and complex application procedures, and to deliver applications in person.[2] The choice-based system was especially challenging for those entering the system for the first time or moving back to New Orleans. They did not know, often until late into the spring, whether their children would get into *any school* to which they had applied. The local OPSB and state RSD made provisions for families who received no acceptance letters, but that meant another long process and more uncertainty. In the end, they might still have to send their children to a school on the other side of town, or to one they did not want.

The choice process also created challenges for schools. Some school leaders complained that handling admissions was an enormous amount of work: communicating the rules, processing all the applications, managing selection decisions, taking calls from families trying to bypass the lottery, and communicating the results to families. And while some students were not accepted to any schools, others received admittance letters from multiple schools, registered at more than one of them, and selected the one to attend on the first day of school, leaving the other schools in a lurch. School leaders could not be certain how many students would show up, which, with funding tied directly to enrollment, meant they could not be sure how much money they would have for the year. This complication forced schools to keep more money in reserve to avoid last-minute staff dismissals.[3]

The uncertainty was worse, though, for families. Schools at least benefited from the law of large numbers. Some students would not show up, but others they did not expect would come anyway. With hundreds of slots, any random fluctuations that might affect specific families would likely average out for each school. But for families, it was a single coin flip for each child. I know of families who ended up moving to the suburbs partly because they could not be assured in advance that their children would get into one of their few top choices. Relying on these lotteries was too risky.

All of this additional work and uncertainty was a natural by-product of giving schools autonomy over the choice process. Under the System, student enrollment had been much simpler. There was really one rule — attend the school in your neighborhood. Complex application and selection processes were unnecessary, and schools knew fairly precisely how many students would show up on the first day of class. In contrast, decentralized school choice was time-consuming, full of uncertainty, and sometimes unfair. Could it be improved?

The Shift to Centralized Enrollment

Decentralized enrollment created problems for students and parents, and a political problem for the RSD.[4] Though control had shifted to the state, which was more insulated from local pressures than the school district had been, no politician or bureaucrat likes bad headlines. The decentralized enrollment process created many of them.

As with student discipline, the state decided to centralize the enrollment process.[5] John White, in his time in New York City, had seen just such a system in place for that city's high schools. In the first step of the new enrollment process, which came to be called OneApp, each family submitted a single application form to the state for each child in which it ranked schools in order of preference. A computer algorithm then used families' rankings to make school assignments. In a perfect world, every family would get its top-ranked choice. If more parents ranked a school first than the school had seats available, the priority categories (e.g., having a sibling in the school) would be considered.[6] To deal with the excess demand in certain schools, the algorithm assigned a lottery number to each student and essentially flipped a coin to determine who received the remaining seats.[7]

All RSD-authorized schools were required to participate in OneApp, and eventually all the OPSB schools would as well. Centralized enrollment helped address many of the problems of the decentralized version: Parents could fill out one form with one deadline and know that seats would really be assigned by lottery. Schools knew well in advance how many students would show up — the algorithm assigned each student to exactly one school, so students could not make last-minute switches.[8] If students showed up to the wrong school on the first day of class, the school could call the RSD and quickly learn where to send them. Perhaps most important, the combination of ranked family preferences, lottery numbers, and the computer algorithm helped shift the balance of power so that families were choosing schools more than schools were choosing students.

The OneApp approach is also arguably more efficient. When applications were submitted one by one, individual schools had no way of knowing which schools students desperately wanted to attend and which schools they saw as backups. Even if the school leaders knew families' top choices, they had no incentive to take them into account when making admission decisions, especially when the schools themselves preferred certain students. Even if schools wanted to take into account families' preferences, doing so would be extremely difficult to coordinate across so many schools. And had they been willing to accept the substantial coordination costs, the best they could do would produce the same result as the OneApp algorithm. It would have been slower and more costly for school staff to do what computers are designed for. OneApp efficiently coordinated the matching of students to schools and helped ensure access for students to all participating schools.[9] As John White put it, "Systematizing choice or bringing some level of transparency and order to the market was something that we had to do because it was fair to kids."[10] It was fair, transparent, and efficient.

The OneApp system also had some less obvious benefits. With decentralized enrollment, the RSD could not see when students transferred, were expelled, or dropped out of schools. With OneApp in place, it could track what was happening and provide oversight to prevent schools from unfairly excluding or pushing out students. The centralized enrollment, transfer, and expulsion systems were interconnected and required centralized data collection.

Centralizing the enrollment process and data also meant that the RSD could see the open seats in the schools under its authority. This was helpful for the small number of students who had to be placed manually, by RSD staff, for instance, when students arrived in the city in the middle of the school year. This gave the state RSD a way to prevent charter schools from pushing students out and then leaving the seats empty—another of the tools of exclusion listed in chapter 6.

Perhaps the least obvious benefit of OneApp came with the closure and takeover of charter schools that failed to perform. What would happen to students in the affected schools? With OneApp, the RSD could give them priority in the choice process, so they could get into a different school that they really wanted. "We could never have done all the high school phaseouts [closures and takeovers] without having [a centralized] enrollment system," White told me.[11]

These advantages did come with some practical problems. The One-App algorithm, based on ideas from Nobel Prize–winning economist Alvin Roth, is so cryptic that the state RSD, which was initially in charge of implementing OneApp, could not explain it to families. The complexity led to misunderstanding, which led families to make mistakes, such as ranking too few schools or thinking, falsely, they could game the system by ranking their actual first preference as second or third—which in reality only reduced their chances of getting their true top choice. In focus groups during the first year OneApp was used, parents expressed confusion and frustration.[12] Some parents mistakenly thought that phone calls they had made to well-connected friends had aided their children's acceptances into specific schools. Sitting in restaurants and coffee shops, I often heard animated conversations blasting the OneApp. Three years after its introduction, 53 percent of its users were still dissatisfied with OneApp.[13]

Even after all of this careful thought by the state RSD, parents at the public events my research team and I organized still reported that the "choice" system gave them few real options. How could this be? Attendance zones had been all but eliminated. The process had been taken out of the hands of school leaders so they could not select students themselves. Families could list up to eight options on the OneApp form. How could parents still feel like they had no real choices? Clearly, computers can only go so far in solving difficult human problems.

Making Choice Real?

Part of the reason parents perceived limits on choice harkens back to our discussion of the Armstrong and Saenger schools. The two schools were in very different tiers, with very different reputations. More broadly, and despite the substantial improvement on a variety of outcomes, 36 percent

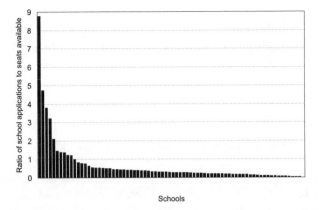

FIGURE 7.1. Most schools were in low demand. *Source*: Analysis by the author and Catherine Balfe of OneApp data in Public information about school demand is available at EnrollNola, "Fall 2017 Enroll-NOLA Annual Report Appendix." *Notes*: The figure reports, for each school, the number of applicants who ranked a school first in OneApp for kindergarten or ninth grade, divided by the number of seats available in those grades. Lower rankings of schools—families could list up to eight in order of preference—are not reflected here. Schools not using OneApp are excluded for lack of data, except for Saenger School, mentioned in chapter 5, which handled its enrollments on its own. This may slightly exaggerate the demand for Saenger relative to schools using the centralized system, because those applying to Saenger might not have thought of it as their first choice (anecdotally, however, few applicants accepted to Saenger turned down the offer).

of schools in the city still had letter grades in the D or F range as of 2014.[14] Naturally, the top-tier schools were in much higher demand than the others. Saenger School, as noted earlier, had at least four times as many applicants as seats. As figure 7.1 shows, another dozen schools had more applications than seats, and the remaining schools—the vast majority— had demand well below their availability (i.e., a ratio less than one).

Roughly 60 percent of families got their first choice.[15] But the majority of those who listed high-demand schools at the top came away disappointed, ending up at their second, third, or fourth choice. Getting the second choice out of sixty-plus elementary schools sounds good—it could have been a lot worse—but to parents it felt like failure. For some students, going from the first- to the second-ranked school was a big step down, especially when parents had been told they could choose what they wanted.[16] It is therefore no surprise that nearly half of families reported that they had trouble finding schools that were a good fit.[17] One school leader told me that most of the students attending her school did not want to be there.

Even with this sophisticated choice-based system, then, there was clearly a big difference for parents between freely ranking their preferences and actually getting what they wanted. Competition did not push out the worst schools, in part because parents had to send their children somewhere. This is one unusual market.

What Schools Do Families Want (and Why)?

Centralized enrollment, for all its flaws and inherent difficulties, did give families some opportunity to choose what they wanted. So what did families want? The OneApp data proved useful here as well. We studied the relationship between parents' school rankings and the characteristics of schools being ranked. If highly rated schools tend to have something in common, then we can infer that this is what families are looking for, especially if we also account for other school characteristics at the same time.

We focused on a long list of school factors that had been the topic of prior research and that parents were most likely to know about. The New Orleans Parents' Guide included more than a hundred pieces of information about every school, such as program offerings, admission requirements, and state-mandated school report card data, including the School Performance Score calculated and reported each year by the Louisiana Department of Education. The school letter grades calculated from these scores—from A down to F—were also sometimes included in the OneApp form. As families picked schools, the letter grades were right in front of them. The Parents' Guide was designed to provide extensive information for parents and the public at large about what schools said they offered, data that were partly corroborated by the guide's publisher.

The results from our OneApp/Parents' Guide analysis confirmed what we heard in our public events and what we expected from prior research: that families wanted higher-quality school options (as measured by both school grades and student growth measures).[18] They also favored schools closer to home. Distance is critical given that parents have to get their children to school every day and sometimes get there themselves.

Our analysis also allowed us to consider a wide range of other factors and to break the results down for different types of families. For families looking for elementary schools, the OneApp results showed that they focused especially on distance from home to school, as well as the availability of after-school care. This was not surprising. Families do not want their seven-year-olds to have to sit on the bus for an hour every day to get to school. In interviews, New Orleans school leaders reported that transportation was one of the topics parents brought up most often when inquiring about their schools.[19] This highlights the importance of practical, as opposed to narrowly educational, considerations in schooling choices.

At the high school level, distance mattered less and extracurricular activities more, especially the most popular activities in New Orleans: band and football. Louisiana sends a larger share of young people to the National Football League than any other state. The New Orleans Saints are the second most popular professional sports team in the country—in any sport—with more than 80 percent of local adults having watched or attended a game in any given year.[20] It was not just boys wanting to play football that mattered, but the entertainment value and camaraderie of Friday night football games.

The unique cultural feature of New Orleans, though, is the holiday celebrated here unlike anywhere else. Mardi Gras is an almost four-week extravaganza with upward of thirty parades, each with a two-hour procession of marchers and floats. At the center of the Mardi Gras festivities are high school bands—the large parades have five to eight bands each. The best high school bands are in high demand, and the schools are paid for their time. In most high schools nationally, an extracurricular activity like band might draw an audience of a few dozen parents and friends. In New Orleans, being in the high school band means an audience of a quarter million people. The flip side is this: attending a high school without a band means no Mardi Gras marching.

In addition to looking for certain product traits, consumers tend to buy a "brand they can trust." Some people are not comfortable buying generic medicines, for example, because their health is paramount and not something to take chances with. This is especially true with our children. Families have good reason to pay attention to school choices, not only because of short-term happiness and the obvious long-term social and economic consequences for their children, but because schools become a lifelong part of our identities. Parents knew that their children, once they became adults, would get the quintessential New Orleans question: "What school did you go to?" They knew the school name would be called out at Mardi Gras balls. They wanted their children to have a good answer.

For all of these reasons, parents may have wanted to send their children to schools that were familiar, comfortable, and reputable, perhaps even the ones they had attended themselves. In our analysis, we therefore considered whether families had a preference for sending their children to schools that had long local histories and traditions, by studying whether schools used a pre-Katrina "legacy" school name as part of their new names. Early on, the reformers were trying to establish their own reputations and seemed to assume the System had been so bad that the citizens of New Orleans would only view the old names negatively—as bad brands. This may have been true for some families, but not on average. Even after accounting for all other differences, we found that schools, especially high schools, with legacy names were preferred. Recall that it took a full decade before the local black community started to think that the post-reform schools were better than the ones they replaced. Their old schools were often not a bad brand in their eyes.

Collectively these factors—practical considerations like distance and after-school care, activities like football and band, and school legacies—seemed to overwhelm the role of academic quality. Yes, students were traveling a lot farther, but this was substantially because the themes of nearby schools were a poor fit or they could not get into the schools in their neighborhood. Also, while families reported that academic quality was the most important factor they considered, only half said they considered school letter grades or, implicitly, the test scores on which they are mainly based.[21]

We can gauge the role of different factors by considering them in different combinations, or packages. For example, the average parent in our data preferred an elementary school that was right across the street from the family's house, had free after-care, and a C letter grade, over a school that was two miles away with no after-school care and a B grade. Likewise, a high school with a legacy status, football and band, and a C grade would typically be preferred to one with no legacy status, no football or band, and a B letter grade.[22] Academics mattered, but this was just one factor in a more complex personal equation.

Our ability to analyze the combination of OneApp data and Parents' Guide came with some big advantages. We did not have to worry about the problems plaguing prior research that had relied on surveys of parents or their enrollment patterns.[23] But there was one thing we could not do: study parent preferences for schools that did not exist. In a 2011 survey, 82 percent of New Orleans parents reported that it was important for children to attend neighborhood schools like those that had been there prior to the reforms.[24] Some wanted their children to attend schools with the children down the block, schools that served as community anchors, schools that offered a wider variety of extracurricular options, and schools that focused less on high-stakes testing. In other words, they wanted the types of schools that charter and choice-based systems are ill-designed to provide and that they had no opportunity to rank.

In my conversations with Ashana Bigard, I asked her about the choice system. She summed up the problem this way:

> It sorts parents into schools that they don't want their children to go to. You have parents who have three small children going to three different schools. If we had a district school, at least my three children could go to their district [school].[25]

There were provisions in OneApp that guaranteed siblings could stay together in these situations, although this often meant going to school that was even further from the ideal. Making allowance for siblings also made the OneApp process even more complicated than it already was.

Finding Niches, Defining Brands

The analysis above focuses on what parents want and shows that they consider a wide variety of factors when choosing schools. Another part of the market theory is that students also have different needs and preferences, and that markets will create a variety of options to meet them. Did this happen? To answer this, we turned again to data from the New Orleans Parents' Guide.

The top section of figure 7.2 shows that New Orleans charter schools often choose a specific theme or curricular specialization—something traditional public schools rarely do. Consistent with the interviews in which school leaders told us that they tried to differentiate themselves from the pack, only about 20 percent of elementary/middle and high schools had no clear theme (i.e., "none of above" in the figure). In contrast, if we were to create a similar figure for traditional public schools, the vast majority of districts would have no theme, with 0 percent in almost all of the narrow curricular categories. To be clear, traditional public schools often offer some curricula on this list, among many other options. The point here is that they rarely specialize; they vary but not in a coherent way.

With extracurricular activities, traditional public schools typically offer a bit of everything—all of those listed in the middle section of figure 7.2 (except perhaps service learning and character development). Both their smaller size and penchant for specialization, however, made it harder for charter schools to offer as many extracurricular activities. As predicted, figure 7.2 shows that most charter schools offered most activities, but many chose not to offer some, like certain high school sports and drama, which had been nearly universal under the System.

Some variation in schools is not reflected in this figure. There were five alternative charter schools; many large school districts have such high schools to serve students who have been expelled from, or otherwise struggled badly in, regular schools. In New Orleans, one of the five was also a middle school that served only about thirty students, all of whom had severe mental health issues.[26] Seven other schools emphasized their diverse student bodies. Four schools had language immersion programs. Another focused on preparing students for jobs in the technology sector. Several schools, especially high schools still governed by the Orleans Parish School Board, also operated in most respects like traditional public schools, offering a wide variety of academic and extracurricular options and trying to hire career teachers trained in university schools of education. Four schools even re-unionized.

While figure 7.1 reflects only New Orleans, our additional analyses show at least as much variety in New Orleans as in other cities similar in size and demographics.[27] In fact, the extent of variety was directly proportional to the number of charter schools in these cities. We cannot prove that this pattern was caused by the introduction of charter schools—correlation is not causation—but the likelihood seems high given that school leaders said they were doing just what the theory predicted: they were trying to be distinctive.

In other respects, there was less choice in New Orleans than it seems. Schools have incentives to make it appear that they are distinct even

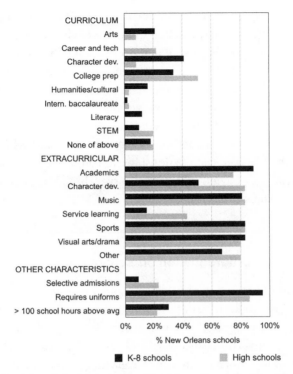

FIGURE 7.2. The variety of schools in post-reform New Orleans. *Sources*: Analyses of the New Orleans Parents Guide by the author (bottom section) and the Center for Reinventing Public Education (top two sections). Betheny Gross et al., "Are City Schools Becoming Monolithic? Analyzing the Diversity of Options in Denver, New Orleans, and Washington, D.C." (Center for Reinventing Public Education, University of Washington, 2017). *Notes*: The bottom section is from the 2014–2015 school year, the top two sections from the 2015–2016 school year. The categories are formally nonexclusive (i.e., schools can be in more than one category at the same time), though this is less common in the curriculum section.

when they are really the same. Rarely does an advertisement say, "Come to us. We are just like everyone else." It could be that the variety seen in figure 7.1 reflected factors that are not that important to families, or factors that are important but that the Parents' Guide represented poorly—it was perhaps more of a marketing device than a descriptive catalog. From the parents we spoke with, and even some of the reform leaders, the message seemed to be: you can't judge these books by their covers.

The idea of "school choice" also usually refers to choice *between* schools, but choice *within* schools is at least as important. Charter schools tend be smaller and more specialized, which creates more between-school choice, but traditional public schools, though derided as cafeterias, typically have more within-school choice. That is a key advantage—you can be fairly sure that everyone will find something they like in a traditional public school. It is not just extracurricular activities. Any given traditional public school has options specifically designed for students with disabilities and those without them, for students who like sports and those who do not, for students who are especially interested in math and those who are not. Given the costs that come with switching schools—the loss of social relationships and adjustments to new school rules and norms—having each school serve a broad range of needs and interests has some real advantages.

Differentiation on School Culture

So far, I have treated differentiation as something that can be done in a piecemeal fashion, by offering a specific academic theme or clearly identifiable course, program, or activity. But some aspects of schools are more amorphous—they reflect a school's essence and nature. We usually call this "culture," and it is suffused in everything that happens in schools.

Much of the evidence presented over the past several chapters pertains to school culture, even if I did not call it that. While there was no typical school in New Orleans, teaching after the reforms tended to be more structured and management more businesslike than it had been before. Interactions among students, teachers, and administrators tended to be more transactional and conservative. Student discipline was stricter. All of these are elements of school culture.

The culture of the communities that people grow up in—their language, values, traditions, and histories—also infuse school culture. When I first started studying charter schools, the three closest to my home (in Michigan) were named National Heritage Academy, Cesar Chavez Academy, and El-Shabazz Academy—attended almost exclusively by white, Hispanic, and black students, respectively. Such culturally themed schools did not arise in New Orleans, but the debate about white, outside teachers was clearly part of the same storyline. Race and ethnicity are also intertwined with one's culture.

Also recall that people are generally more comfortable being with others like themselves. Churches, for example, remain among society's most racially segregated institutions. Schools are right there with them. White flight from traditional public schools in New Orleans, precipitated by the *Brown v. Board of Education* decision, meant that white families left their local public schools, often for suburban public schools or religious schools tied to their churches, whose members looked like themselves and had the incomes to pay private school tuition.

Those of different cultures also tend to have different schooling preferences. In New Orleans at least, the new, more instructionally conservative schools typically serve lower-income minority families. Meanwhile, language immersion programs, Montessori, and other programs considered to be more progressive, are more likely to serve white and higher-income populations. We found evidence in New Orleans that preferences for schools varied by family income,[28] and other evidence suggests that black families and those in Southern states have greater preference for strict discipline.[29]

To be clear, there is probably much more variation in preference within racial/ethnic groups than between them, but even small differences become amplified by segregation in society as a whole. The fact that people are more comfortable with others like themselves, and the fact that neighborhoods tend to tip toward similar racial, ethnic, and income groups, means that schools tend to segregate. Private schools tend to be somewhat more segregated than traditional public schools because all the usual cultural differences are correlated with race and income, and the ability to pay private school tuition.[30] When schools segregate, they take on the identity of their dominant groups. And that identity makes them segregate even more, attracting some, excluding others, and shaping schools in powerful ways.

Policy, Access, and Segregation

The social and economic forces undergirding segregation are clearly powerful. Also, as we saw in chapters 2 and 6, segregation means schools end up in different tiers, which translate into unequal access to quality education. The question is, can we design government policies to counteract these forces? If policies were designed to at least ensure that families were the ones doing the choosing—that they had equitable access to schools—would this lead to less segregation and more equitable access?

The New Orleans school reformers recognized that low-income families lived further from high-quality schools and were particularly constrained by a lack of transportation, greater distances from the schools in highest demand, and the need for free after-school care.[31] So the reformers required schools to provide transportation. They recognized that schools had incentives to exclude certain students and that, with autonomy over school design and discipline, they had the means to do so. So they instituted centralized enrollment and expulsion systems. More broadly, the state sent a message that equity mattered.

If these policies had an effect on access to schools, then we might see signs of increased enrollment of disadvantaged students in top-tier schools. One way to study this is through measures of segregation. While this term usually implies a discussion of race, I mean something broader here: the concentration of any types of students in particular schools. If, for example, centralized enrollment made it easier for low-scoring students to attend high-quality schools, then that change might show up as a reduction in cross-school segregation of low-scoring students.[32]

We considered the trends in segregation for ten different student subgroups, by race, income, disability, English learning status, and achievement, in each case making separate calculations for elementary/middle and high schools. We also considered two different measures that capture different aspects of segregation and used the same type of analyses discussed in chapter 4, comparing New Orleans to other districts, before and after the reforms.[33] All told, we ended up with forty different segregation measures.[34]

New Orleans was highly segregated to begin with. There was a clear opportunity for improvement here, just as there had been with the city's very low test scores and other academic measures. However, we see no evidence that the reforms improved matters. No clear changes in the direction of segregation were evident for thirty-two of the forty groups/measures, while seven measures implied increased segregation: for low-income students in both elementary and high schools, for white and Hispanic elementary students, and for black, white, and Hispanic high-school students. We saw a decline in segregation for only one subgroup (high-achieving elementary students). These patterns were generally reinforced by analysis of student transfers between schools.[35]

The stagnation of segregation is noteworthy given just how segregated New Orleans schools were to start with and the intense efforts of the RSD to improve access.[36] We did not see any clear breaks, for example, in segregation trends after the centralized enrollment and transfer policies were put in place. It might be too early to tell, or that the policies did not apply to all schools (especially the high-demand schools), or that improved access might not show up in these segregation measures. Alternatively, it could be that even carefully constructed choice policies are insufficient to overcome the unusual features of the schooling market and other factors — self-segregation, housing policy, and the tipping point phenomenon — working against access. Clearly, there are powerful forces at work that even the best laid plans of school policy may struggle to address.

Theory versus Reality of Choice, Revisited

One of the main arguments for market-based school reform is that it extends choice — and thus educational opportunity — to families who cannot otherwise afford to exit traditional public schools for private schools. The results in this and the previous chapter provide support for one part of this theory: choice created a wide range of higher-performing schools throughout the city.

However, the existence of better and more varied schools, and a sophisticated system for gaining access to them, was not enough to make people feel they had real or equitable access to school quality. There were simply too few schools that were both high quality and able to satisfy parents' practical needs, such as being close to home and providing services like after-care. The natural tiers of the schooling market meant that some schools were in very high demand, so many did not get what they said they wanted on their OneApp forms. Schools also still had almost 20 different ways to select students.

Some of the schools families wanted simply did not exist. This was true of the many longtime New Orleanians we spoke with. It was also true of the reformers themselves, some of whom fretted privately that they would not send their own children to the schools they had created. Critics of urban traditional public schools often point to the fact that the teachers in public schools send their own children to private ones, but this was equally the case with New Orleans charter schools. The reformers knew this was a problem and struggled to fix it.

Calling it a choice system also seems to have implied a promise that the reforms could not keep. When people hear the word "choice," they have certain expectations, formed by years of acting as consumers in other markets. But creating real choice in schooling is clearly difficult. The unusual features of the schooling market seem almost to preclude typical consumer choice. This is the frustration we heard anytime someone mentioned the term "OneApp." Families did not feel like they had real choices, or that the Superman in the documentary had come to save them. If the goal was to provide excellent education to all children, there were many signs that something had gone wrong.

Traditional public schools might even have one advantage over charter schools when it comes to choice. Many families wanted neighborhood schools that were close to home and offered a variety of options within a single school, through wide-ranging elective courses and extracurricular programs. While reformers sometimes derided this "cafeteria" approach, choice between schools requires students to take the costly step of transferring schools if they find they are not getting what they want. This is apparently why parents displayed such mixed emotions about choice: while more than 80 percent of parents said they wanted neighborhood schools, almost the exact same percentage wanted choice.[37] Many apparently did not recognize that moving toward one of these meant moving away from the other.

What does all of this tell us about how the New Orleans reforms generated such large measurable effects on student outcomes? The reality is that the improvements were not driven by parents and students, nor by a competitive process that pushed out low-performing or unwanted schools. Parents and students could choose the schools they wanted, in theory, but they did not always want what the reformers made available, and they were choosing as much based on practical considerations and extracurricular activities that were detached from academic measures. This, in turn, led to school responses that were superficial.

But choice did matter in at least one, more indirect, way: it allowed families to find a better fit and therefore made New Orleans an attractive environment for charter operators. It is hard to see how KIPP could have functioned with its largely no-excuses approach if its schools had been forced to accept all students living in the immediate vicinity, including those who strongly opposed no-excuses.

As the subsequent chapters further reinforce, the improvement in student outcomes was not driven mainly or directly by choice or competition. Nor was the reduction in achievement gaps driven by increased access of disadvantaged students to relatively high-performing schools. The effects were driven not by parents and students on the demand side but, as we will see more later, by the supply side — especially by what government officials and reform leaders thought was best.

CHAPTER 8

Cooperation: A (Partial) Way to Soften the Market's Hard Edges

Even the most ardent supporters of markets recognize that problems can emerge from market competition. Few would endorse how some schools selected or pushed students out. No one liked the fact that having more independent organizations running schools meant having to spend so much on management and transportation.

Yet, many reform advocates saw these as acceptable sacrifices because the principles of parent choice, school autonomy, and performance-based accountability would help the schools self-correct. Unbounded by rules and regulations, education leaders could, in theory, work together and find creative ways to address the worst effects of competition — smoothing out the rough edges. Local reform advocates Leslie Jacobs and Mary Landrieu certainly believed as much. They even had a name for their happy mixture of competition and cooperation: "coopetition."

It all sounded good and hopeful, but this modified theory turned out to be as much a mixed success as competition had been. Competition, even when mixed with a spirit of public service, is still competition, which means the interests of schools are often not aligned. Even when mutually beneficial solutions exist, so that cooperation is theoretically possible, it is unclear whether, in a decentralized system, the large number of educational actors could come to agreement in a way that served students well. Could schools both compete and cooperate at the same

time? Could they use their sense of mission and commitment to public service in ways that made government regulation unnecessary? New
Orleans provides at least a partial answer, as the leaders of the effort were
conscious of the problems and were asking these same questions themselves.

I start here by introducing the main methods of cooperation at educators' disposal: banding together in informal networks, contracting out
between charter schools and third parties, and merging schools into
charter management organizations (CMOs). I then describe how these
played out in New Orleans, including the cooperative roles played by the
Cowen Institute, New Schools for New Orleans (NSNO), and contractors. I identify some specific problems that predictably emerged in New
Orleans and consider whether the three cooperative methods were adequate to solve them. It turns out that the interests of school leaders, in a
market setting, are not sufficiently aligned in most cases, and even when
they are, the costs of negotiating and enforcing agreements across groups
works against the best of intentions. The analysis highlights the potential
of cooperation but also the narrow circumstances and limited number of
problems where that potential is likely to manifest.

Paradoxically, the effort that went into cooperation, which often met
with limited immediate success, still seems to have paved the way for successful *involuntary* government oversight later on. This may have been
the most important, albeit indirect, contribution of cooperation.

Cooperation versus Hierarchy

Perhaps the most familiar means of cooperation occurs when organizations join forces by *contracting out* services to third parties. This approach
is a logical extension of market competition itself. The government contracts out to charter operators to run schools. Schools and CMOs can
then turn around and contract out some activities to others, purchasing
them at the market price. School districts, too, contract out on a regular
basis, especially for non-instructional services such as busing, food service, textbooks, and office supplies. Again, this is all voluntary. Schools
can decide to provide or produce these things themselves or decide, of
their own accord, to write a contract with someone else.

One advantage of contracting is that the contractor can specialize and take advantage of economies of scale; many schools can choose the same contractor. *Mergers* have the same advantages. Schools, in other words, could voluntarily join forces through charter management organizations (CMOs) to share fixed costs such as bus transportation, information technology, accounting and budgeting, curriculum planning, and so on, and create specialized expertise at the CMO level. Indeed, some initially independent New Orleans charter schools concluded that it was too difficult and inefficient to operate on their own and voluntarily approached CMOs. As with contracting, the merger approach was voluntary, in the sense that schools could decide to merge with these other organizations, or not, at their own discretion.

The final, and perhaps most intuitive, mechanism of cooperation is the *informal network*. These were numerous in New Orleans, with the Cowen Institute and NSNO being prime examples. Instead of contractual relationships, these groups would bring school leaders together periodically, and informally, to talk about specific problems and solutions. Schools did not have to pay one another or sign agreements to engage in this last form of cooperation.

With its decentralized structure, the New Orleans reforms were more dependent on all of these forms of cooperation than are more hierarchical school districts. This is not to say that people in school districts did not cooperate with one another; they simply have less of a need and opportunity for it. In a school district hierarchy, everyone recognizes that the superintendent is in charge and coordinates resources across units. Coordination, by definition, is less voluntary than cooperation.

The top chart in figure 8.1 highlights the structure of the New Orleans Public Schools prior to the reforms.[1] It shows a traditional hierarchy where solid lines indicate the authority of the board over the superintendent and the superintendent over the district's various departments and schools.

The bottom chart in figure 8.1 illustrates the more decentralized and cooperative nature of schools after the reforms. Here, there are only two solid lines—between the CMO and the schools it operates. The dashed lines between the authorizer and the charter schools indicate that the government agency has governing authority, but no authority over the day-to-day management, of charter schools. Finally, the dotted lines indicate voluntary relationships between schools, contractors, and informal networks, such as the Cowen Institute and NSNO.

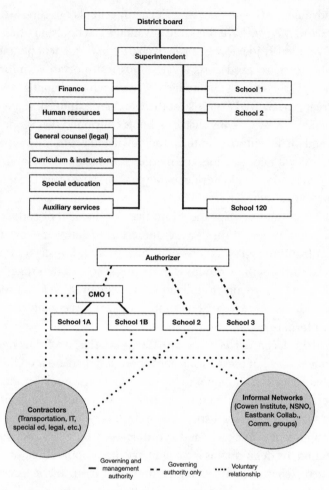

FIGURE 8.1. Authority and cooperative relationships in traditional school districts (top) and New Orleans schools after the reform (bottom).

The first visual difference between the two charts is in the types of relationships between organizations. In bureaucracies, power is vested at the top, in the board and superintendent. Under the reforms, most of the lines are dashed and dotted, indicating less formal, more voluntary relationships.

The second, and less evident, difference is that the reforms entail a much larger number of relationships in total. A more complete version of the bottom chart, for New Orleans, would break out all of the separate contractors and informal networks, including the relationship of each one to each school, like a large spider web. It is this combination of more, and more voluntary, relationships that led the reformers to talk about their approach as an "ecosystem," that is, complex networks of interconnected actors commingling in a single environment.

The solid lines from CMOs to their schools reflect the fact that CMOs are like mini-school districts. A CMO has its own (appointed) boards, which hires a CEO who in turn hires individual school leaders. While some stand-alone charter schools voluntarily chose to join a CMO, to take advantage of expertise and economies of scale, the subsequent relationship was more hierarchical. In New Orleans, a decade after the reforms started, just over half of charter school students were in schools that operated within CMOs.[2] Many school leaders reported that CMOs, like traditional school districts, set salary schedules and established policies that all of their schools were required to attend to.[3]

To simplify matters, I have left certain pieces out of these charts.[4] In particular, there are the organizations that affect or circumscribe all the various relationships. Under the reforms, the reform family—Patrick Dobard, Leslie Jacobs, Sarah Usdin, Paul Vallas, John White, and others—affected everything, from the initial reform design to the creation of new nonprofits to the approval of charter applications to the RSD policies, not to mention all aspects of implementation.

In the top chart, a similar broad role is played by teacher unions. Both groups might bristle at the comparison. Many reformers will object that they had no direct financial interest in the reforms the way the unions did, while unions may object that they were actually elected by teachers to represent them, who were the experts and knew most about the needs of their students. The disparate groups put their power to very different purposes, to be sure, but this misses the point: unions and reformers had in common a broad and deep reach throughout most aspects of school governance and management. The roles of the unions and the reform family were all-encompassing.

Ultimately, we are interested in this chapter not just in illustrating the differences between the System and the reforms, but in understanding how well the decentralized reforms were able to leverage the three mechanisms of cooperation—mergers, contracts, and networks—to address the problems created by competition. As we have already seen, with the large increase in spending on administration and transportation, cooperation was only partly successful in addressing the loss of economies of scale. In what follows, I elaborate further and try to explain why cooperation was also insufficient to deal with problems such as equitable access to schools.

Conditions for Effective Cooperation

When is cooperation among autonomous actors likely to succeed or fail? Two general types of answers stand out in academic research. First, the general conditions have to be ripe for cooperation. In particular, the various actors—the potential collaborators—have to trust one another. They need to know each other, share similar values, have similar levels of power, and believe that the other potential partners will follow through on their commitments.[5] Without trust, it is unlikely that the key players necessary to solve a problem will even start the conversation and come to the negotiating table.

Even when these general conditions hold, the potential for cooperation also depends on the nature of the problem. I focus on three aspects of the problem that are likely to matter most:

- PROBLEMS ARE SEEN AS SEVERE. Some, though not necessarily all, of the key actors need to believe a problem meaningfully harms their interests or missions. To the degree that schools see themselves as public entities, cooperation is more likely to work when the issue is a matter of significant public concern. When journalists report on an issue in newspapers and on the television news, when community groups and activists protest, and when elected officials draw attention to a problem in their campaigns, key actors are generally willing to go to greater lengths to solve it.

- COSTS OF REACHING AGREEMENT (TRANSACTION COSTS) ARE LOW. In some cases, a solution to the problem might exist that everyone would find beneficial. Even then, however, it can be difficult to find that solution and negotiate specific agreements that satisfy everyone. Cooperation takes time: identifying the key stakeholders, defining the problem, identifying potential solutions, negotiating roles, and so on. The complexity and costs of this process increase exponentially—and the probability of success decreases—with the number of stakeholders and level of resources involved. Also, in almost every negotiation, the costs and benefits of solving a problem are higher for certain actors. The key actors need to take the time to agree on how everyone benefits in order to allocate the costs of cooperation in a way that seems fair.

- POTENTIAL EXISTS TO ALIGN INTERESTS (LOW ENFORCE-MENT COSTS). Suppose there were a solution that everyone agreed on; if everyone then followed through on their promises, everyone would be better off. The issue is the "if." The various groups would have to promise to act, and in some cases, it may be difficult to observe whether they have followed through or decided to "free ride" on the contributions of others. This may require what economists call enforcement or monitoring costs. If the enforcement costs are not too high, then cooperation might be possible. This threat to cooperation is lessened when the necessary actions are easily visible.

Unless *all* of these conditions are met, it is unlikely that stakeholders will even attempt cooperation, let alone succeed in it.

The above conditions for cooperation also highlight a deeper conflict within the larger competitive environment. We cannot compartmentalize the two elements of "coopetition" because competition creates the conditions—divergent interests, mistrust, and a less public focus—that preclude cooperation. Competition and cooperation do not always fit neatly together.

Addressing Specific Problems in the Schooling Market

The degree to which cooperation can be effective, then, depends on the nature of the problem stakeholders are trying to solve and the potential set of solutions. It is worth considering some specific problems that we have already seen arise under market-based school reforms, and how much cooperation would reasonably resolve them.

UNFAIR ENROLLMENT PRACTICES. Chapters 2 and 6 showed that schools—especially those in the top tier with high demand—have incentives to select their preferred students. This is a significant problem not only for equity, but for efficiency. The ability to select students misdirects school leaders' competitive energies toward "glossification" or surface-level improvement. Genuine school improvement can get lost.

Unfortunately, this analysis also points to why cooperation is not likely to solve the problem. Schools in the top tiers, like Saenger School, have an incentive not to cooperate because they tend to benefit from what other schools see as a problem. Lower-tier schools, like Armstrong School, should be more willing to cooperate, as they are already more engaged in fair practices—they are simply trying to attract enough students to survive. But it does little good for schools already using fair practices to band together when it is the selective ones that are the problem. Also, any agreement would be costly to enforce because it is difficult to monitor enrollment practices, especially with the more subtle tools that schools use to exclude certain students.

SPECIALIZED SERVICES. A growing share of the US student population has special needs. This includes English language learners and children with learning disabilities and mental health issues. Urban districts, where market-based school reforms are most common, usually have a disproportionate share of these students. New Orleans, in particular, has long been near the top nationally in the rate of extreme poverty, murder, and crime, all of which create trauma and therefore a need for mental health services.[6] Hurricane Katrina only made matters worse.[7] Mental health was an issue many school leaders raised but seemed to have few answers for.

The interests of schools, unfortunately, were not well aligned on this. Government programs generally provide insufficient funds to support quality specialized services, so schools wishing to provide them have to pull resources from the general education programs. Some of the new charter schools served students with special needs out of a sense of mission, but not enough to fill local needs—as the SPLC lawsuit, filed on behalf of a group of special education students, clearly highlighted. Specialized services are expensive and therefore increase the transaction costs involved in pooling resources. The focus on test scores and poor design of state accountability metrics made matters worse by punishing schools that served these students, giving them lower School Performance Scores, even when educators did their job effectively. The most obvious strategy for many schools was to push these students to other schools.

SCHOOL BUILDINGS. The most important resource in schools is teachers, but they still cannot do their work without appropriate school buildings. The question is, how do school leaders gain access to these essential assets? At first blush, this should not seem like a problem for charter schools. It is common for small businesses and NGOs to seek loans to purchase or construct buildings. When an organization has a stable source of revenue, banks are willing to extend loans, using the building itself as collateral. If a business fails, the bank can sell the building to someone else for other purposes.

The problem is that schools do not work this way. Charter and private schools, especially in their early years, have limited financial stability and lack the reserves generally needed for such large, long-term investments—school buildings cost at least $10 million. This is especially problematic for stand-alone charter schools, whose enrollments can be unpredictable. When the repayment of funds is contingent on receipt of future government funding, the problems are compounded. This is because, in addition to the usual market instability, shifting political winds can affect a school's financial security and therefore its ability to repay the loans. As we will see in the next chapter, uncertainty about government decisions was a real concern because the state regularly took over New Orleans charter schools. Banks do not like to take risks.

The risk for banks is lower when the building can be easily reused for other purposes, but this condition is also more problematic for schools. School buildings can of course be put to other uses but not without substantial renovations, which reduces their value and increases the chance that the building investment will be wasted. Renting school buildings, as an alternative to purchasing them, is unlikely to be a productive solution for the same reason: there are rarely buildings designed for schooling that are available to rent. An exception is in large cities that have seen declining population and enrollments, where old school buildings often sit dormant, but even then, such buildings are usually owned by school districts, which have little incentive to cooperate with competing charter schools.

Individual schools or CMOs operating on their own in the market cannot deal with such situations well, nor can they easily cooperate. Suppose school operators banded together to purchase or construct buildings. In theory, this has promise because, while each individual school has uncertain future funding, the collection of schools, with fixed demand, has almost guaranteed long-term stability. However, all the school leaders would have to agree on which CMOs would get which buildings, even though some buildings and locations would be far more beneficial than others.

Cooperation among schools is therefore unlikely to provide access to school buildings. It is a significant potential problem with limited enforcement costs, but the transaction costs to cooperation would be enormous. In addition to the vast sums of money involved, school buildings, and their locations, are a core basis for competition between schools. Governments, in contrast, can coordinate resources directly, can spread the risk and borrow money for construction at lower interest rates, and can more easily purchase property on which buildings can be constructed.

One theme across all of the above examples—enrollment, specialized services, and school buildings—is that the costs and other impediments to reaching agreement are high, especially in decentralized settings with many competing organizations. A second theme is that cooperation is unlikely to significantly address the important goal of equity. The problems of unfair enrollment systems and specialized services hit hardest for the most disadvantaged students. The above analysis shows that, even with the strong equity mission of reformers, they would be hamstrung trying to solve these problems on their own, given conflicting interests and high transaction and enforcement costs.

In none of these examples does it seem likely that cooperation will succeed in solving the specified problems. All of the above conditions arguably have to be met before there is any real chance of success, yet, more often, none of the above conditions hold. The deck is stacked against cooperative solutions.

Cooperation in New Orleans?

The previous chapters tested the market theory presented in chapter 2. Here it is useful to follow suit, albeit with more qualitative than statistical analysis, and see whether the predictions about cooperation among autonomous organizations held true.

If ever there was a situation where cooperation across organizations in a schooling market could work, this was it. The New Orleans reformers had created so much trust that I have been able to write about them as a reform *family*. This tight bond was possible for several reasons: First, New Orleans is relatively small—much smaller than earlier reform cities like Chicago and New York City. It is also a social place—reformers ran into each other at coffee shops, bars, and Mardi Gras parades.

Second, many of the reformers had started with a common connection through their work in Teach for America. Recall that the organization's purpose was to build a corps of educational leaders who shared reform-oriented view and a sense of mission to improve schooling, especially for disadvantaged students. Many also went on to hold key leadership posts in the network of nonprofits and the RSD. Because of TFA, the reform leaders not only knew each other, but had shared experiences and values.

Third, the Cowen Institute provided office space for the entire network of nonprofits. New Schools for New Orleans, TeachNOLA, the Louisiana Association for Public Charter Schools, and the Cowen Institute itself were all located in the same building. They later moved, still together, to another building located across the street from the state RSD, making collaboration easy and facilitating new relationships.

Fourth, when John White arrived, he instituted regular meetings with school and CMO leaders to develop relationships and solve problems. He did not absolutely require their support for his own initiatives, but he thought this more collaborative approach was the best path to long-term success.[8]

As a result, dozens of key reform leaders got to know and trust one other—to an unusual degree, considering the competitive climate. The conditions were ripe, but did this translate into actual cooperation to solve the problems the market had created?

COOPERATION ON UNFAIR ENROLLMENT PRACTICES IN NEW ORLEANS. There was essentially no cooperation to solve the unfair enrollment practices, for all the reasons mentioned above. Decentralized enrollment created negative headlines about how schools were choosing whichever student they pleased, but this was not enough to get schools to correct the problem. The top-tier schools had no incentive to change their ways, and there was no way to monitor each school's enrollment practices. For this reason, one of White's first moves as RSD superintendent was to begin to *require* schools to participate in centralized enrollment (OneApp).

Transfers and disciplinary policies are also connected to admissions—and are among the tools of exclusion discussed in chapter 6. But cooperation was insufficient to address these exclusionary practices either, which is why the state eventually intervened.

COOPERATION ON SPECIAL EDUCATION AND MENTAL HEALTH IN NEW ORLEANS. Some progress was made on special education. The former director of special education for the district started her own nonprofit that contracted these services to schools. Since most schools had a small number of students needing these services, the contractor could then rotate across schools to provide the services more efficiently. Indeed, this is the way it works in most school districts. The difference of course—and a nontrivial one when you talk with school leaders—is that the charter schools could end their relationships with contractors if the services were inadequate. Under the district model, at least in New Orleans, there was limited accountability when the various departments (see figure 8.1a) failed in their jobs.

Contracting is only a partial solution, however. Given the high cost of services for students with severe mental health needs, the state RSD stepped in to fund a separate nonprofit center to provide mental health services to students with the most severe needs. This program has continued to expand, basing some of its services in a local children's hospital.

COOPERATION ON SCHOOL BUILDINGS IN NEW ORLEANS. Various options existed for ensuring that buildings were available and well maintained. The state, for example, could have disbursed capital funds to schools on a per-student basis, as is done with operating funds. The schools and CMOs could then use their autonomy, as they did with school discipline and other matters, to find and pay for buildings as they saw fit.

But in all the interviews and conversations I had, over many years, this idea never came up. The reform leaders, though they prized school autonomy, seemed to recognize that school buildings were best left in the hands of state and local governments. The initial legislation, which turned control of most schools over to the state, also turned control of school buildings over to the state. In addition, the state superintendent created an oversight committee to ensure that the construction and renovation work proceeded effectively, something that continued well after turning the schools over to charter managers.[9]

SUMMARY. It is no coincidence that the state intervened in the market where it did. Enrollment, transfers, discipline, specialized services for disadvantaged students, and school buildings are among the areas in which problems are the most likely to arise in a schooling market, and the least likely to be solved by cooperation. In contrast, schools did often contract out services like arts and physical education, tutoring, counseling, security, and even some aspects of discipline.[10]

These are not the only forms of cooperation that emerged. The New Orleans Arts Education Alliance emerged to provide professional development for arts educators and to advocate for expanded arts offerings. The College and Career Counselors Collaborative, organized by the Cowen Institute, brought school counselors together to discuss shared challenges. A group of schools that remained under district control joined together into what was later called the Greater New Orleans Collaborative of Charter Schools, which advocated for their schools with district officials and engaged in coordinated professional development and other areas of common interest. Is it unclear how much they achieved, but a clear spirit of collaboration did emerge.

Might Cooperation Degenerate into Collusion?

The focus of this chapter is on how the large number of separate organizations might work together to solve problems. The first potential complication with this, however, as I have shown, is that the effort might not work as intended simply because cooperation is difficult.

Another possibility is that it might work *too well*—that a small number of people might work together to impose their own vision and interests on the city. The fact that we could characterize the reformers as a reform family (see chapter 3) certainly suggests this possibility. In the worst case, these relationships among people and organizations can degenerate into what economists call *collusion*. Matthew Candler, who had helped incubate charter schools under New Schools for New Orleans, and later ran another innovation incubator, had a different name for it:

As a market, we can't let this become an oligarchy. That's starting to emerge.[11]

He was particularly concerned about an "oligarchy" of charter operators. A few individuals served on the boards of directors of almost all the major nonprofits.

The reform family also became politically powerful. Although they were formerly sleepy affairs to which few paid attention, New Orleans school board elections in the reform era drew upward of $300,000 in campaign donations, many times more than had been seen before the reforms or in other districts.[12] State board campaigns, once under the radar, involved even larger sums. Whereas out-of-state political support is rare in school board elections, the New Orleans campaigns in the post-reform era received upward of 25 percent from outsiders.[13] As those funds overwhelmingly went to pro-reform candidates, the reform family was able to maintain slim majorities on the state and local district boards that were the key to their successes.

In addition to working together to ensure sympathetic leaders in key elected positions, the reform family worked together to shape the reform's public image. Jacobs gathered funds for some of the polling discussed in chapter 4 and to create and distribute flyers and brochures with positive messages and news throughout the city, especially during election season and just before key votes in the legislature.

Whatever we might think of the appropriateness of these activities, cooperative efforts had an important side benefit. They allowed reformers to develop close relationships and a degree of trust. School leaders felt they could depend on most of the RSD superintendents—and that school leaders could support proposed regulations. The centralized enrollment system, centralized transfer, centralized expulsion, mandatory busing, and school funding formula are all important examples where the state stepped in with limited opposition from the schools themselves.[14] School and CMO leaders had developed a sense that the RSD shared their goals and trusted the regulations would respect their autonomy to the extent possible.

This too might seem like a form of collusion. Regulated groups should not have the power to sign off on regulations. But giving them some voice in the process had some benefits: it ensured that the state understood the consequences of regulation, that the rules were not just sent down, ill-informed from on high; it meant that schools likely would be more willing to comply with any regulations that did go into effect, because they had had a chance to participate in the process and understood the reasoning; and, finally, it prevented the eruption of public political battles that would have undermined the reforms as a whole.

It can be hard to distinguish selfish collusion from mission-driven cooperation, for the simple reason that every policy change benefits some schools more than others. What is more apparent is that even failed cooperation can build relationships that facilitate productive, albeit less-voluntary, solutions. School leaders could start by saying, "Let's see if we can fix this problem ourselves," and, if they failed, they could accept the state stepping in to force a resolution.

The Potential and Limits of Cooperation

When supporters of market-based school reforms outline their arguments, they usually focus on how autonomy and accountability allow and encourage schools to improve from within. This chapter shows a different, less widely recognized, potential mechanism. The same autonomy and accountability meant to drive changes within organizations could, in theory, allow them to work together to solve problems *across* organizations, or even to create new groups. Instead of the single, strict institutional hierarchy that typified school districts, the post-reform New Orleans schools were characterized by large numbers of loose relationships, allowing people to band together in informal networks, contracts, and charter management organizations.

Could these mechanisms succeed in softening the hard edges of the market? Could they keep administrative costs down? Could they keep schools from choosing families, and ensure that students with special needs were well served? Would they successfully engage in "coopetition"?

Apparently, not much. While the reformers had shared values and trust, most of the problems created by markets are the sort that cooperation cannot solve. The competition among schools, and the difficulty of coming to agreements and monitoring practices among so many diffuse actors, proved a difficult barrier to overcome. Loose networks might be able to solve easier problems but apparently not those that most plague the schooling market. In some cases where groups were able to work together, it was not necessarily in ways that made the system better. Perhaps the greatest benefit was unintentional: facilitating relationships for effective government regulation.

More broadly, nothing we have seen so far would explain the fast rise in student outcomes—not choice, not competition, and not cooperation. They all contributed some, but when it comes to understanding the effects of the reforms on measurable student outcomes, one additional factor stands out above all others.

CHAPTER 9

The Impact of Government Oversight and Charter Authorization

The discussion of autonomy for charter schools, and choice for families, might create the impression that the New Orleans school reforms simply represented a reduction in the role of government. This is certainly true in the sense that parents were no longer locked into attendance zones, and the district and state relinquished almost all authority over school personnel, curriculum, textbooks, instruction, budgeting, school hours, and really every decision that directly affected students. Power was pushed down to CMOs, charter schools, and parents, and taken on by a new network of philanthropically funded nonprofits that could cooperate to solve the problems that emerged. In the prior chapters, however, I showed that these mechanisms had real limitations. Competition between schools and choice for families solved some problems but also created some new ones that cooperation could not solve.

But the government did not go away by any means. In addition to regulating enrollment, transfer, transportation, and discipline, as school districts always had, the government actually gained authority through the New Orleans reforms. The agencies that oversee charter schools, called authorizers, have considerable power both to open new schools and to close and take over the ones under their control. When government authorizers intervene in this way, schools are either closed completely or handed over to a new charter board or CMO that brings in its own team and plan. The political design of school districts essentially precludes district leaders from having an equivalent power. Traditional public schools do close, but rarely based on performance, and they cannot be turned over to other groups of educators because district leaders have so little control over personnel.[1]

This power to close or take over charter schools is rooted in the performance contracts between charter organizations and the government authorizers. After discussing some basic principles of government contracting, or what critics call privatization, I consider how the various parts of the process played out in practice in New Orleans. How did charter authorizing/contracting work in the immediate hurricane aftermath when the charter applicants had limited track records? How did the state, as the main authorizer, react after observing the actual performance of the schools it had approved? How many mistakes did state agencies make when they were first selecting charter schools, and how did they respond to those errors? What contributed to the successes and failures of the authorization process?

Given the tremendous power that the state had as the main authorizer, and how actively state leaders exercised that power, it may come as no surprise that charter authorization had a major influence on what happened in schools and on what students experienced. The government, in the end, was the most direct and immediate cause of students' measurable academic improvement.

When Contracting Entire Schools Can Work (and Fail)

The logic of contracting is based on what social scientists call *principal-agent theory*.[2] With private enterprise, the company owner is the principal and hires employees as agents to provide a good or service on the owner's behalf. The "problem," as it were, is that the principal's goals are not aligned with those of the agent. The owner is trying to earn a profit, while the workers are only concerned with their own well-being. Moreover, employees can take advantage of the fact that the owner cannot easily measure worker performance; if the owner does not know how hard or how effectively her employees are working, then she cannot easily punish those who are low-performing. The question is, what does the principal—in this case, the government—need to do to get what it wants from its hired agents, such as charter schools?

Most of the conditions for effective contracting echo the basic assumptions of free markets. It requires having a reasonable number of
potential contractors, the ability to switch easily between them, and
good information about performance. If there were only one available
contractor, that would be a monopoly, and the contractor could take
advantage of taxpayers and sacrifice quality for personal financial gain.
Even when we have many potential contractors, success is not guaranteed because of how difficult it is to measure performance. In education, as we saw in chapter 2, we have a large number of somewhat amorphous goals for students; all are difficult to measure and attribute to the
schools, and all can become distorted by the pressure schools face to increase them. As a result, contractors can look good when they are actually bad.

Even when performance can be measured well, and when there are
many contractors to choose from, it can be costly for the government—
and for students—to change contractors. This is a common problem with
contracting because governments, almost by definition, provide the most
basic of human services. Interruptions in essential services can be a real
problem, allowing the contractor to hold the government hostage with
threats of sudden departure.

But school districts contract out for things like computers, janito-
rial service, and bus drivers all the time. So surely contracting can work
just fine when hiring someone to run schools, right? Not exactly. Other
goods and services are bought and sold in separate, competitive markets.
Dozens of companies make computers, and millions of people, mostly
outside the government, are interested in buying them. It would make
no sense under these conditions for the government to produce its own
computers. Rather, the government can take advantage of market forces
by contracting out to established producers.

These examples, of goods like computers (and services from janitors
and bus drivers), also have simple, definable goals and performance measures. Students need to be able to type on the computer, access the internet, and print. It is easy to determine when the equipment is working,
and when it fails, the school or district can take it back to the vendor. Life
gets much more complicated for those running schools because schools
as a whole are ultimately responsible for students' livelihoods—not for
whether the computers work, but for keeping children safe, teaching
skills and knowledge, and instilling values. Computers, buses, and food

are only tools in the much broader process of achieving these fundamental, and hard-to-measure, objectives.

Can contracting out the entire enterprise of schooling to organizations like charter management organizations work effectively in this unusual market of schooling? How would the reformers in New Orleans avoid the predictable problems?

The Initial Choice of Charter Schools in New Orleans

Clearly, many things could have gone wrong with charter authorization in New Orleans. To test whether they did go wrong, and how much the contracting process contributed to the city's apparent success, we first documented the process of charter approval, collecting all available charter applications submitted to the state board and RSD, and subsequently linked the applications to the future performance of approved schools, to allow us to examine how well the RSD picked effective contractors.[3]

The authorization process can be separated into four formal phases: (1) The state solicited applications with a public call for proposals. (2) Nonprofits like New Schools for New Orleans (led by Matthew Candler in the early years) incubated many of the charter aspirants. (3) Perhaps in part because the RSD was so new and had little experience with contracting, and to minimize political pressures, state law required a third-party evaluation of each charter application. Initially, the state board chose the National Association of Charter School Authorizers (NACSA), a Chicago-based organization that provided external reviewers on a contract basis. NACSA's review included in-person interviews with the leadership teams for each application.[4] Finally, (4) with NACSA's evaluations and recommendations in hand, the state decided which applications to accept.[5]

Given that the charter sector was still developing, both locally and nationally, this process could have ended badly. Most applicants had a limited track record of relevant performance. Choosing an up-and-coming charter operator is like choosing an entry-level employee from a group of recent college graduates. We can try to predict their effectiveness based on resumes, interviews, and calls to prior employers and references, but because they lack the most relevant job experience, such information is only weakly predictive of performance for most careers.

In light of the inherently limited information, the outcome of the RSD contracting still might be judged a modest success. Thanks partly to NSNO's incubation efforts, the RSD and state board ended up with far more applications—at least a hundred between 2007 and 2012—than they could reasonably accept. NACSA's reviewers collected an enormous amount of information, well beyond the written applications, and seemed to carefully consider what they learned. The state followed NACSA's recommendations, almost without exception, and eventually authorized more than forty different organizations to run schools. Partly as a result, 75 percent of the initially authorized charters—especially those with higher NACSA ratings—reached levels of performance that allowed their contracts to be renewed. There were also some signs that the NACSA ratings were positively associated with growth in student achievement in the newly opened schools.[6] These are all note-worthy signs.

Still, the initial authorization process was imperfect, and the prior evidence on contracting suggests that some of the more than eighty charters would fail. With so many organizations running schools, and so many applicants in reserve, the state would certainly have the opportunity to take over low-performing schools and turn them over to other charter operators. But would they do so? In how many cases? More importantly, *which* schools would be taken over and what would this mean for students?

State Responses to Failed Charter Contracts

If the initial application process counts as a modest success on measurable outcomes, the renewal stage was, by standard measures, a resounding success. Louisiana law required that contracts with state-authorized charter schools be renewed if they were high-performing but allowed some discretion for low-performing schools. As it turned out, the RSD moved aggressively, shutting down schools with the lowest School Performance Scores on a regular basis. More than forty of the initially opened schools were replaced between 2007 and 2016; to put that in perspective, there were only eighty-three schools operating in 2016. The RSD also turned over more and more charter contracts to the most successful operators.[7] The process worked just as its advocates intended.

Even this did not guarantee that students would benefit, however. As critics were quick to point out, school closure and takeover is disruptive for students, as they are forced to move to new schools. They lose friends, have to learn new sets of school rules and norms, and, because schools organize the curriculum in different ways, may miss important content or see the same material two or three times. Ashana Bigard's daughter had exactly this experience when she switched schools:

> They weren't puttin' her in her right classes. She was like, "I took these classes already."[8]

Almost all US-based studies conducted on school closure and takeover before we started our work had found no positive effects for elementary students, and large negative effects for high school students.[9]

In New Orleans, however, we found that school takeover had substantial *positive* effects on student outcomes, even among students who were in the schools at the time they were being taken over.[10] (Since the vast majority of responses to low-performing schools were takeovers, I do not mention closures in the rest of the chapter.[11]) We evaluated the effects of takeovers by comparing test scores for students attending schools at the time they were taken over with the scores of similar students in low-performing schools that were not taken over (similar to the difference-in-differences method used to study student outcomes in chapter 4). Figure 9.1 shows a sharp increase in test scores for elementary students in the takeover schools.[12]

The results were not as positive for high schools. In general, we saw positive effects on high school graduation, but no effects on college entry.[13] One reason is that, unlike with elementary and middle schools, the reformers, by their own admission, struggled to move students into better high schools. We identified several reasons why, even in the best of circumstances, the disruptive effects of school takeovers might be generally larger in high schools.[14]

Overall, the results were still much better in New Orleans than they had been in other cities that had taken over schools. Why? The main reason is simple: in New Orleans, schools were taken over based on performance, and this meant that students ended up in better schools.[15] For both elementary and (to a lesser extent) high schools, improvements in school quality meant better outcomes for students. In contrast, in other

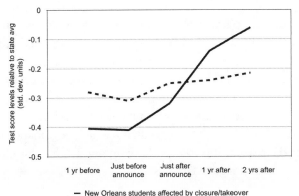

FIGURE 9.1. School takeover increased achievement for students attending affected schools. *Source*: Whitney Bross and Douglas N. Harris, "The Effects of Performance-Based School Closure and Take-over on Student Performance" (New Orleans: Education Research Alliance for New Orleans, Tulane University, 2016). *Notes*: The figure shows the changes in math scores for students who experienced takeovers and others in New Orleans who never did, over the period 2008–2104. The matched comparison group was identified first by finding similar schools and, second, finding similar students within those schools (in both cases based on pre-intervention test scores). The equivalent difference-in-difference estimates yield statistically significant positive effects of takeover on students in the schools at the time of intervention, and pass parallel trends test.

cities studied by other researchers, schools were apparently taken over for other reasons—district finances, building age/quality, or politics—and students, more often than not, ended up in even worse schools than where they started.[16] When the worst-performing schools (on a given measure) are taken over, students are very likely to do better on that measure in the year or two that follow.

The long run was likely to be even better. Successfully taking over a low-performing school means that the menu of options in a choice system is better for *future* students as well—far more students than are in the school at the time of a takeover. These future students would have the benefit of better options but without the disruption.

Students clearly benefit when low-performing schools are turned over to high-performing operators, but what about the schools that stay open, what we call "persisting schools"? We might expect that the strong threat of takeover would induce them to improve too. Instead of "teach like a champion," their motto might become "teach like your contract depends on it."

To test this, we separated the overall improvement described in chapter 4 into two parts: replacing low-performing schools and improving persisting schools. Somewhat surprisingly, we found that persisting schools did not improve after their first year. This means the takeover process was responsible for the vast majority of the measurable improvement in student outcomes in the post-reform period. This may be because the pressure from the threat of takeover was relatively weak for the majority of schools, which were well above the performance threshold. Whatever the reason, this is a key finding, not just for this chapter, but for the entire story of New Orleans.

The Skill (and Luck) of New Orleans Charter Authorization

That authorizers will fulfill their responsibilities well enough to produce such results is not guaranteed.[17] Measuring performance is a challenge, and the political pressures that come with large contracts to private organizations can be powerful. Similar efforts had not worked well elsewhere. Why was New Orleans so different? The short answer is that the charter authorization process was carried out fairly well at every stage. NSNO developed a competitive process for selecting proposals to incubate and provided support for creating schools. Though most applicants had limited track records, the RSD, with NACSA's help, had partial success predicting which prospective schools would be most effective. When it came time to renew charters, the state focused on their recent performance and took over the worst schools. They also allowed many different operators to run schools, avoiding the monopoly conditions that often pervade public-sector contracting. But this just begs the question, why did the RSD make better decisions than school districts typically do?

First, the RSD had many strong proposals to choose from. Having a good authorization process would have done little good if there had been few applications, or if a large share had failed to meet their standards. The RSD also had a backup plan. If it did not find suitable charter operators, it maintained the capacity to run the schools itself. While few would argue the state was especially good at running schools, retaining some minimal capability bought the RSD time and discouraged desperate moves to accept ill-conceived charters. The surest way for an organization to avoid being held hostage by a contractor is to be willing and able to do the work in-house. This option, along with outside support leading to a large number of applicants, allowed the RSD to be patient and work to ensure quality in the long run.

The state also anticipated that students in schools that were being taken over might be harmed by the disruption and took steps to offset the damage. While not available during the initial round of takeovers, the centralized enrollment system (OneApp) came online in 2012. This allowed RSD officials to give priority in the school choice process to students affected by takeovers, increasing their chances of getting into one of their preferred alternatives. Later, when OPSB also started to take over schools, the district contracted with a nonprofit called EdNavigator to provide counselors to assist families in finding new and better schools. All of this would have been more difficult in a decentralized enrollment system. Placing enrollment control in the hands of individual schools made it almost impossible for the authorizer to support individual students in coordinated ways. This interplay between contracting and centralized enrollment, as well as NSNO's help in generating applications, highlights the connections among the various actors (charter schools, the state, and system-level nonprofits), as well as the teamwork surrounding policy and implementation decisions.

A third factor in the contracting success was that the state limited the organizations that could serve as authorizers to just school districts and the state board.[18] Other states opened up authorizing more broadly, for example, to mayors or universities. The issue here is not just who the authorizers are but *how many* authorizers are operating in any given locale. In Michigan, for example, a state law allowing universities to authorize charter schools has led to at least ten different authorizers governing schools in Detroit alone. While it might seem that this would create an additional, potentially productive form of competition, between authorizers, this is very different from competition among schools. The problem is, with a multitude of authorizers, charter schools are encouraged to shop for the one that will give them the best deal, which may include weak enforcement of performance standards and rules (e.g., allowing schools to ignore fair enrollment policies and exclude certain students). Low-performing schools might persist because of strong political connections. If the goal is to create an alternative to traditional public schools, there generally has to be at least one authorizer other than the district, but having more than one nondistrict authorizer may be counterproductive, sparking a race to the bottom.[19]

In some respects, then, the authorization process was well designed and implemented. In other ways, the RSD was lucky. The state-defined School Performance Scores used as the primary determinant of renewal were based on student test scores, not the more relevant student *growth* measures. This means they ran the risk of taking over schools because students had low initial scores, even if those schools were contributing a great deal to student learning. The selective-admissions schools, meanwhile, had high test scores mainly because they admitted only students who already scored high. The reformers were fortunate, then, that School Performance Scores and student growth were more positively correlated in New Orleans than in many other places.[20] This meant that they were truly targeting the lowest-performing schools for takeover.

On a broader scale, NSNO's aggressive pursuit of charter applicants also benefited from national interest in the New Orleans reform experiment. National CMOs with aspirations to expand and make a name for themselves wanted to establish a presence in the city that was clearly becoming the Silicon Valley of school reform.

It would take both skill and luck to make the New Orleans reforms work the way they did. The reformers created NSNO to build an ample supply of applicants; the state bought itself time by running schools until it found good charter operators; lawmakers designed the policy to prevent a race to the bottom with authorizer shopping; and the state was willing and able to accept its initial chartering mistakes and take over low-performing schools. Those were good decisions, but the reformers were also fortunate in having a first-mover advantage that other cities lacked and not having to suffer the consequences of their flawed performance measures.

It is better to be lucky than good, so the saying goes. It is even better to be both, as was the case in New Orleans.

Distorted Outcomes, Costs, and Fraud?

There was one other way in which the reformers skillfully handled the application and authorization process. Prior research in many industries consistently shows that measurable outcomes improve, and costs decline, when governments contract out to private companies.[21] While this might sound like success, it is often unclear whether these supposed improvements are genuine. Firms want to increase profits and, with contract revenue fixed, the only way to do that is to cut costs. Unless the firm can come up with some new and innovative way to do that, quality is inevitably reduced. Firms can get away with this by either distorting the measures in the contracts or by ignoring obviously important elements of quality that are not in the contracts at all. The problem, a variation of Campbell's Law discussed in chapters 2, is what I will call the Law of Contracts: *the results of contracts are not as positive as they seem because outcome measures are distorted and narrow.*[22]

In New Orleans we were dealing with nonprofits rather than for-profits, and we saw improvements even on low-stakes measures like college outcomes and parent satisfaction. Did the Law of Contracts not apply here? Perhaps not completely—these leaders were on a mission to help students and not mainly to make a buck. On the other hand, we know the test score improvements at least partly reflected teaching to the test and a shift away from untested outcomes, such as the arts—to what extent is hard to tell. Moreover, the marked increase in administrative spending and decrease in instructional spending suggest that the nonprofit leaders may have benefited even without explicit profits. The Law of Contracts is clearly a powerful force.[23]

Another potential way to profit is through fraud. Because the vast majority of school spending goes to pay educators, the main opportunities for misappropriation in the charter world generally come from other expenditures, especially large ones like buildings and management services.[24] Many cases have arisen, nationally, where CMO leaders or board members have owned buildings or for-profit management companies have made large profits by pushing their schools into contracts with complex fine print.[25] Such activities are often technically legal, but it is easy to question the ethics and conflicts of interest.

Unfortunately, it is hard to gauge the frequency of any of these actions because CMOs are private organizations and, as such, are not subject to public records laws that apply to government agencies, such as school districts. For example, prior to Katrina, a New Orleans school board member was convicted of taking $100,000 in bribes to support a particular vendor's curriculum. But when private organizations like charters are contracting, such payments can be made to charter leaders, in at least ostensibly legal ways, for example, by paying charter leaders as "consultants." What we call corruption in government can be cast as simply supply and demand when private organizations do the same. Such payments are often legal, accepted, and almost impossible to track because of weak public records laws. While charter schools are required to have annual audits by approved accounting firms, the schools can pick any firm they want, and audit results explicitly state that they cannot account for fraud.

Despite the difficulties, we searched for reports of fraud from the Louisiana legislative auditor, the media, and academic experts, before and after the reforms, and found a dozen instances of fraud and other potential financial mismanagement in the post-reform years. In dollar value, the largest focused on the ability of the RSD to track property—mostly computers and related equipment. It is not clear, however, whether there was any fraud or whether this was just a record-keeping issue. (Many organizations have trouble tracking equipment such as laptop computers that are not used in a fixed location.) In sum, the total reported fraud in the pre-reform era was at least ten times larger than in the post-reform era. Given what we know about the pre-reform school district—for instance, that the FBI established a field office within the district offices to deal with all the corruption cases—the apparent reduction in fraud is perhaps not surprising.

Aside from the inherent challenge of financial accountability with private organizations, the New Orleans reforms were generally well designed to avoid fraud. Turning control of buildings over to the state RSD may partly explain why we heard no allegations or reports of building-related fraud.

The state also appeared to actively avoid charter applications involving for-profit charter managers, where such problems are likely to be worse. Matthew Candler had played a central role in incubating schools and had inside knowledge of the operations of some charter schools in other states that were trying to enter the city:

I knew the games for-profit charter organizations played with their sponsor boards. I knew the games they played with balance sheets and facilities and profit and loss statements. I knew the games they played with, "Oh, our fee? We'll defer it. Oh, you're short on working capital? I'll give you a working capital loan. Oh, you don't have a building? I'll lease you my building." They could get you three ways. [They would take] close to 20 or 25 percent [of revenue] off the top for the most naïve board. . . . I felt it was my mission to protect local boards from that kind of abuse.[26]

So while the power of the reform family worked to keep the community out, it also protected the community from fraud and other shenanigans. Even if they had been so inclined, most schools were under so much pressure to improve test scores and graduation rates that it would have been difficult to misuse funds and still generate strong enough student outcomes and enrollments to continue operating.

Racial Equity and Community Engagement in the Authorization Process

In many respects, the charter authorization process yielded wise decisions that ultimately were the driving force behind the measurable improvement. In other respects, those same processes led to perceptions of unfair discrimination that still linger today. Perhaps more than any other part of this story, the authorization process shows the dominance of young white outsiders over more experienced black locals, especially in the early years. To get under the surface, to really understand the implementation of this seemingly objective process, I turn now to interviews with those involved.

At least one person in the reform family tried to influence NACSA and the state superintendent by providing additional information meant to undermine proposals from certain charter applicants. Another reform leader also suggested to me that NACSA had been replaced as the outside evaluator because its assessments were too objective and did not sufficiently account for what those in power wanted. We saw evidence of pressure to influence charter approvals from other sources as well. One black charter applicant who was not approved put it this way:

It was a sham. A flat out sham! We kept going back and forth with these people. They'd tell us change this. We'd change it. They'd tell us do this. And we'd do [it]. We did all they asked for and still got denied. After all of that. It was exhausting and heartbreaking.[27]

Though the NACSA review teams were demographically diverse and included some local members, the process still seemed to favor white outsiders over local black applicants. Another black charter applicant explained:

> We tried. We really did. But it became clear they didn't want *us*. We didn't have a board made up of people who weren't from New Orleans or who only taught for two years. You'd think that would be a good thing, huh? But nope! (laughter) We represented a failed, bloated black bureaucracy ... controlling and operating schools isn't for us. It's for them.[28]

When I raised the issues of fairness and potential discrimination with Candler, who led the charter recruiting and incubation process for New Schools for New Orleans, he agreed that it was a real concern:

> I think the tragedy is, at that time at NSNO, we were losing grip on the reality or the opportunity—the window of inviting local New Orleanians or people with experience with these kids, even maybe folks who were let go from their [teaching] jobs and knew these kids. It was a check against them [in the charter applications] if they were local and had worked in the existing setting.[29]

It was not that Candler saw no role for the community in those early years; he just thought it was best for that role to be limited:

> I wasn't very open to community groups as [school] operators. I saw them as our partners in enhancing parent capacity to choose and know what their options are and navigate as consumers. I confess that I did not really think about local [community members as] "producers" or potential school leaders. . . . I was like, "I think I know what works. Let me bring it to you."

Candler regretted this approach. Some others did as well, but this was not true of everyone in the reform family. Others seemed to view it as a necessary evil. Either way, experience with the old system and local heritage was highly correlated with race. Black locals were being shut out.

This perspective of the reformers also seemed to carry over to local community engagement in the authorization process. In theory, the state

RSD, as authorizer, could seek and take into account community input through public meetings, like those Tulane president Scott Cowen had organized after the storm. But this did not occur either in the early years. To the extent that local input was gathered in the first five years, the RSD's promises to the community were frequently broken.

It did not have to be that way. The person who proved this was one I introduced at the start of chapter 1. Patrick Dobard and his family had serious concerns about the local school district and the schools they governed and had opted for a prestigious local private high school instead. But he still thought the reforms could and should involve substantial community engagement. Once he moved up to the ranks to become RSD superintendent in 2013, he had a chance to show this could be done:

> I think he [another reform leader] started to understand my thinking around the community and the political landscape and how, while he might have the right idea [about the design of the system], there's a way to do it *with* the community and not *to* the community.[30]

Dobard developed a new approach. As RSD superintendent, when he knew a school was going to have a new operator in the near future, he began identifying groups of educators and community members to create a shared vision for the school and to recommend school operators to the RSD. Dobard generally followed the community's recommendation. The state still held considerable power because only charter operators the state had already approved were on the menu the community board could choose from, and the community-driven process was not applied to many school operator decisions, but it was still an advance over what had happened in the past and over what authorizers typically did nationally.

Such community engagement might also mitigate problems from earlier stages. Previous applicants who viewed the process as a sham are unlikely to submit future applications, but they might if they start to feel someone is listening. Whether Dobard's level of engagement will last, and actually have these broader effects, remains to be seen.

What is clear is that "taking the politics out" of school reform, a rallying cry for school reformers for more than a century, is essentially impossible. Where there is government funding, there is politics. Where there is charter authorization, there is politics too. The issue is, as always, who wields the political power and how.

Conclusion: The Important Role of Government

After considering many possibilities, this chapter finally provides us with the main driver of the improvements in measurable student outcomes described in chapter 4. The state did not just take over schools once, in the initial post-Katrina aftermath, but in some cases, multiple times, until reformers thought they had it right. If not for the takeover process, this would be a book not about how the reformers raised student outcomes but about why the reforms failed.

Extreme steps like school takeover and closure are not guaranteed to work. In fact, past national evidence suggests they generally do not. What are the keys to success and how did these play out differently in New Orleans? There seem to be six answers:

- BEING WILLING AND ABLE TO TAKE OVER SCHOOLS. In traditional school districts, small groups of students, parents, teachers, and voters have a powerful voice to oppose such moves. In New Orleans, state control limited critics' power.

- SELECTING THE TRULY LOWEST-PERFORMING SCHOOLS FOR INTERVENTION. Closing just any school can easily backfire. In this case, the contracting process provided built-in means to end contracts and take over schools based on poor performance. Given the political interests involved, there was no guarantee the state would follow through, but it held charters to the terms of their contracts.

- ADMITTING MISTAKES WHEN SCHOOLS FAIL. When a charter operator selected by the state produced poor results, it (implicitly) admitted the error and tried again. This is really a corollary of the lesson above but warrants separate emphasis because it is difficult for people, including those in government agencies, to admit mistakes.

- ENSURING AN AMPLE SUPPLY OF QUALITY OPERATORS READY TO FILL THE VOID WHEN SCHOOLS ARE TAKEN OVER. New Schools for New Orleans recruited successful CMOs like KIPP and incubated new ones. The state ended up with far more applications than were needed.

- SELECTING NEW OPERATORS CAREFULLY AND CAUTIOUSLY. The state had a third party evaluate the applications and almost always followed that evaluator's recommendations. Moreover, in the early years, the state maintained some capacity to operate schools directly, so that it did not have to rush and bring in questionable charter organizations.

- SOFTENING THE BLOW FOR STUDENTS IN AFFECTED SCHOOLS. Making use of the centralized enrollment system, the state gave students in affected schools first priority in selecting the schools they would move to, which eased the transitions for students and their families.

The architects of the reforms were both lucky and good, and as a result, the majority of students, even in takeover schools, were better off academically.

Nonetheless, critics of the New Orleans approach pose some reasonable questions. First, was the process truly fair? Yes and no. The fact that the state used a third-party reviewer and followed its recommendations was helpful; however, the reform family had intervened in the process and influenced the pool of applications even before they reached the state and were submitted to review. NSNO was part of the reform family, which provided support and funding to their favored applicants. Moreover, there was bias against those who were from New Orleans and had worked within the traditional public schools. As a result, local, experienced black educators were mostly rejected when they applied through the authorization process.

Second, were there unintended consequences? Almost certainly. While difficult to observe, the reforms probably led to unhealthy forms of teaching to the test. Also, contracting was likely a key driving force behind the shift to more structured teaching and businesslike management. Government contracts require objective measures, which almost by definition align best to more basic content and teaching strategies. Teachers had to teach like their school's contract depended on it, but that can also work against the ultimate goal—what is best for students. By forcing schools to focus on what could be measured, the reformers may have lost sight of equally important outcomes that are harder to measure, such as the city's rich tradition in the arts, making schooling uninspiring for students and teaching less attractive to the most skilled teachers.

A third question emerges for those who would have preferred an even more market-oriented approach. Would the initial set of charter schools have been taken over without the intervention of the state? Would markets alone have had the same effect? The answer is, almost certainly not.

The probability that the government would renew a contract was almost completely unrelated to our best (but still imperfect) measure of market success—enrollment levels.[31] As I showed in chapter 7, the constraints of distance, and the fact that families had to send their children somewhere, meant that even low-performing schools could attract ample enrollments.[32] The mix of schools would have looked very different under a market-only regime, and likely would not have had such large effects on measurable student outcomes.

We have finally come to the main explanation behind the marked improvement in New Orleans's schools. Though the reforms were accurately characterized as market-oriented, it was the new role of government, as authorizer and contractor, that was key to measurable improvement. In theory, traditional school districts could also intervene aggressively based on school performance, but the System was designed to prevent such action. Instead, school districts tried a more piecemeal approach with changes in the school principal or curriculum, but this practice rarely had measurable effects; or, worse, local districts closed schools that were better than the ones they left open. This is partly why New Orleans district schools were mired near the bottom of the state for so long before the reforms.

All schools should continually seek to improve, but doing so with existing personnel and systems can be a tall task. There comes a point when stronger measures, unpopular though they may be, may be the only path to real improvement. We cannot fire our way to success, but it can be an important tool of last resort.

PART 3

Rethinking the Roles of Markets, Governments, and Nonprofits

CHAPTER 10

How the New Orleans Results Fit the National Picture

The New Orleans experience presents a unique opportunity to see how an intense reform based on the principles of school autonomy, parental choice, and government accountability works in practice. The effects on measurable student outcomes have been positive and substantial, driven mostly by the supply side of the market—that is, by the reform family and the strong new role for government in authorizing, contracting, and oversight. Autonomy and choice also played roles, but more indirectly.

But clearly, with more than fourteen thousand school districts across the country, operating over a century's time, and with hundreds, if not thousands, of other studies on related reforms, it would be unwise to draw broad conclusions about school reform and the role of markets and government based on the experience of just this one city, especially one that seems, at first glance, to be an outlier. Few, if any, cities had, before the period analyzed here, seen the sort of improvement New Orleans did.

A burgeoning body of evidence suggests, however, that the New Orleans experience is not an outlier but part of a larger pattern. The evidence on charter schools, no-excuses urban school reform, effective schools, and school closures and takeovers all showed ways that schools could be improved. New Orleans combined them all, and the government intervened to address predictable market failures. The city's positive results are therefore less surprising than they first seemed.

Since this is a book about the roles of markets and governments, it is also important to consider evidence on an even more free market-oriented approach to reforms: school vouchers. The conventional wisdom has long been that private schools are better than public schools, implying that vouchers subsidizing attendance in private schools should lead to clear improvements in student outcomes. Milton Friedman tapped into that belief when he proposed the broad outline of vouchers back in 1955 and when he reiterated that proposal for New Orleans in 2005. The discussion of vouchers here might seem unnecessary, given the focus of the book on charter schools, but the charter and voucher debates are closely intertwined, representing two different, but related, strategies for going forward. The implications of the New Orleans charter reforms therefore depend on the voucher evidence too.

Based on the theories discussed in chapter 2 about what can go wrong with free markets, and the results presented in the subsequent chapters, however, Leslie Jacobs and the reformers were probably right to reject Friedman's proposal. Though it can be difficult to compare results for charter schools with those for private school voucher programs, the evidence provides little reason to think that vouchers would be a more effective means of improving student outcomes; where traditional public schools have failed, the evidence I discuss below suggests that some types of regulations, such as those often applied to charter schools, are a more viable alternative.

Charter Effectiveness in Other Cities

Charter schools had taken off nationally well before Hurricane Katrina, and more than seven thousand now dot the American schooling landscape. With so many charter schools, some having operated over many decades, the number of studies about them has likewise grown.

On student test scores, the most broad-based evidence comes from the Center for Research on Education Outcomes (CREDO), which has gathered data from the majority of charter schools across the country. The CREDO results suggest that, on the basis of test scores, charter schools now slightly outperform the traditional public schools from which they draw students.[1] This does not seem to be a case of correlation-is-not-causation. The CREDO studies appropriately focus on growth in student achievement, which provides some confidence that the results are not due to the ways schools select students. Studies where students have been randomly assigned to schools tend to yield similar results when the same schools are studied with CREDO's methods.[2]

Charter performance has also steadily improved over time.[3] One study, relying only on charter schools where students were assigned by lottery in the years 2005–2007, found no effects.[4] The early CREDO results also suggested that, in the earlier years of the movement, charter schools actually performed somewhat worse than traditional public schools, before turning positive.[5] The contrast between studies of older and newer charter schools provides some indication that charter schools are getting better.

The gradual improvement in charter school test score results is not especially surprising. Nationally, as in New Orleans, charter schools were being created from scratch. Many of the New Orleans leaders I have heard talk about the early years, especially those who previously had limited experience running schools, admit that they were full of ideas and a sense of mission but did not really know what they were doing at first. As the charter sector developed, its teachers, leaders, and authorizers learned from experience. The resulting improvement is a sign that the charter community has been learning how to run these new kinds of schools, that charter authorizers have learned how to close down the low-performers, that families' choices have pushed out low-performing schools, or all of the above. The improvements have been small, to be sure, but again, charter schools do now seem better on average than traditional public schools, and that advantage seems to be slowly growing over time.

Much less evidence exists on the effects of charter schools on longer-term student outcomes. A few studies of state- or district-specific samples have found substantial positive effects on students' college outcomes when compared with traditional public schools,[6] while another study found that charter schools only shifted students from two-year to four-year colleges, with no overall effect on college enrollment.[7] A handful of studies on students' subsequent earnings in the labor market have found a mix of positive and negative effects.[8] It will be some years before we have a clear picture of the long-term effects.

Advocates of market reform have also argued that charter schools create greater variety and fit. As in New Orleans, the national charter sector has seemingly succeeded on this dimension as well. Charter policies exist in more than forty states, and each state is different. Within each state, given the autonomy granted to school leaders, there is also considerable variety in school offerings—not always as much as we found within New Orleans, nor as much as some might wish, but certainly far more than between traditional public school districts. Two national analyses have come to a similar conclusion.[9]

These individual findings regarding charter schools are important in themselves, but more so when we consider them together. It is good news for charter schools that they generate similar or somewhat higher measured outcomes for students than traditional public schools, at least with regard to test scores and college outcomes. It is good that the results are progressing over time. If we accept the objectives of the reforms, then it is also good that charter students and schools are achieving these higher standardized metrics amid varying and nonstandard themes and educational missions. The real feat, though, was doing it all at once. We might have expected some schools to focus on basic academic content and better test scores, while other schools focused on sports, art, or ethnicity-focused curricula, and perhaps sacrificed standardized tests. But this sacrifice did not arise.

Charter schools now seem to have created a wider variety of options and generated somewhat more positive, and gradually improving, academic results. This is a noteworthy combination and a possible leading indicator of more positive results in the future.

Research on Private School Vouchers

School vouchers differ from charter schools in that they involve much less government intervention. With both charters and vouchers, the government role starts with providing funding that follows students to whichever schools they choose. With vouchers, this is also where the role of government mostly ends. With charter schools, the government imposes more rules and performance-based accountability. If these charter regulations present an undue burden, and do not help improve education as intended, then we would expect private schools that accept vouchers, with limited regulations, to outperform both traditional public schools and charter schools.

Our interest in both charters and vouchers—and the larger issue of markets versus governments—makes the New Orleans case that much more compelling because the state also instituted a school voucher program, called the Louisiana Scholarship Program. Students from low-income families could use these vouchers, equal to 90 percent of state and local public school spending (up to the school's total tuition, whichever is lower), at any participating private school (religious or secular).[10] The program started as a pilot in 2008 in New Orleans and expanded statewide in 2012. As of 2016, the program included more than seven thousand students statewide.[11]

The effects of the Louisiana vouchers depend on what outcome we focus on. Research led by Patrick Wolf and one of my research team's postdoctoral fellows, Jonathan Mills, suggests that the state's voucher program has likely *reduced* student test scores or, at best, had no effect.[12] It is highly unusual to find negative effects like this in any type of education program. The results in this case are also especially persuasive because the study is based on students who were *randomly assigned* to receive a voucher.[13] The same finding was corroborated by a second team, led by researchers at Duke and MIT.[14]

This pattern also emerged in studies of test scores from statewide voucher programs in three other states. A study in Florida was inconclusive, but those in Indiana and Ohio initially showed large negative effects.[15] The Indiana and Louisiana programs did show some improvement in the second year. This may suggest that private schools were learning and getting better, as charter schools have, though, as many of these schools had been operating for decades, they should not have had the same learning curve as charter operators. Yet they were still producing negative effects.

A large-scale review of earlier evidence from mostly city-specific voucher programs was somewhat more positive. The researchers showed that the average effect of US-based voucher programs on student achievement has been perhaps slightly positive, but still indistinguishable from zero.[16] The results look better when limited only to students who remain enrolled in private schools over many years, but such analyses are not very informative about the overall effects of vouchers.[17] The results look considerably worse when factoring in the often-negative statewide studies discussed earlier.

In contrast to charter schools, voucher effectiveness has also been mostly worsening over time. Washington, DC, provides the clearest case of this. The first rigorous study of vouchers in the city suggested positive effects on student achievement, but these have turned negative after the aggressive expansion of high-performing charter schools. It was apparently harder for vouchers to look good against this stiffer competition from charters.

A small but growing number of studies have examined the long-term effects of vouchers on measures like high school graduation and college entry. One of these, focused on the Louisiana voucher program, shows that the outcomes are nearly identical for the randomly selected voucher recipients as for the nonrecipients.[18] Similarly, results from New York City show no average effect on college-going.[19]

In contrast, studies from Florida, Milwaukee, and Washington, DC, do show positive effects of vouchers on college-going.[20] The Florida voucher program increased college entry and raised college graduation by 1–2 percentage points.[21] The Florida results are noteworthy as the only instance where a statewide program has yielded positive effects on any outcome.

We still have much to learn about vouchers. Twenty-six states now have voucher programs, and the US secretary of education, Betsy DeVos, is pushing for more at the federal level. This will yield a steady flow of studies testing whether vouchers can produce results at scale. The results so far, however, do not provide much confidence that they can perform better, or even on par, with charter schools.

Challenges in Comparing Traditional Public Schools, Charters, and Voucher Programs

The discussion above focuses on studies comparing vouchers with traditional public schools. However, though the researchers have been careful in their work, research to date is limited in several important ways. I start by considering three factors that give an unfair advantage of sorts to vouchers that researchers cannot easily account for:

- SELECTING STUDENTS. While there is some selection of students by traditional public schools (especially in who is able to move into a school district and selective magnet schools), the potential for selection is still greater with private schools, where admission rules are common and expected. Differences in student outcomes thus may not reflect school performance so much as students' prior abilities. To account for this, I gave more weight above to the most rigorous research, which used random assignment of students to voucher programs, though even this is insufficient. To the extent that private schools select students, we can expect voucher results to look better for reasons that have nothing to do with private school effectiveness.

- CLASSMATE EFFECTS. It is not just that private schools can select voucher students; they also select and serve tuition-paying students who are likely to exert positive classmate effects on voucher students.
- LEARNING CURVE. The vast majority of voucher schools have been open for many years, having operated first as tuition-paying schools. As we have seen, schools, like the teachers who work in them, tend to get better, especially in their first year or two of operation.[22] Charter schools, in contrast, are usually much newer, and their teachers much younger.

A fourth factor sometimes works in favor of vouchers, sometimes against them:

- ALIGNMENT OF SCHOOL MISSION TO OUTCOME METRICS. One objective of market reforms is to give schools autonomy, allowing them to pursue objectives different from those of from traditional public schools. To the extent that schools' missions differ, their alignment with any set of standardized outcome metrics will also diverge. For example, some private schools aim to instill religious values, which are not measured by standardized tests. Which sector gains an advantage depends on which specific metrics are used. While this likely favors traditional public schools in some existing studies, it cannot explain all the negative voucher results that have emerged.[23]

Two additional factors tend to favor traditional public schools:

- SPENDING. Money matters, and private schools usually receive fewer public resources per student than traditional public schools. While this would seem to make it more difficult for private schools to improve student outcomes, such comparisons are difficult. The difference in government funds going to voucher and traditional public schools exaggerate the true, and more relevant, differences in *resources* contributing to voucher student outcomes.[24] For example, private schools often receive large donations from churches and parents, providing resources above and beyond government funds. Overall, students in private schools probably have lower resource levels per student, but the precise amount remains unclear.[25]

- OVER-REGULATION. A second form of selection bias might sometimes be at work. Private schools are probably less likely to participate in voucher programs that come with more strings attached. If the highest-quality private schools are the ones most likely to be driven away by regulation, this will reduce the measured effectiveness of voucher schools relative to traditional public schools. Research on vouchers under these conditions will only capture the effectiveness of the lower-performing private schools that do choose to participate.

This last point, on over-regulation, warrants more attention. While regulation almost certainly dissuades some private schools, the key question is, does regulation keep out the *highest-quality* private schools? There is little reason to think so based on evidence to date. Arguably the only study on this topic found no relationship between private school participation in voucher programs and the one, albeit imperfect, quality measure the researchers had available, pertaining to parent satisfaction with private schools.[26]

The reasons why private schools opt out is also instructive. In one survey, the top five concerns private schools had about voucher participation included "the effect [of government regulation] on our school's admissions policies," "students might not be prepared for our academic rigor," and "the effect on our independence, character, or identity."[27] A subsequent study by the same research team came to a similar conclusion.[28]

These results are not surprising. Given what we learned in chapter 2 about classmate effects, we would expect private schools, especially the most exclusive and expensive schools, to consider "admission standards" and "character" when selecting students. But this is less a sign of over-regulation than it is that nonparticipating schools are focused on educating only certain types of students. Again, this is not because private school educators care less about disadvantaged students, but because the private school business model requires it. The implication is that voucher

TABLE 10.1. Unfair advantages of different sectors in studies of school participation effects

Type of advantage	Sector(s) with likely unfair advantage
Student selection	Private, Charter
Classmate effects	Private, Charter
Learning curve	Private, Traditional
Metric alignment	Charter, Traditional
Funding	Traditional (?)
Regulation/school selection	Traditional

programs are unlikely to induce the best private schools to participate and serve those students held up as having too little choice in the public sector—regulation or not.[29]

Without regulation, we would also have no way of knowing whether private schools participating in voucher programs are effective. Data reporting requirements are the most common and basic elements of regulation. Standardized test scores, for example, are used to create school letter grades for parents, and to carry out the kind of research I have emphasized throughout this book. Without those requirements, it would be difficult for parents and policymakers to draw conclusions about alternatives to traditional public schools. Paradoxically, then, we cannot evaluate the effects of regulation without at least some regulation.

As a general rule, the above advantages and disadvantages of private schools also apply to charter schools, though usually to a lesser extent. Charter schools can—and do, according to one national study[30]—select students, but these schools are usually required to use lotteries, and authorizers exist (in theory) to enforce this. Their advantage in terms of classmate effects is smaller both for this reason and because they do not have tuition-paying students. Similarly, funding mechanisms probably place charter schools at some disadvantage, and regulations may drive out potentially high-performing charter operators.[31] Private schools that decide to add voucher students also get a bit of a head start over charter schools because they have developed over many years, while charter schools are usually starting from scratch.

Table 10.1 summarizes the above analysis, listing which sector or sectors are likely to enjoy an advantage in terms of each of these six factors that are difficult for research to account for (the first sector listed likely has the largest advantage). One important observation is that every sector has unfair advantages in several of these areas, so we cannot say definitively that research generally tilts one way or the other.

The table also suggests, however, that charter schools have fewer unfair advantages than private schools. (The only exception is with mission-metric alignment.) This implies that, to the degree we are interested in comparing charter and private voucher schools, charter schools are at a bit of a disadvantage, the size of which depends on how authorizers intervene to prevent schools from selecting students, and how state law dictates funding allocations.

So far, this analysis may seem somewhat speculative and theoretical. How large are these sector-specific advantages in practice? It is difficult to know, but as I explain below, these complications make the New Orleans experience even more relevant than it may have seemed at first glance.

Charter Schools and Vouchers in New Orleans

One purpose of the above analysis is to point us toward the most convincing evidence—that is, evidence based on research that has done the most to place the different school sectors on an even playing field. It turns out that the evidence on charter schools and vouchers in New Orleans and Louisiana is perhaps the most convincing of all. This is arguably the only single location for which we have rigorous evidence regarding both charter schools *and* voucher programs.

Louisiana is also the place where research has been able to address the largest number of unfair advantages. The state's voucher evidence is based on random selection of students, and the charter evidence is based on a convincing research design, which compares the same outcomes before and after reform for multiple matched comparison groups. Since we studied charter schools over a ten-year span, we largely sidestep private schools' potential advantage on the learning-curve problem. Moreover, the funding design allowed private schools to receive 90 percent of the funding of traditional public schools (excluding capital funding), placing them on a relatively even playing field on this dimension as well.

Most importantly, we have some alignment between mission and metrics. The Louisiana Department of Education provides public reports on the test scores for private voucher students (by school), making the tests partially high-stakes for all schools. In addition, we have rigorous evidence for both programs on college attendance—a key goal for all types of schools, and one that cannot be manipulated the way test scores can.

New Orleans is also useful for understanding the role of government because, even setting aside the official voucher program, the city showed us three types of government intervention, operating in short succession, at scale. We started with traditional public schools before Katrina. In the first phase of reforms, charter schools were established and left largely on their own, with limited oversight and accountability. In the second phase, vouchers were added to the mix, likewise with limited oversight and accountability. But in the third, the RSD stepped in for a reinvigorated government role with charter schools. The charter results improved between phases one and two, and again between two and three, providing some suggestive evidence that regulation—performance-based contracts and centralized enrollment, expulsion, and building ownership—helped, or at least did not hinder, school success.

In light of the significant challenges involved when comparing schools across sectors—the built-in advantages and disadvantages of each sector—New Orleans is even more important to the national experience than it initially seemed. To date, the city has had the most even playing field imaginable for comparing charter schools and vouchers, and here again, the results seemed to favor charter schools. This reinforces the idea that a strong role for government can complement market-based reforms.

The Role of Competition

So far, I have focused on evidence about differences in the performance of individual charter and voucher schools, vis-à-vis nearby traditional public schools. Another part of the market theory holds that allowing families to choose schools will pressure all schools to improve on a systemwide scale—indeed, this has been one of the main arguments for a market-based approach since Milton Friedman. When schools perform poorly, families will presumably vote with their feet and the low-performers will shut down, giving all schools a strong incentive to improve.

We have already seen some evidence of competitive effects in New Orleans (e.g., school principals could name their specific competitors and their responses), though it is difficult to gauge the impact of these effects on student outcomes, as they are mixed up with the other mechanisms. In other cities, researchers have compared outcomes in traditional public schools before and after individual charter schools located nearby, allowing them to test for the effects of competition. Evidence from these studies suggests that competition following the introduction of charter schools or private school vouchers generally improves, albeit to a small degree, the measurable student outcomes in traditional public schools.[32]

This finding is important in part because market critics argue that charters and vouchers hurt traditional public schools by taking away their money and perhaps their better students. This is often true. Indeed, for its advocates, that is the whole point of school choice, to allow students — and their associated public subsidies — to leave for other schools that use public funds more wisely. The schools that serve students should receive the money to cover their costs. On the other hand, because of economies of scale, taking money away from traditional public schools makes it harder for them to function, creating a countervailing force that could, in theory, undermine traditional public schools — and competition more broadly. The fact that the net competitive effect is slightly positive suggests that competition more than offsets any such negative effects for students who remain in traditional public schools.

Perhaps more than any other, the argument that competitive effects are important makes educators bristle because it seems to suggest that educators are lazy and need external pressure to do what is in the best interests of children. But this is another case where the clunky language of economics can get in the way of a useful interpretation. Competition can work in many ways. Choice can give families a greater sense of control and agency over their children's educations, provide information to schools about what families are looking for, encourage schools to focus more on parents' wants and needs, and create a better fit between school programs and student needs. Perhaps "competitive effect" is not the right term. In any event, the evidence on this phenomenon seems clear. The introduction of charters and vouchers does not seem to harm traditional public schools on the whole, and it may help their students slightly.

Innovative Systems, Conservative Schools

Markets have many potential advantages. To this point, I have focused especially on competition and fit, i.e., the ways schools operate autonomously can increase the variety of schooling options available and allow families to choose those best suited to their children. But there is one more potential advantage I have so far largely ignored: innovation. In most markets, companies invest in finding ways to produce their existing products more efficiently and to develop entirely new products.

As with other aspects of the schooling market, though, there are many reasons to expect that a free market in schooling would not be very innovative. Parents generally want schools that are familiar and have a sense of permanence—schools that have stood the test of time. This is understandable considering the great responsibility parents are giving schools when they have them take care of their children. A related issue is that parents are uncertain about the aptitudes and long-term interests of their children; not many adults end up doing the things they dreamed about as children. Under such circumstances, perhaps the best approach is to have children experience a wide variety of activities and subjects, consistent with the cafeteria style of traditional public schools. Almost no one would send their children to a school that teaches only math, for example. Parents (and voters and policymakers) want it all, which greatly limits the potential for innovation.

When schools do try to innovate, especially with the curriculum, they run into a different problem. Schools might be the main, and most intuitive, source of student outcomes, but parents matter a great deal too. Teachers teach, but so do mothers and fathers, and siblings, in the evenings and on weekends when students work on their homework. If they do not understand what their children are learning, or how it is being taught, then families' inability to support students may not only create frustration but undermine schools' credibility. Schools can only deviate so far from established parental expectations.

Pressures against innovation are also felt on the supply side. Schooling is a social enterprise at heart, and there are only so many ways to innovate in social relationships. Even among for-profit schools, which have especially strong incentives, such innovations would be hard to capitalize on. Educational entrepreneurs, when they think about potential innovations, ask: Where's the intellectual property? In other words, how can they create something that they alone can control and sell to others, with patent or copyright protections? There is some intellectual property with instructional materials, for example, but it is easy for educators to create their own versions of such materials. Even to the degree innovation is possible in a socially driven enterprise, there is not much reason to invest in promising ideas, given the difficulty of profiting from them.

The information problem also inhibits innovation. Entrepreneurs need to show results, but how do they measure quality given how hard it is to connect schooling to students' long-term outcomes and separate out the effects of non-school factors? Schools cannot experiment in a lab the way, say, a pharmaceutical company can experiment with new medicines.

It is not impossible to innovate—in fact, some genuinely innovative ideas did develop in New Orleans[33]—but it is much more difficult in education. No evidence, no proof. No proof, less profit. Of course, educators innovate in small ways all the time, and share what they have learned without the expectation of remuneration, but we do not need a free market in schooling for that.

With neither pressure from the demand side nor opportunities on the supply side, we would not expect much innovation. Is there any reason to expect that government helps or hinders on this count? The answer is unclear. On the one hand, intense performance-based contracts force schools to find some way to be effective. On the other hand, this pressure also forces schools to focus on a narrow range of outcomes, limiting the range of potential innovation.

I put this question to Walter Isaacson, the native New Orleanian who helped lead the committee in charge of rebuilding Louisiana after Hurricane Katrina. Among his best-selling books have been biographies of innovators such as Apple founder Steve Jobs. In what ways did Isaacson think the New Orleans reforms were innovative?

> They [the reformers] were all willing to innovate and try but not innovate too much. They weren't going to experiment on kids, but they were going to say, "All right, if somebody's got a good school coming in and parents want it, we're going to try to make it so that the rules aren't too difficult."
>
> You don't want to experiment on humans, especially on young kids'

education. You had to limit it, to some extent. If people came up with wacky things, you had to say no. They have to be able to pass reading tests. People said, "Well, why are you doing so much testing?" Because you couldn't have experimentation unless you had some accountability.[34]

What this implies is that the innovation in New Orleans was in the system—in implementation of choice, autonomy, and accountability—more than in the schools. The reformers relaxed some of the rules (e.g., around personnel) so that schools could recruit, hire, develop, reward, and retain the best teachers, but the charter authorization process and performance contracts restricted how far schools could stray, and how much harm they could do if an experiment went wrong. The result was that this innovative system produced mostly retro schools—not so much twenty-first-century marvels as better versions of the conservative schools idealized in the nineteenth century. Under the New Orleans reforms, the three Rs and strict discipline were schools' calling cards.

In many respects, even the new system of schools was a throwback to earlier times. Before the System, back in the early 1900s, each school had its own board and operated independently. Teachers lacked the job protections and bargaining power provided by union contracts and tenure, and could be fired for any reason. They had little training, and most stayed for only a few years. Teachers were judged, often harshly, based on standardized tests or public recitations and spelling bees, so they crammed in additional reviews to make sure their students performed well.[35] This all sounds very familiar. The schools of a century ago did not quite follow the no-excuses script, which involves higher expectations and more data than the schools of earlier eras, but they were in the same genre.

The same seems to be true of charter and private schools nationally. Charter school advocates fret about the lack of innovation and the difficulty in defining it.[36] Private schools tend to look the same as public schools serving the same populations.[37] This is not necessarily a problem. Maybe we are not looking for innovation so much as high-quality and varied options. Creating schools that are very good at getting the basics right, especially for disadvantaged students, would be a significant accomplishment by itself.

The Alignment of Evidence on No-Excuses, Effective Schools, and More

The New Orleans reforms were throwbacks to earlier times, and it is tempting to think this makes them unwise. However, studies in other cities have consistently shown that such no-excuses schools are more effective in raising scores than other types of charter schools.[38] Efforts to extend the no-excuses approach to traditional public schools have showed some signs of success.[39] The no-excuses approach is also consistent with the "effective schools" studies, dating back to the early 1970s.[40] While the studies were not very sophisticated research by today's standards, their conclusion was basically the same: that effective schools focus on basic skills, strong administrative leadership, high expectations, an orderly atmosphere, school autonomy, and frequent monitoring of pupil progress.

The research on instructional methods is also relevant here. Direct instruction is a teacher-driven model, where the teacher largely delivers content to students. While not all charter schools use direct instruction, it is implied by the methods listed in *Teach Like a Champion* and in the test-driven mentality more generally. In contrast, inquiry-based learning relies on teachers presenting questions, problems, and scenarios, thereby facilitating students' discovery of the knowledge they need to respond to such prompts. Research shows that direct instruction generally does more to improve test scores than other approaches.[41] Many of the whole school reforms that have proven successful over several decades also rely on direct instruction.[42]

When we step back and take a global perspective on school policy, the conclusion seems similar. In an extensive study using data from the Program in International Student Assessment (PISA), researchers found that schools generate higher test scores when accountability provisions "are in place that aim at students (external exit exams), teachers (monitoring of lessons), and schools (assessment-based comparisons)." They also found that accountability was more effective when schools have "hiring autonomy" and are located in "urban areas."[43] This almost exactly echoes the prior conclusions, emphasizing school autonomy and accountability. Further, the authors of this international study found that "students perform better in countries with more choice and competition as measured by the share of privately managed schools . . . [and that] the performance advantage of privately operated schools within countries is stronger where schools face external accountability measures."[44] In other words, the market-based approach seems to work better in conjunction with government-imposed accountability.

If the goal is to increase student achievement, then we have an increasingly good idea what to do. The combination of school autonomy, high expectations, and measurement-based accountability leads schools toward certain instructional practices that raise those scores.

Market Reforms Seem to Work Better in Urban Locations

School reforms, of any sort, might also work differently depending on *where* they are implemented. In chapter 2, I discussed the importance of geography in relation to economic theory. Since more choice is possible in large, high-density populations, we might expect school choice policies to be most effective in urban areas.

The results are also likely to be more positive in urban locations because this is where traditional public schools seem to be lowest-performing. While the degree of urban school failure has been greatly exaggerated, due to a misleading focus on test scores and neglect of the influence of concentrated poverty, the general conclusion that urban schools are lower-performing also seems to hold when using more sophisticated analysis based on student achievement growth.[45]

This theory about the role of geography is consistent with the patterns of evidence. In addition to the international study mentioned above, two studies using random assignment have found market-based school reforms to have more positive effects in urban areas relative to other locations within Massachusetts,[46] and another found the same with a national sample of lottery-assignment charter schools.[47] Some of the strongest evidence of positive effects on students' long-term outcomes is from another city, Boston.[48] A randomized trial of schools in urban areas also found strong positive effects.[49] The CREDO charter school study covered almost the entire country and showed positive (and improving) effects on achievement on average also looked at the issue by location; it too found the most positive effects in urban locations, followed, in order, by suburban and rural charters.[50] I have found only one exception, pertaining to a single charter management organization.[51] New Orleans is apparently not the only urban area where this general type of reforms has been especially effective.[52]

I put this question about the viability of New Orleans–style reform outside urban locations to Louisiana state superintendent John White. His response? "You can't imagine it in a rural parish in Louisiana. You just can't."[53] The role of context, then, is crucial. If this is true—that market-based reforms really only have the potential to work well in urban locations—then it may be better to think of this combination of school autonomy, parental choice, and government accountability as a targeted intervention that may work in certain situations rather than as an organizing principle for broad-based school improvement.

Conclusion: Markets and Governments Need Each Other

Throughout this book, I have argued that the application of market principles to schooling by itself is unlikely to yield the results its advocates promise and hope for, or that we usually observe in other markets. The New Orleans evidence is consistent with this conclusion, as is the broad body of evidence nationally.

Neither charter schools nor vouchers have shown the success we would expect if the piercing criticisms of school districts were generally on the mark. Also, the evidence for charter schools is at least as positive as that for voucher programs, reinforcing the conclusion that "getting the government out" is probably not the answer. Because of the various unfair advantages in these programs that researchers struggle to incorporate in their results, it is difficult to compare results across these different systems. Yet the charter evidence is also more positive than the voucher evidence in Louisiana—one of the only places where we can make a head-to-head comparison of charters and vouchers on a fairly even playing field. Charter schools are at least as effective as voucher programs in this case, and charters are getting better as they scale up over time. The voucher results, on the other hand, are less positive and getting worse.

Voucher supporters might object by pointing to the survey indicating that some private schools are not participating in voucher programs because of government rules, especially those designed to ensure equitable access or basic accountability. But if a goal of vouchers is to provide greater access to disadvantaged students—a worthy goal—then perhaps the more relevant question is this: Among those schools focused on the public ends that regulations are intended to pursue, which type of school system seems most effective? Charter schools faced far more regulation, and the positive results in New Orleans continued even after more rules were put in place.

Even if we ignore the extremely poor results in statewide voucher programs, which may not be as bad as they seem, the best we can say is that vouchers have measurably positive effects for black students in urban areas and probably for students in Florida. Charter schools also seem to work better in urban areas, but, unlike vouchers, they also seem slightly more effective even in statewide programs that include large numbers of rural and suburban schools.

Both the theory and evidence, then, seem to point toward a conclusion that neither of the typical sides of the political debate is likely to be comfortable with. On the one hand, it is hard to make a case for maintaining traditional public school districts that are demonstrably failing, such as the pre-Katrina school district of New Orleans. At the same time, it is hard to argue we should turn over public funds to private schools with limited government oversight, as vouchers seem no better than charter schools on some dimensions and worse on others, and private schools often seem less interested in serving students with the most challenges. In this case, the invisible hand of markets benefits from a visible hand of government, though perhaps in a form different from the System. What remains is to identify the appropriate nature and scope of that government involvement.

CHAPTER 11

Democratic Choice: The Fundamental Roles for Government in the Market for Schooling

The New Orleans school reforms are unprecedented. Partly because of this, they provide a unique window into the roles of markets and governments in schooling. As I have shown, schooling is a market but a highly unusual one. A free market in schooling would be undercut by limited options, poor information, and inequity, among other problems. If ever there were a market in need of government, this would be it. Yet, we have also seen that not just any role for government will do. School districts are capable of producing both excellent and poor results. The supposed advantages of the System—coordination, expertise, scale, and democratic accountability—can, in some cases, degenerate into a political bureaucracy that is moribund, corrupt, and ineffective. Moreover, school districts are designed to restrict the freedom of families to choose schools and the freedom of schools to pursue distinctive and coherent missions.

So what are the appropriate roles for markets and governments, and what can we do to ensure each fulfills its purposes? Are there general principles that we can follow across essentially all circumstances? Does the New Orleans experience help us, in at least some small way, to answer these questions?

In this chapter, I argue that the New Orleans experience, combined with evidence from across the country over several decades, suggests that at least some failing school districts may benefit from a different path—

neither market nor district alone. Even with a heavily market-driven system, the government, in conjunction with the third sector of NGOs, still needs to play an important role, what we might call the market-maker. Specifically, based on the prior analysis, I identify five fundamental roles for government in schools: accountability, access, transparency, engagement, and choice. By "fundamental," I mean roles for government that are important under almost all plausible conditions.

New Orleans is significant in part because it was the first to adopt an approach that built in most of the five fundamental roles for government within a market framework. Leslie Jacobs and the reform family created a network of public and nonprofit organizations to govern and guide a new type of school system—really a system of independent schools—one that greatly improved average outcomes and reduced achievement gaps. But the system in New Orleans was far from perfect. Transparency and engagement with the community remained especially weak. I am therefore not making the case that all, or most, or even some, cities should adopt New Orleans–style policies as is. To take this a step further, I am not even arguing that the New Orleans model is best for New Orleans.

I am also not espousing particular strategies or policies. The evidence does not support it, and it seems clear that our school systems need to be as diverse as our states, cities, and small towns. Replacing the one best system of American education with another best system would be unwise. The five fundamental roles need not, and should not, be carried out the same way everywhere. There is certainly a role for broad federal guidelines, especially in protecting the rights of children, but as different places live under different conditions, we need different ways of governing and running schools to match local circumstances.

These five roles for government are derived from the theory and evidence presented in this book, as well as more philosophical considerations that I have only touched on to this point. Appropriate policy design depends both on evidence, such as I have presented throughout this book, and on the *values* through which we interpret it. I therefore start this chapter by explaining how these five roles for government are based on four core values: freedom, efficiency, equity, and community. I then explain how these values, combined with the theory and evidence, lead to the fundamental roles for government. Finally, I discuss which public institutions are best suited for which roles, and consider some of the most likely counterarguments.

The Four Core Values

The four values listed above—freedom, efficiency, equity, and community—are not new. Henry Levin, a well-known economist and education scholar, has outlined a similar framework and applied it to evaluate school vouchers.[1] While some might emphasize one value over others, they are, as a group, widely held.

The four values can be usefully separated into two groups. For opponents of the System, efficiency and freedom—the more private-oriented values—are usually seen as pointing toward the necessity of individual education decisions made through markets. For supporters of the System, equity and community—the more public-oriented values—take precedence and provide a strong case for public, democratic governance.

FREEDOM. A core American value, freedom might seem the simplest of the four. But it actually has two very different meanings that are rarely distinguished. Market advocates usually focus on what I will call *freedom from constraint*.[2] In the present context, New Orleans families, rather than being locked into neighborhood attendance zones, should be able to apply to any publicly funded school in the city. Rather than being beholden to a faraway district, state and federal officials, and union contracts, New Orleans school leaders should choose their schools' paths, and choose their personnel.

But what are we to make of the fact that the schooling market, for most families, cannot offer many options? Are low-income families, for example, really freer in a "free market"? Perhaps not when we consider the word's second meaning. As I explained in chapters 2 and 7, economies of scale, the geography of choice, the information problem, and incentives for cream-skimming all prevent choice from being real for many families. School choices may be free from constraints but still provide little *freedom of opportunity*.[3] The difference between these two forms of freedom is crucial because theory and evidence are really only relevant to freedom of opportunity, and the two can be in conflict. One of the fundamental problems with the theory of schooling markets is that reducing constraints may mean reducing opportunity for certain groups. Families might have freedom to choose schools in theory, but their particular opportunities may be limited.

EFFICIENCY. The success of any system in generating freedom from constraint is intertwined with the market conditions that lead to efficiency. Market logic dictates that, when consumers and producers are left to make their own decisions, consumers will choose what is best for themselves; and the process of competition and innovation will (usually) yield outcomes that maximize social well-being, defined as the sum of well-being across all individuals. Centralized governments are not omniscient; they cannot know each individual's circumstances and preferences. The effect of government regulation, then, is to constrain individuals in unhelpful ways, reducing efficiency in the process.[4] Individuals can make better decisions for themselves, on their own. Again, this logic seems to hold in the vast majority of cases. Markets can be powerful tools for increasing social well-being.

But the market logic quickly falls apart with schooling. Classmate effects mean that families have incentives to choose schools based on who else attends them, rather than the quality of instruction and curriculum. Further, if families lack any real opportunity to choose schools, and have limited information with which to judge performance, then the competitive process and efficiency are stunted. The market will not be able to solve these problems on its own. Even in cases where local leaders try to work together voluntarily, the challenges to cooperation across a large number of organizations create substantial hurdles and costs. The fact that a free market in schooling is inefficient in these ways is worrisome considering that efficiency is usually the main strength of markets.

EQUITY. Even if the schooling market were efficient, almost all participants in schooling debates believe that equity is important too. The problem is that the same factors that tend to make markets more efficient also make them less equitable. Even if government funding were exactly equal for every student, free markets naturally tend toward tiers of quality and toward segregation. The geography of quality schools limits options, not just on average, but disproportionately for low-income and minority families. Cream-skimming, by definition, does not occur randomly, but targets those who are already most vulnerable. Consumers are not equally misinformed about school quality, but rather low-income and less-educated parents tend to have less information.

Different people may define equity in different ways, but such definitions do not matter much for the argument at hand. Free markets will be inequitable by any reasonable definition. This is what markets do. As we have seen, schools select some students and exclude those most in need.

COMMUNITY. One of Paul Hill's main arguments for a more market-based approach is that it provides autonomy for school leaders, who can set their own distinctive missions, select their own teachers, and build strong school cultures around common values, beliefs, and norms. In other words, they can create strong school communities.

But school communities are not the only ones that matter. Students spend a lot of time in school, but they live, and spend even more time, in neighborhoods. As school district defenders correctly point out, neighborhood schools facilitate relations and closer bonds with the people next door. This was illuminated for me in a conversation with a friend whose son attended one of the handful of schools that still had neighborhood attendance zones in post-reform New Orleans. When walking the neighborhood for Halloween trick-or-treating, he and his family knocked on the doors of families with children from the school their child attended and were invited into each to join the party going on inside. In contrast, my neighborhood, like most of the rest of the city, lacked such school zones. Some families still held Halloween parties, but attending them meant driving all over town, something few actually did. It weakened our neighborhood.

Schools also have the potential to be community anchors for neighborhood activities and events, and for optional services like pre-kindergarten and adult education. While recognizing the importance of such activities, New Orleans school leaders questioned how they would help their particular schools. A leader of local adult education programs, for example, explained to me that she wanted to host events at charter schools for the growing number of non-English-speaking adults, but was rebuffed.[5] Charter leaders generally did not seem to view their schools as public places with neighborhood-based missions.

This loss of geographic community and public functioning is a real concern given today's social dilemmas. People increasingly tend to experience life on their own, "bowling alone," caught up in television and smart phones, or isolated in the filter bubble of the internet.[6] Indeed, in using school choice to create school communities with like-minded people, we may further isolate ourselves from our neighbors and those whose views differ from our own. Such isolation may be a particular issue in high-poverty urban areas where people are more dependent on friends and neighbors to get by.

The democratic character of American schools is another aspect of community. Education, early in American history, was broadly considered essential for binding together a nation of immigrants and teaching democratic values that were not natural and ingrained. Children have to be taught that they, and everyone else, have self-determination and rights, to free speech and religion, among others. Democratic citizens tolerate differences, recognize and value the public good over their own individual interests, and seek equality before the law for all people. To really learn democracy and put its values into practice, people also need to participate as citizens—seeking out divergent views in order to become informed, making their voices heard on matters of public import, participating in reasoned public discourse, campaigning for and otherwise supporting candidates for elected office, and of course voting for representatives in elections. Given the current political tenor, it may be that the need for schools to teach and demonstrate democratic values is greater than ever.

THE FOUR VALUES TOGETHER. It should be clear that we can, at least partly, measure to what extent schooling is consistent with these values. Analyses of school spending and families' school choices, for example, tell us something about how well these policies succeed in achieving efficiency and freedom of opportunity. Analyses of achievement gaps, segregation, and exclusionary practices tell us something about our success in improving equity. The description of the reform process—the role of Jacobs and, subsequently, those of the authorizer and districts—tells us about how the reforms largely failed to involve or build on New Orleans's strong sense of community. We pursued such an extensive empirical analysis in New Orleans because we believed the results meant something in the pursuit of these four values.

Bringing in all of the values, and evidence regarding each, might sound like an effort to please everyone, to forge a compromise with an overly large philosophical tent. But these values are widely held. We expect our schools to pursue many interconnected, and sometimes conflicting, aims. The framework is meant to highlight trade-offs and find ways to balance them, so that we can develop a system of schooling that can endure and stand firm against the political winds. Traditional school districts have lasted for over a century and continue to command public support and resources because the System has engaged the community and responded to local needs. Losing broad political support, as polling data suggests happened in pre-Katrina New Orleans (chapter 4), is perhaps one of the greatest risks to any schooling system in the long run. For any policy strategy to be both politically sustainable and educationally sound, it has to be attuned to our core values, and to the facts.

Democratic Choice and the Five Fundamental Roles for Government

What does all of this tell us about the future of schooling? I argue that the four core values—overlaid on the New Orleans experience, and combined with economic theory and decades of education evidence from across the country—point to a new way of thinking about markets. Moreover, they point to five fundamental roles for government, an approach that I call Democratic Choice.

ACCOUNTABILITY. Given the extreme imperfections of the schooling market, and the likelihood that undesirable, low-performing schools would survive in a free market, it is important that some public institution actively ensure that schools are of high quality, so that families have good options to choose from and tax dollars are used wisely. Even Milton Friedman, in his argument for school vouchers, acknowledged the need for "minimum standards" for participating schools.[7] Given that disadvantaged students are more likely to end up in low-performing schools, this is important for both efficiency and equity.

Louisiana's Recovery School District (RSD) was both lucky and good in its New Orleans accountability efforts, putting in place policies to facilitate objective reviews of charter applications, following the third-party recommendations, acknowledging errors, and taking over schools it had opened when they turned out to be low-performing. Our research suggests that market accountability alone would not have shut down these low-performing schools.

School districts, especially operating on their own, have not been adept at holding schools accountable either. Local politics and union contracts leave few options for identifying failure and improving on it. Before state and federal accountability policies were implemented, it was difficult to compare schools and therefore to determine which were really failing. Yet the government accountability we have now has many flaws, especially in the narrow focus on test scores and the failure of their performance measures to distinguish what schools contribute to student outcomes from what students themselves contribute. Nor have these past government efforts led to the closure or takeover even of persistently failing schools.

This is not to say that the New Orleans approach to accountability is the best one. Taking over half of all schools in one decade is not something we would hope for as standard operating procedure. Also, accountability does not have to focus on academic outcomes, or really any measurable outcomes, in the way it did in New Orleans. It would probably be useful to account for factors like parent satisfaction, which capture a wide range of hard-to-quantify contributions that schools make to student well-being. Accountability could be based on subjective measures, using what economists call implicit contracts, in which two parties continue to work together until one decides not to. Schools could decide to stop operating, or the government could, as a last resort, decide to stop funding them, for reasons that do not involve specific metrics.

No approach or set of measures will ever be perfect, but government accountability seems a necessary countermeasure to the considerable flaws of the market and to the rule-compliance and input-orientation of other forms of government action.

ACCESS. One of the unusual flaws of the schooling market I have highlighted here is that schools have strong incentives to recruit and choose the students they prefer, especially students who are well-behaved, high achieving, and inexpensive to educate. These incentives, combined with geographic constraints, are why a free market in schooling will generate a tiered system of schools, the same division of haves and have-nots that we are trying to fix in traditional school districts. Disadvantaged students are likely to be excluded from the upper-tier schools, making the term "school choice" a misnomer.

Broad and equitable access to high-quality schools requires public oversight over five main areas: enrollment, transfer, discipline, transportation, and special education. Again, New Orleans leaders handled these fairly well. In a city with poor mass transit, they required schools to provide bus transportation, so that the city's overwhelmingly low-income student population could get to the schools they wanted. They created rules and processes for expulsions. To address the issue of dropouts, they solicited and accepted charter applications for alternative schools—schools of last resort for students who struggled in more typical school settings. These activities sent a message to the entire community, and to school leaders, that access is an important objective.

In traditional school districts, all students are guaranteed slots in their neighborhood schools. School districts can pool resources, develop more advanced expertise, and provide a wide range of services in essentially all of their schools. Federal regulation regarding special education services provided through districts has unquestionably improved access to quality education for students with disabilities, as well as English language learners.[8]

Government efforts to make schools accessible are necessary to achieve any form of equity. In more market-oriented systems, such efforts also encourage efficiency, as more access for everyone means easier movement to preferred schools and more competition. When schools are accessible, they have to compete based on the quality of their instruction and curriculum, not just on the types of students they can attract and select.

TRANSPARENCY. Neither the market nor democracy functions well without good information, something markets themselves often fail to provide on their own. Standardized testing, though sometimes controversial, is meant precisely for this purpose: to provide information about school performance that is comparable across schools. Transparency in governance also requires this type of information. More broadly, parents and citizens should know what programs are available and to what extent they are meeting student needs, and taxpayers and policymakers should know how tax dollars are being used.

Here, New Orleans was a more modest success. While the New Orleans Parents' Guide, combined with standardized state accountability metrics, provided well-rounded information about educational programs and outcomes, school governance and financial matters were anything but transparent. Many questioned the accuracy of the Parents' Guide and saw it more as a marketing device for schools. Also, little is known about conflicts of interest in the city's schools, in part because charter schools, as private organizations, are not required to make public the financial and contractual information that would be required to identify them.

Whether a system is more government- or market-driven, a good rule of thumb is, the more information and transparency the better. This along with the first two roles—accountability and access—are what I call government's three core market-maker roles. These roles are necessary to make markets function in ways consistent with all the core values.

ENGAGEMENT. Given the importance of developing community, it is important that the community be involved in critical education decisions. Transparency is a first step, but information is not useful to the community if people have no authority to use it. Engagement is about involving families and communities in key decision-making processes; it is about soliciting and responding to feedback and ideas from those within and outside school walls.

Of all the core functions, this is clearly the one where New Orleans was least successful. Community engagement was minimal during the first phase, when the general direction of the reforms was being discussed. Cowen's committee held many public meetings, just as we might have expected a school board to do. However, this input seems to have had little bearing on the reform design. Jacobs and other reform leaders made their decisions behind closed doors. As Candler described it, his job was delivering canned solutions.

Things did not get much better in the second phase, as the shift to charter schools began. Charter boards rarely posted or disseminated their meeting times, locations, and agendas — or even the names of board members. Such information often was released only in response to pressure from community organizations. Local community members were led on through an endless process of tinkering with their charter applications without ever getting them approved. Without a school board or superintendent in charge, community members did not know whom to talk with when they did not like the menu of options before them. People had something to say, but the reforms were designed so that no one was designated to listen or respond. Even when the RSD was listening, it made promises it did not keep.

Eventually, the third RSD superintendent, New Orleans native Patrick Dobard, tried to change the direction and involve the community more in selecting school operators. Instead of doing school reform "to the community," as he put it, Dobard engaged and worked "with the community" in choosing some school operators.[9] But even in this case, the RSD selected the community members it wanted involved and gave the group a restricted set of options to choose from. For most policy decisions, even these limited steps were not taken.

In a public event we organized, a school leader put it this way:

> I wish that there was a greater influence of those community individuals from neighborhoods, making decisions about what happens with schools. I think there is a dead voice there, if I'm just being brutally honest. [We need] individuals that are community advocates that are engrossed, actually able to make [education] decisions about their children.[10]

The System, in contrast, engages the community through democratic elections, legally mandated open meetings where citizens have a right to speak, and open-records laws. It is understood that board members are to listen to the community. In addition to having to answer for their actions at the ballot box, board members have to answer for them in the grocery store, where they regularly run into constituents. When I was growing up, my father was the school board president, and it was hard to leave the house without his bumping into someone who wanted to talk about a school issue. As economist Albert O. Hirschman pointed out, both exit and voice can be valuable.

CHOICE. Choice is fundamental to freedom, and perhaps in some cases necessary to efficiency, as it provides an additional form of accountability—market accountability—with advantages and disadvantages that differ from government accountability. For both legal and political reasons, governments rely on objective measures to make decisions. In the case of education, however, this can be counterproductive because we cannot directly measure what we think is most important. In contrast, when families make choices, they can pay some attention to objective measures, but their contract with schools is implicit, allowing them to consider any factor they wish when deciding whether to exit to other schools. Allowing choice between schools can therefore offset the problem created by the Law of Contracts. If schools cheat or distort their explicit performance metrics, or go too far in ignoring important unmeasurables, there will be consequences, as parents have at least some power to respond by sending their children elsewhere.

So it would seem that "school choice" is fundamental. But it is clear by now that allowing choice between schools also limits freedom and efficiency in other ways. Many parents are constrained by geography and the costs of switching schools. School choice is also unlikely to create the kind of neighborhood public schools that 80 percent of New Orleans families said they wanted: schools tied to tight-knit geographic communities, in convenient locations, with cafeteria-like menu options. Moreover, choice *within* schools may be just as important as choice between them, providing students with more options but with lower administrative and transportation costs.

So yes, schools should endeavor to provide choice, but this term should not be confined narrowly to the choice *between* schools. Many communities may reasonably choose to limit choice between schools because of geographic and transportation considerations, and in order to ensure that families get the neighborhood schools they prefer.

AUTONOMY? Given the success of the New Orleans experience, it is tempting to add autonomy for school leaders as a sixth fundamental role. However, the prior analysis has shown several reasons why such a role is both ambiguous and, in some ways, problematic. First, we have to ask, autonomy for whom? The System provides autonomy to teachers. With job security, teachers can experiment with new ideas without the looming threat of being fired. Giving teachers autonomy seems natural given that they work in isolation; autonomy is also an attractive feature of the job for thoughtful and able teachers—people who value exercising their own judgment.

When reformers talk about autonomy, however, they are talking not about teachers but about school leaders. There is a certain organizational logic to this—to allowing school leaders to coordinate activities within their schools and manage their personnel without undue restraints. However, given that schools and classrooms are loosely coupled, and teaching is complex, observing performance is a challenge. Even good teachers may run afoul of school leaders or principals. More broadly, if we turn teaching into just another occupation, where the bosses call the shots and pay is low, then teaching may become less attractive to the very people who would make the best teachers. This is why autonomy is not among the core roles. It is not that obvious which educators should be in charge of key educational decisions.

To summarize, Democratic Choice is a broad concept encompassing five roles for government. It embraces different forms of choice and a role for democratic participation based on transparent community engagement and accompanied by accountability for schools and access for all children. The five roles are meant to be specific enough to guide policy and practice, but general enough to allow for needed experimentation and to account for the diverse circumstances across the country, from farming communities to big cities.

By now, it should be clear where the New Orleans reforms fit into these principles—the reformers were strong on accountability, access, and choice, but weak on transparency and engagement. Traditional school districts, too, can be consistent with these principles. The System *can* provide accountability and engagement through elections and public meetings; provide transparency through public records laws; provide access through funding rules that ensure most schools have adequate resources and that all schools provide a wide range of services; and provide choice between and/or within most schools. But obviously, in the pre-Katrina period, the district did none of these things well.

These roles for government also exclude some policy options. A universal, full-scale voucher program, in particular, would not fit within Democratic Choice because, by definition, such an approach precludes these five roles for government—and the market itself lacks the capacity to carry them out on its own. This is why it appears vouchers, in their pure form, would be inconsistent with the underlying core values.

Later, I will consider potential responses to these arguments from advocates of school vouchers. But first it is important to consider roles for other institutions, beyond markets and governments, in Democratic Choice.

The Roles of Nongovernmental Organizations

Democratic Choice is fundamentally about the role of government. Chapter 8 also showed, however, that there is a role for a third type of institution: nonprofits, or what I will simply call nongovernmental organization (NGOs). These organizations have long played a greater role in public life in the United States than in other countries, and there are potentially untapped roles in education as well. Below, I distinguish two types of NGOs that can play an important role under Democratic Choice: the boards of privately operated schools and intermediary organizations like those that facilitated the operation of schools in New Orleans, even without a direct hand in running them.

CHARTER BOARDS. Nonprofit organizations are generally legally required to have governing boards, and charter schools are no exception. The role of charter boards is quite different, however, from those of elected government boards. NGOs are responsible for ensuring that organizational managers use their funds well and in line with the public interest as stated in their missions. This is different, however, from a broad duty to the public interest.[11] Nonprofit charter board members are like elected boards in their duty to a public mission, but also like corporate boards in being primarily responsible for ensuring the success of their organizations.

It is possible to design charter board laws to encourage governance that is consistent with democratic principles and the public interest. Transparency, again, is the watchword. Charter boards have been known to meet rarely, and behind closed doors; moreover, they effectively allow their CEOs effectively choose their own board members. One New Orleans CMO leader acknowledged to me that he simply put his friends on his board. In other cases, the same members served on many different boards at the same time. This is problematic given that one of the main functions of the boards is to help prevent conflicts of interest.

Rules regarding the composition of boards and how they carry out their work can help address these problems. Charter boards, as with authorizers, should be required to follow open meetings laws in ways similar to school boards. Board members should be required to disclose personal and financial relationships with the school itself, other board members, and charter administrators. It may also be wise to require that some board members be students, parents, teachers, and representatives of neighborhood groups, and to prevent people from serving on multiple boards simultaneously. Such requirements send the important message that charter boards are there to serve the entire community and to help prevent boards from becoming irrelevant, inbred, or cloistered.

These issues are likely to be worse in the case of for-profit charter organizations, which need not have any public mission guiding their thinking. As Candler explained, the for-profit charters he encountered were also apt to playing financial games to increase profits, largely at the expense of school quality. For-profits struggle to produce high-quality schools because outcomes are not clearly defined or easily measured; the Law of Contracts takes over and quality suffers. In this respect, the New Orleans reformers were probably wise in keeping out for-profit organizations.

In other respects, however, the New Orleans approach faltered. With little encouragement from the RSD, even the nonprofit charter boards were too cozy with their leaders and did little to engage the community.

INTERMEDIARY NONPROFITS. Other nonprofits, beyond charter boards, also had roles in New Orleans. NSNO incubated charter schools, recruited educators, and provided direct support to schools to help them improve; the Cowen Institute surveyed parents and developed informal networks; and both organizations advocated for system improvement. Philanthropists helped fund their efforts, which not only brought more resources in total but helped sidestep the transaction costs that come when many organizations are involved. The question here is, to what degree can these organizations assist with the five government roles?

Again, consider transparency. Standardized test scores and graduation data are useful—in fact, the government is uniquely positioned to gather information like this that is comparable across schools. The Cowen Institute also took on responsibility for summarizing these data and working with local leaders to identify issues of concern.

Those more critical of the reforms also had an important role to play. The Southern Poverty Law Center helped to unearth problems with the treatment of students with disabilities and used what it found to bring suit against the government. The media also played a key role, with frequent front-page stories and exposés. An informal network of volunteers emerged to attend charter board meetings and report publicly on their discussions. When something went wrong, the public often learned of it quickly.

More deliberate engagement with the community is a second role, especially when the NGOs have credibility as advocates for community and neighborhood needs. The Orleans Parish Education Network (OPEN) has seemed to fit this description most closely. Without local elected representatives to contact, OPEN became a hub to which parents and other community members could bring complaints. A more recent group, Black Education for New Orleans (BENOLA), pursues the goal of "build[ing] the capacity of Black-led efforts to enhance the pace of educational success in New Orleans."[12] The leaders of these organizations served as liaisons to bring concerns to government officials. One parent, Ashana Bigard, also functioned as an informal advocate for parents.

These organizations and individuals had little real authority, though, and certainly could not manage or even guide the market effectively on their own. The role of the SPLC and the media, in particular, were contingent on government rules and regulations that gave them standing to file lawsuits and demand information that schools were not providing on their own.

NGOs, charities, and the press—sometimes called institutions of civil society—have a greater presence in the United States than in other countries. It is worth considering, in the case of schooling, how they might be useful partners with government to make the market work.

Distinguishing Public Ends from Public Means in Accountability

There are clearly limits to what private organizations can do. Some critics go a step further and raise a more fundamental concern: that, as private organizations, NGOs have their own interests and cannot serve public ends.

But the problem may not be as large as it seems. Whether private means can be used to pursue public ends depends on at least three key questions: First, to what degree are the private goals of families consistent with the public goals? If families place a high value on their children learning democratic values and practices, for example, there might not be a conflict.

Second, to what degree are the goals of schools driven by families, as opposed to educators? Even if families do not happen to place much value on the public aims of education, teachers and school leaders often feel passionately about these ends and may pursue them anyway. The goodwill of educators is an essential asset to the success of any school system.

Third, to what degree can public and private aims be brought into further alignment through nontraditional democratic accountability and contracting? The government can, in theory, write contracts with privately-operated schools that prioritize public goals. In fact, this has been the main purpose of state and federal standards and accountability all along. States set academic standards and require schools to test students because public officials believe the material covered by the tests is important to the public interest. Social studies standards include, among other things, learning about American history, the Declaration of Independence, the Constitution, and other aspects of civic life. Beyond contracting, charter boards and the media can also place pressures on schools to serve public ends.

Implicit, then, in my argument for Democratic Choice is that there are other combinations of public and private processes—combining market pressures, government contracting, charter boards, the press, and more—that might be more successful than local school districts. If choice pulls private and public goals apart, then the hard power of contracts, combined with the soft pressure of NGOs, might bring them back together.[13]

In the New Orleans case, the democratic side of Democratic Choice fell short. Local charter schools were authorized by officials elected by citizens throughout Louisiana—the *state* Board of Elementary and Secondary Education—giving New Orleans voters little real political power or voice in their own schools. The participation of citizens in the democratic process is both more feasible and influential at the local level.[14] Accountability is different when you know your elected representatives personally and see them in the neighborhood. Also, if the goal is to teach democracy, there may be no substitute for seeing it in action with one's own schools. Local voices are stronger voices.

A further implication of this decline in local democratic governance is the depleted political power of the city's largely African American citizenry. The reforms were created and managed by white leaders. Three out of four teachers fired were black, compared with fewer than half of those subsequently hired. The charter authorization process, deliberately or otherwise, favored outside white groups over local community groups.[15] This is no doubt partly why a split in public opinion between white and black voters persists.

To many in the local black community, this felt like more of the new Jim Crow.[16] The reforms did not prevent black citizens from voting per se, but their votes mattered far less in the statewide balloting that selected the state board, which selected the state superintendent, who selected the RSD superintendent, who had ultimate authority over New Orleans schools. Moreover, recall that research suggests that market-based reforms may be most effective in urban areas. We therefore face a conundrum: the place where these reforms seem to work best, on measurable outcomes, are precisely the places where the threat to minority political disenfranchisement is greatest. The increase in choice for African American families, and perhaps better schools, help to make up for that, but whether this does more to pursue public ends, as viewed by the African American community, is unclear.

Addressing Potential Responses

My main argument in this book, informed by the New Orleans experience, is that government and nonprofit organizations have important roles to play in schooling. This is why Democratic Choice involves five roles for government. Below, I consider potential responses from supporters of the System and from various of its opponents, including voucher supporters and those, especially Paul Hill, who conceptualized the portfolio model.[17]

RESPONSES FROM SUPPORTERS OF THE SYSTEM. Many defenders of traditional public schools argue, essentially, that there is no other viable system of public education. My argument is that, while the System has many advantages, other institutional arrangements might be more consistent with the four core values, at least in situations where urban districts have been clearly and persistently failing.

I have already outlined several substantive arguments in favor of the System: Public means, such as elected boards overseeing local school districts, are most likely to facilitate public ends. Private operation of schools, in contrast, will turn key stakeholders into private actors focused on private ends. Schools will select students, leaving disadvantaged students ill-served and segregated in separate schools, possibly more than they are now. The mix of available schools will not match what families and communities really want. Neighborhoods will suffer.

Defenders of traditional public school might argue that the roles I have outlined for government (and NGOs) will be insufficient to counteract these unfortunate market forces. This might be true in some cases, though the New Orleans experience shows that the fundamental roles of government—roles that districts now perform—can, potentially, be carried out in other ways.

Some defend the System as part of a larger desire for progressive schools and a more professional (less occupational) structure of teaching. It is difficult to know, however, what kinds of schools Democratic

Choice might generate once we add in greater community engagement and transparency—the elements that were missing in New Orleans. Some communities might advocate for progressive approaches and pressure governments to contract with private organizations to build such schools. Others might implement versions of Democratic Choice that are built less around test-based contracts. While the New Orleans reform version was clearly more conservative, there are other versions where the progressive-conservative outcome is less clear.

RESPONSES FROM VOUCHER SUPPORTERS (LIBERTARIAN VERSION). Libertarians such as Milton Friedman prize individual liberty—especially freedom from constraint—above all other values and acknowledge little role for government beyond protecting property and civil rights. With regard to education, one libertarian argument holds that traditional public schools force people to think in a particular way, restricting freedom of conscience. However, some common beliefs are necessary for a society to function; it is not clear, for example, how democracy could work if citizens did not believe in its underpinnings. A key goal of public schooling is thus to inculcate democratic virtues and values, such as tolerance for divergent views and the belief that individuals are equal before the law. Also, though all schools clearly influence what students believe, it is hard to argue that traditional public schools require students to believe much. They do tend to expose students to a wide variety of ideas, which would seem necessary for freedom of thought generally. People cannot be free to follow their conscience if they are not aware of the moral frameworks from which they are choosing.

Some adherents to libertarianism also argue their case on the basis of efficiency, asserting that liberty yields better results.[18] Here theory and evidence come back into play. As I have shown, the simple market logic falls far short when we consider the very unusual features of schooling. Moreover, research evidence provides little reason to believe vouchers would yield better measurable outcomes than, say, charter schools. It is possible that the government will get some things wrong under Democratic Choice, but this seems even more likely with the market.

The libertarian argument entails a value judgment that freedom from constraint is an end in itself—the foremost value. For this reason, libertarians would likely prefer Democratic Choice to school districts, even if neither would be high on their list. Still, libertarianism requires a narrow view of the world, one that hones in on only one particular aspect of just one of the four core values. If a system does not generate quality schools that are accessible and serve community needs, then telling people they are free from constraints will be cold comfort.

RESPONSES FROM VOUCHER SUPPORTERS (CONSERVATIVE VERSION).[19] An alternative case for vouchers comes from the political philosophy of conservatism. This is quite different from libertarianism in many respects, though the two groups often support vouchers and oppose traditional school districts for reasons that at least sound similar.

A core principle of conservatism is that most decisions should be left to the most localized group possible—usually families. Those best situated to make schooling decisions are parents who have close bonds with, responsibility for, and knowledge of their children. When children are placed in schools, the educators in those schools, while subsidiary to families, are the next best group to which authority should be assigned, especially if families have the power (choice) to decide which schools their children will attend. Government bureaucrats, such as charter authorizers, are more remote and prone to imposing one-size-fits-all rules that do not account for local circumstances and needs. Therefore, while the reasoning differs, both conservatives and libertarians both want families to choose schools.

Conservatives also value morality and religion. Many fret about the separation of church and state, and rules against prayer in traditional public schools.[20] Some favor vouchers because they will allow religious communities to create schools that hew to their beliefs; this is a particular concern among Catholics and some other religious faiths as their schools have experienced steadily declining enrollments, driven partly by the rise of charter schools.[21] Libertarians, by contrast, do not make their argument on the basis of religion, but do generally believe that people should be able to follow their own individual consciences.

Other conservative beliefs cut in multiple directions and even suggest a defense for school districts. Conservatives value tradition, which would seem to conflict with the progressive thinking that goes on in university schools of education and gets transferred into traditional public schools. On the other hand, the System has been around for over a century—it has become its own tradition, which conservatives would typically defend. As I have said, these are *traditional* public schools.

Finally, the conservative principle of local decision-making (subsidiarity) reinforces the role of both families and local communities. If conservatives value neighborhood communities more than school communities (see chapter 7), then the idea of a neighborhood school is also conservative. This valuing of localness, combined with that of tradition, seems to provide a defense of school districts as much as an argument against them.

Where conservatives come down on either school districts or Democratic Choice is therefore unclear, as the value accorded to family and religion may clash with that ascribed to tradition and neighborhood community.

RESPONSES FROM PURE CONTRACTING AND PORTFOLIO SUPPORTERS. Democratic Choice is consistent in many ways with Paul Hill's portfolio model approach, so it is important to consider the two main differences, and how Hill's adherents might respond differently than voucher supporters.

The first and most obvious difference is that Democratic Choice is a set of principles, whereas Hill's portfolio model is, as the name implies, a model or blueprint for policy. It is much more specific.

Second, I have left school autonomy off the list of government roles. Hill argues that the school is the fundamental unit of organization, so that school-level autonomy is central. What I have shown, however, is that autonomy at that level often means less autonomy for teachers, which may make teaching less attractive, even to the best teachers. While I believe union contracts and tenure provisions can and should be improved, the issue of autonomy is more complicated than it seems.

The second substantive difference between Democratic Choice and the portfolio model is that Hill's early writings do not suggest a viable role for school districts. While his subsequent work has included collaborations with districts, this has not come with a substantive defense of their roles. My proposal, in contrast, explicitly affirms the role of districts and suggests maintaining them where they seem to be working well. As I have argued, school districts have certain advantages: the ability to build local support, provide local democratic control, take advantage of economies of scale, facilitate coordination, and provide certainty to parents and teachers. These strengths should not be shed lightly.

Conclusion: Toward Better School Systems

No system of schooling can be perfectly consistent with all the values of efficiency, freedom, equity, and community, or with every educational philosophy. Public policy is also a limited tool, meaning that, while we can set the priorities, conditions, and resources for those who do the real work, students, parents, teachers, and leaders are ultimately responsible for their implementation, and for dealing with the inherent trade-offs involved in the everyday life of classrooms.

Yet there do seem to be policies that are likely to improve schools broadly, across all of these dimensions. The five fundamental roles for government—what I collectively refer to as Democratic Choice—are reinforced by social science theory and, generally speaking, the empirical evidence I have presented. Markets create specific kinds of problems, and the five roles for government are designed to create targeted solutions to solve them. Rather than more versus less government, the argument for Democratic Choice is about what kind of government we need. Much of what we think of as "market" activity in everyday life actually involves a quiet and healthy dose of government, and that seems even more necessary with schools.

One option is to maintain the System. The analysis throughout this book suggests that, in most places, that is probably the right strategy. The advantages that led to the System's creation remain today. While not the focus here, there are also ways to improve school districts from within and to rethink some of the ways in which they have evolved and become increasingly detached from schools and parents. Federal, state, and district leaders should consider cutting down on the rules and regulations that constrain educators. Teacher unions, likewise, should take a close look at what they ask for when negotiating with school districts and charter schools and consider the unintended consequences even for their own members.

Sometimes districts will succeed, sometimes not. When one fails, clearly and persistently, something needs to be changed. One alternative, at the opposite end of the government-market spectrum, is to have private organizations run schools with public funding and largely without constraint. Parents, not the government, are given the responsibility for holding schools accountable, based on which schools they choose. This voucher strategy, however, gives rise to many predictable problems:

muted and distorted competition, schools choosing students instead of students choosing schools, and a menu of schooling options that does not line up with what families really want. Innovation of the sort that typical markets create is unlikely to arise.

I therefore argue here for Democratic Choice as a third approach in which families exercise school choice while government performs certain roles designed to address market flaws through targeted rules. In some ways, the government's role is increased; the ability to select and take over schools based on performance is something local school districts have lacked. In other ways, the role of government is lessened, especially with respect to the day-to-day operations of schools. New Orleans was not quite a Democratic Choice approach, as it lacked transparency and engagement, but it is probably the closest any district has ever come on the other roles.

This analysis does not tell us what to do (no reasonable analysis can), but at the very least, it can help us move beyond unproductive and superficial debates about "public education," "privatization," and "government monopolies"—terms that, at best, roughly characterize, or caricature, markets and government. The term privatization is narrowly accurate in describing contracting with private organizations but fails to reflect that contracting actually increases government power in some ways. The term public education, likewise, has become almost synonymous with school districts, and fails to account for the roles of parents, other government agencies, and nongovernmental public institutions, or the fact that districts sometimes fail to meet their expected public ends.

If nothing else, my hope is that this discussion helps build a different, clearer, and more productive language to reason through our many expectations for schools and the many roles entailed in meeting them.

CHAPTER 12

New Orleans and the Future of America's Schools

It has been a century now, a century of political bureaucracy and local school districts and superintendents and teacher unions, the key actors in traditional public schools. Has the one best system's time finally come to an end? Has the world passed it by? From the analysis in this book, I argue that the answer to these questions is, probably not.

This may seem a surprising conclusion to a book about a revolutionary school reform that represented a sharp break from the past and had such success. New Orleans has shown us a new kind of schooling system—built around the principles of school autonomy, parental choice, and government accountability—that, unlike the vast majority of reform efforts over the past half century, led to substantial improvements on almost every measurable educational dimension. The city offers hope that we can get closer to the high and elusive bar of competing with the best in the world and, simultaneously, serve as the nation's great equalizer, so that all children have a reasonable chance to succeed in life.

But there are two versions of every story. Ashana Bigard's and Patrick Dobard's. Conservative and progressive. Insider and outsider. Local and state. Black and white. Bridging these differences, over such a long period and through changing times, has been one of the System's signature attributes. In post-reform New Orleans, the bridge may be missing. While survey data suggest a clear majority of support in the city, we might have expected more universal approval for a reform that generated so much measurable improvement.

Such skepticism is a product of the many slights and errors the reformers made along the way: the dominance of a small number of white
leaders in its design. The firing of all the black teachers without cause. The
pushing away of local black educators in the charter authorization process. The lack of community engagement. Patrick Dobard recognized the
problem and tried to bring the community back in, but there was only
so much he could do. Even if he had been inclined to do so, he could not
give the community control that the law did not allow.

What then should other places take from this? In what other cities—
and suburbs and towns—might similar reforms improve measurable outcomes? Can these reforms be designed and implemented in a way that is
more locally rooted? More broadly, how might the New Orleans reforms
be remembered in the long arc of the history and future of American
schooling? To answer these questions, we have to be clear about the realities of traditional school districts and of the alternatives.

Dispelling Myths of the One Best System

Let us start by summarizing the misunderstandings about the System
that I have examined so far.

No, traditional school districts are not government monopolies. They
involve the interplay of local government with housing and labor markets. Families already vote with their feet by moving between districts
and neighborhoods. As a matter of basic economics, monopolies produce
too little of the good or service in question. Yet one of the main successes
of American school districts is that they have succeeded in producing
so much formal education—and the most productive workforce in the
world. Monopolies are also inefficient, but the above analysis (of economies of scale, expertise, and transportation costs) calls that into question
as well in the case of schooling. If they were really as bad as their critics
assert, traditional school districts would not have lasted more than a century, and with such widespread support. Four out of every five New Orleanians said they wanted neighborhood schools even after the otherwise
successful reforms that had eliminated them; and three out of four parents
nationally say they prefer good neighborhood schools to more choice.[1]

No, the world has not passed the System by. It has adapted all along to the social and economic upheaval going on around us, offering more advanced courses, extending opportunity to more students, updating curricula with the latest scientific discoveries, and adding the latest technology to classrooms, in order to deliver instruction and teach students how to use the tools of the future. Today's classroom teaching would be unrecognizable to the teachers of a century ago. At the same time, we can appreciate the ways in which our traditional public schools have been islands of stability, helping to pull us together when social media, technology, politics, and other social forces are pulling us apart. We should not wish for schools that blow in the wind, changing what they are doing every time a new occupation or technology emerges. The demand for skill in the workplace has been rising slowly and steadily, but the best evidence suggests that the academic, cognitive, and technical skills of the System have generally kept pace.[2]

No, the fact that classrooms look the same now as they did a century ago, with rows of desks, stacks of textbooks, and teachers at the front of the room, is not a sign that school districts have failed to adapt. There have been many attempts to change the way classrooms look—schools without walls, open classrooms—almost all of which came to be derided as failures. It is ironic that the look of classrooms is invoked as evidence of school districts' lack of experimentation with the latest ideas, when the reality is that setting desks in rows is the result of just such experimentation. If this usual classroom setup is so bad, it is worth asking, why does almost every classroom on earth, in public and private schools alike, repeat it? Maybe it just works. The same could be said of other aspects of traditional public schools that have not changed. Our schools have changed in some ways and stayed the same in others, mostly in ways we should embrace.

No, public schools do not offer a cookie-cutter approach that treats all the students the same. Special education, gifted, and advanced courses are designed to address distinctive student needs. Students can also choose among electives and extracurricular activities, and select specific teachers. The choices within schools may be less extensive, and the compilation less cohesive, than some might wish, but choosing options within schools is far less disruptive and less costly than switching schools.

No, when school districts fail, it is not mainly because they are too focused on "adult issues" as opposed to childrens' issues. Even with this most radical of reforms, the leaders are still struggling with adult issues, and they always will because educators' needs are intertwined with those of the children they serve. As Jacobs and White emphasized, reformers have struggled to find ways to make teaching attractive, especially once educators have families and mortgages to worry about. Organizations cannot thrive unless their employees do too, and that means school reformers need to find a way to make teaching manageable and fulfilling for talented young people.

There are two sides to every story, and the truth is usually somewhere in the middle. School districts maintain most of the strengths that led to their widespread adoption: scale, expertise, choice within schools, neighborhood attendance zones, and democratic accountability. The job protections that come with tenure and union contracts—the most derided aspects of traditional public schools—lend job security, head off misguided attempts to precisely measure and reward teacher performance, provide a degree of teacher autonomy, and make the jobs more attractive. If we are going to pay people with bachelor's degrees salaries below what they could earn elsewhere, then we need to find other ways to make it worthwhile. The System is one way to do that.

The idea of the traditional school district is not broken, though certain specific systems (small s) certainly are. New Orleans was persistently failing in 2005. Of the nation's fourteen thousand school districts, others are probably broken as well. Often, even after repeated attempts, school districts are unable to right the ship. What then?

Scaling Improvement

The reforms worked in New Orleans by almost every measure. Could they work elsewhere? Could this be a broadly effective strategy for fixing failing schools and districts? Again, the answer is, probably not.

Jacobs and the other reforms leaders recognized that they had considerable advantages. They could build the reforms without organized political opposition, and with a leg up on the most important task of all: attracting teachers and leaders. New Orleans receives more than ten million visitors per year. The music and food and festivals are world-renowned. That national familiarity and appreciation for the city, combined with a desire to help it rebuild in the horrific aftermath of Katrina, generated an almost missionary zeal. People wanted to save this great American city.

Even that enthusiasm probably would not have been enough if not for the reforms themselves. It quickly became clear that New Orleans was going to be the Silicon Valley of school reform—the place where ambitious entrepreneurs, wishing to make a name for themselves, would join together. If local leaders had simply hired teachers back into the old system based on seniority, this energy would have been lost. The result, in Jacobs's words, was that "on a per-capita basis we have a higher level of educator talent than probably any city."[3]

The reforms attracted resources as well from local property taxes and philanthropists. With enough local support, other cities might be similarly able to boost property tax revenue. The philanthropic funding, on the other hand, is unlikely to be there in other places. New Orleans drew national interest, and funding from ultra-wealthy donors, in part because this was a first-of-its-kind reform, what Paul Hill called a "green field" opportunity. Those that follow cannot be first, and there is only so much philanthropic funding to go around.

Perhaps most important of all was the very low starting point for student outcomes. New Orleans was the second lowest-performing district in the second lowest-performing state in the country. With nowhere to go but up, and with our analyses measuring changes from this initial low starting point, it is perhaps not surprising that we saw significant improvement in this particular case.

A few other large cities might be in similar situations—again, recall the urban advantage with charter schools and private schools generally—but perhaps no city, and certainly no suburb or town, will ever have them all. The effects we have seen in New Orleans therefore probably represent the best-case scenario. Other districts will have to create versions of reform that best fit their contexts.

A Retro Reform Effort

Whether the reforms can be sustained in New Orleans or scaled to other places is one question, but the heart of the debate is a philosophical one—whether they *should* be extended. Do we want to send our children to schools that are progressive and caring—that are, as Ashana Bigard put it, like sending them to "auntie's house"? Or are we more concerned with measurable student achievement, with factors like those that led Patrick Dobard's family to send him to private schools?

The long arc of history has gradually bent from conservative toward progressive teaching. In the 1800s and early 1900s, teachers ruled their classrooms, directing students to memorize facts and keeping order through corporal punishment. This conservative approach gave way, gradually, to schools built around students' needs. Reflecting broader trends in society, discipline became more relaxed. Teachers began covering a wider variety of more advanced (nonreligious) material, often using more student-centered projects and inquiry.

A second, parallel arc has seen teaching shift from an occupation to a profession. Teachers went from being at-will employees with little training a century ago to being professionals whose jobs were protected by tenure and union contracts. The training institutes (called "normal schools") that some teachers attended a century ago evolved into university-based schools of education that almost anyone who wanted to be a teacher had to attend. By the 1970s, teaching had become a desirable career.

That the occupational-professional arc has coincided with the conservative-progressive one is no coincidence. They are both based on the same underlying logic: conservative teaching fits best with an occupational view, with school leaders directing teachers and teachers directing students in clearly defined tasks, while progressive teaching matches up with the professional view, with teachers using their experience and expertise to work autonomously, make their own judgments, and motivate students to want to learn more. The latter may make teaching more attractive to highly skilled people as a career path, allowing expertise to develop, while the former provides more accountability and can function with less experienced teachers and high turnover.

The New Orleans reforms, therefore, can be viewed as an inflection point on both of these trends, a sharp swing of the pendulum back toward more conservative pedagogy and a more occupational view of teaching. The reformed school organization is also a throwback to earlier times. A century ago, most school districts had only one or two schools and operated more or less autonomously, like CMOs. Each school had its own board. Over time, decision-making authority moved further and further from the schools. Starting in the late 1960s, federal special education laws and programs offering funding for low-income and other students led to more rules. Teacher unions emerged and negotiated contracts. Districts consolidated from more than one hundred thousand at their peak a century ago to only fourteen thousand today. Each of these steps diminished the control of school leaders, especially over personnel.

The New Orleans reforms were not intended as a throwback. The reformers just wanted to provide solid academic skills and discipline, and to give New Orleans students better life opportunities. Few reformers seemed to be aware that they were updating a nineteenth-century model in their pursuit of twenty-first-century schools.

Where Does New Orleans Go from Here?

Schools are rarely static, and this revolutionary reform has not been either. The New Orleans reforms continually evolved, from the chaotic, free-wheeling early days to the later phase, when the state began to re-regulate and soften the hard edges of the market.

As I write this, New Orleans is in the midst of another unprecedented school reform. After going to all that trouble to remove control from the local school district, Jacobs has been working to shift it right back. Why? Because Jacobs knew this would happen eventually. Again, she got out in front of it with carefully crafted legislation. According to the new state law:

> Unless mutually agreed [with schools] . . . the local school board shall not impede the operational autonomy of a charter school under its jurisdiction in the areas of school programming, instruction, curriculum, materials and texts, yearly school calendars and daily schedules, hiring and firing of personnel, employee performance management and evaluation, terms and conditions of employment, teacher or administrator certification, salaries and benefits, retirement, collective bargaining, budgeting, purchasing, procurement, and contracting for services other than capital repairs and facilities construction.[4]

This is clearly not a return to the traditional System. The law bans the district from doing almost all the things districts have typically done. The schools may be returning to the district, but *as charter schools*. At least in the short run, there will still be no attendance zones, no union contracts, and no tenure. Moreover, the reform's institutional foundation remains firmly in place. NGOs like New Schools for New Orleans, the Louisiana Association of Public Charter Schools, the local Teach for America branch, and TeachNOLA had been built to sustain the reforms and insulate schools from unwanted government authority, even after the return to "district governance."

In effect, what Jacobs and the reform family have now done is to create an entirely new type of school district, one intended to entrench school-level autonomy, parental choice, and performance-based accountability. This last point is key. As we have seen, the approval and renewal of charter applications have been critical to the district's measurable success. Traditional school districts rarely close or take over schools, and when they do, the reason is generally severe financial distress, not poor performance. Will this new type of school district be any different? So far, the local district has continued to strictly enforce charter contracts. It is also taking a more hands-on approach, intervening in schools that are not on track to meet their performance thresholds. But it is far too early to predict where this will go.

It is also worth remembering that the reforms do not have universal support and there is a still something of a racial divide. The return to district control could increase community engagement and lead to decisions that are more in line with local preferences. Or the lingering resentment and concern in some segments of the community could turn into organized opposition of the sort that has been sidelined since Katrina. In theory, the district could start turning charter schools back into traditional public schools that the district manages directly. At present, however, the local district, like the RSD in the wake of Katrina, has almost no capacity to do so. The district office has been redesigned to focus on accountability and those specific core elements of regulation that remain (e.g., centralized enrollment and discipline). But all that could change.

Whatever happens next, in what is now an all-charter district, may be just as important as the immediate post-Katrina revolution. The new legislation lays out a plausible legal path for expanding the New Orleans model elsewhere. Perhaps the next revolution will be in a district that embraces the core elements of the New Orleans model, but with a process that embraces engagement and transparency—full Democratic Choice—in the process of reform.

Why New Orleans Matters

New Orleans matters. It matters because its reforms open our eyes to alternative ways of managing and governing schools. It matters because, at least on the usual metrics, the reforms worked very well. It matters because the spark that precipitated the reforms was one of the worst disasters in American history. It matters because many of those affected were vulnerable children who the schools had been serving poorly.

New Orleans also matters beyond New Orleans, in all the school districts, states, and even other countries that have been observing it from afar and considering emulating its approach. At the system design level, more so than in classrooms, the city's reforms are without precedent. They have inspired new thinking. As the reform leaders fan out across the country, they will create versions of what they saw in New Orleans. Few cities are likely to follow its example completely, but they will be hard pressed to avoid being influenced by it. Educators around the country will be talking about, and hearing about, New Orleans for a long time to come.

My main goal here has been to describe what happened in New Orleans and why, as accurately and completely as possible. It is a story worth telling, especially if doing so helps to move school reform forward in some small way, by kindling ambition in our educational goals, creativity in our thinking, and the realism that comes from hard evidence. It is useful to see something that is both new and measurably successful, as it forces us to question things we have long taken for granted. Even if we ultimately decide to stay the course, or go in a completely different direction, it will be from a position of deeper understanding.

Before Katrina, New Orleans may have been the last place on earth to expect anything innovative. Some would say the same right now about the country as a whole. Scholars, experts, and advocates have fretted about how tepidly we pursue even the most modest of educational goals. My hope is that other cities and states will build on the New Orleans experience with a desire to copy not its design and process but its ambition and inventiveness. No system will ever be enough by itself, as each system is what people make of it, but the decisions we make about the roles of governments, markets, and NGOs do shape the character of our schools. These decisions are not to be taken lightly given that the character of schools, in subtle yet powerful ways, shapes the character of the children they serve.

ACKNOWLEDGMENTS

This book has many origins. It is based on five years of research in New Orleans with a large and excellent team of researchers, and another decade before that studying test-based and market-based accountability in education systems around the country. It is also based on my personal experiences as a student, educator, parent, citizen, and school board member, which have influenced me in ways I probably do not fully realize.

Some influences, however, I do recognize. I grew up in the suburbs of Detroit, constantly perplexed by the fact that everyone around me was white and life was safe, stable, and calm. Everyone around me seemed to have money and opportunity, yet the headlines in the newspaper continually focused on this place called Detroit where the opposite seemed to be true. This troubled me. In the back of my mind, I kept asking, why? Why are these places so different? Why can't everyone have the opportunities I had? Why does it seem to matter that I am white and they are black? It seemed unjust, to the say the least, though this was not a word I fully understood at the time.

As a teenager, I went to Detroit every chance I had, seemingly to try and answer these questions. Perhaps I was also drawn by my family roots since my father had grown up there and was saddened by what was happening to the city. I interned in the Detroit City Council, volunteered with grassroots organizations, and started a nonprofit with my family to address homelessness in the city. I thank my family for encouraging me to follow this rather unusual interest. Going to Detroit was not something that most suburban families encouraged.

Growing up, I also got to see firsthand how school boards operate. My father was an elected member of our local board for many years. Everyone in the community seemed to know him. When he was not at school board meetings, he was on endless phone calls dealing with board issues. I realized that some of these issues must be important when my mother got into a physical altercation with a family member of another board member at a meeting. (If you knew my mother, you would find this rather extraordinary.)

In the mid-1990s, these ideas and interests collided. My earlier life experiences led me to study urban economics as a PhD student at Michigan State University when the state's Republican governor, John Engler, and state boosters—especially Betsy DeVos—created one of the nation's first state charter school policies. The fact that I partially owe my involvement in this work to Ms. DeVos would gain an ironic twist years later when she was nominated to be the US secretary of education. As part of my dissertation, I studied the charter schools she helped create.

University schools of education have been much maligned by the leaders of the branch of reform discussed in this book, but in addition to the MSU Department of Economics, I spent a lot of time in the university's top-ranked School of Education—an important contrast that allowed me to appreciate both the arguments for the market-based reforms in economics and the reasonable counterarguments, which I have tried to present faithfully. I particularly thank David Plank for his mentorship, and he and David Arsen for pushing me to think more deeply and broadly about these issues.

Given my family history, this was more than an academic exercise. While completing my dissertation, I joined a neighborhood association and served as liaison with the Lansing School Board. Eventually, I also ran (and lost) a race to become a member of the Lansing School Board. Later, while on the faculty at Florida State University, I did finally follow in my father's footsteps and became a school board member. I continued studying school reform, especially issues like the measurement of teacher and school performance that are the underpinnings of this book's focus on performance-based contracting and today's school reform movement.

Years later, like the rest of the world, I watched on television, transfixed and horrified, as Hurricane Katrina struck the Gulf Coast. I continued watching from afar as the New Orleans school reforms unfolded, and having occasional conversations with researchers about how to study what was happening. I did not expect I would ever be in a position to follow through on my interest in New Orleans, in part because I knew it would take a decade or more to see the results, and that untangling the reform effects from the hurricane effects would be a tall task.

Then came the call from Tulane University. The Department of Economics was looking for an education economist, and Scott Cowen, the university president, wanted an experienced education scholar to study what was happening. Scott and many others at the university provided considerable support over many years to help me build a research center, what became the Education Research Alliance for New Orleans (ERA–New Orleans). For that I am eternally grateful.

By the time I arrived in New Orleans in 2012 to launch ERA–New Orleans, I had been studying school reform for fifteen years and had seen it from seven different angles (i.e., seven different cities). Given the mixed and even negative evidence on school reforms available at the time from other cities and states, I was skeptical that the apparent post-reform successes were real, but I was not sure and kept an open mind. It would take years of research effort to do justice to such an unprecedented reform. It would also take years for me to get beyond my own one-best-system way of thinking to understand what was really happening.

In addition to Tulane's support, my team and I were fortunate to receive substantial grants from various sources (listed below). I appreciate the room these funders gave me to explore such a controversial topic and the trust that entailed. They never urged me to ask particular questions or provide particular answers. They never commented on our conclusions. To this day, I do not know whether they agree with our conclusions or not. That silence has been a real and unusual gift. They let me and my team do our best to let the data speak for themselves.

Running ERA–New Orleans was a difficult balancing act. On the one hand, I wanted to keep my distance from both the reformers and their opponents. I never donated to campaigns or attended events for candidates for the Orleans Parish School Board or state board of education. Thanks to Tulane's support, and funders of my other projects, I was able to avoid taking a salary or compensation for the work reported here, from the foundations that supported ERA–New Orleans or from any other key reform supporters or opponents. Whatever you might think of tenure for university faculty, one of its main benefits is facilitating the free flow of

ideas, even those that may be uncomfortable. I could report results un-
filtered. I never had to ask, "Will I lose my job or income because of this
report?" This is one of many ways universities play an important role in
the world.

On the other hand, I needed to engage both sides of the reform movement—supporters and opponents—to really understand what was happening. It is not possible to understand public policy, or really anything
else, just by analyzing the readily available data, such as test scores and
school finances. One of my first acts after creating ERA–New Orleans
was to create an advisory board of local education leaders, from teacher
union leaders to reform leaders (see list below). I also attended a lot
of meetings organized by my board members, their organizations, and
others in the community. Being embedded in the education community in this way was instrumental to our work and understanding of the
schools and context. Seeing the reforms up close in this way gave me a
much fuller picture, which I have attempted to weave into the discussion.

My goal, ultimately, was to answer the most important empirical
questions using methods that met the highest scientific standards, and to
make our findings accessible to educators and the community. "Objective, rigorous, and useful" was our center's motto. Of course, there is no
way to remove one's perspective completely from research. The reality is
that I and many on our research team were, like many of the reformers,
white, privileged outsiders whose backgrounds and experiences affected
how we thought. Still, it is possible to present well-reasoned opposing
viewpoints, uncover the assumptions and beliefs behind them, test their
implications with data and analysis, and present the findings scientifi-
cally. It is not just the findings of such research that can be powerful; research reports can also help frame conversations in useful ways.

I especially want to thank my entire team at ERA–New Orleans,
listed below, for helping carry out one of the broadest and most intense
evaluations any district has ever seen. They know better than anyone else
how hard this work is. There are reasons we know relatively little about
the successes and failures of the last century of school reform. There are
reasons research is usually not part of the public discourse and policy
conversations. There were some trying times, and I will never forget my
team's commitment and perseverance.

The University of Chicago Press has been an excellent partner in turning all of this into a book. I particularly wish to thank Elizabeth Branch

Dyson for her encouragement and guidance in shaping the manuscript over several years.

More than anyone else, I owe my family. All the work that went into ERA-New Orleans, and this book, meant time away from them. I am deeply appreciative for the love, affection, and support of my wife, Debbi, and daughters, Lyndsey and Norah.

EDUCATION RESEARCH ALLIANCE FOR NEW ORLEANS TEAM. Most of the empirical findings in this book are based on studies carried out under the auspices of ERA-New Orleans, authored by our internal staff of researchers. Jane Arnold Lincove, Nathan Barrett, Lindsay Bell Weixler, Matthew Larsen, Lihan Liu, Jonathan Mills, and Jon Valant all coauthored multiple projects over many years. Jon Valant also read and commented on an entire early draft of this manuscript. Paula Arce-Trigatti, Christian Buerger, Mary (Beth) Glenn, Mónica Hernandez, and Robert Santillano served as postdoctoral fellows and coauthored individual reports.

In most organizations, especially those that publish research, there are many who make important contributions but do not get public recognition as coauthors. ERA-New Orleans is no exception. A special thanks to our outstanding research analysts, Catherine Balfe, Briana Diaz, Alica Gerry, and Fred Sakon. Alica Gerry, in particular, played multiple roles and was instrumental in getting the organization up and running. Deanna Allen provided invaluable administrative assistance, above and beyond the call of duty.

Sara Slaughter, our associate director for operations, finance, and communications, deserves special recognition. A former New Orleans school teacher, she contributed to all of our publications, directly and indirectly, in ways that went well beyond her official responsibilities. She also had a central role in the production of this book, producing the figures, reading chapters, organizing discussions about manuscript drafts with the larger team, and providing invaluable editorial assistance. She has also been the glue that held the entire center together.

ERA-NEW ORLEANS NATIONAL RESEARCH TEAM. In addition to our internal team, I want to thank our national research team of scholars at other universities and research organizations. Deven Carlson, Joshua Cowen, Betheny Gross, Jason Imbrogno, Huriya Jabbar, Jennifer

Jennings, Spiro Maroulis, Julie Marsh, Andrew McEachin, and Katharine Strunk are scholars at other institutions who coauthored studies on the New Orleans reforms. Huriya Jabbar also produced a large number of additional studies of New Orleans, outside the auspices of ERA–New Orleans, that I have incorporated into the text (and cited in the endnotes). Patrick Wolf led a team of researchers on the Louisiana school vouchers, on which our team collaborated. Susan Bush-Mecenas and Alice Huguet and Vivian Wong also coauthored some of the reports.

ERA–NEW ORLEANS GRADUATE STUDENTS AND INTERNS. Whitney Bross coauthored two of our earliest reports and played a key role in building our data sets in the early years. Sarah Woodward studied the status of arts education in the city (see chapter 7). Danica Brown, Brittany (Tait) Kellogg, Estilla Lightfoot, Siyu Quan, and Brigham (Brig) Walker participated in various projects as Tulane PhD students. We had more than thirty interns, of whom Tucker Baker, Haley Kiernan, Elyse Magen, Natalie Phillips, and Patrick Simon made particular contributions to this book. In my undergraduate courses, many students wrote papers about the New Orleans school reforms that were also informative.

ERA–NEW ORLEANS ADVISORY BOARD. Our advisory board reviewed every report we released and provided important feedback at every stage leading up to publication: Louisiana Association of Educators (Debbie Meaux, Grant Schreiner), Louisiana Federation of Teachers (Steve Monaghan, Jim Randels), Orleans Parish Education Network (Deirdre Johnson Burrel, Nahliah Webber), Orleans Parish School Board (Nolan Marshall, Henderson Lewis, Mary Garton, Adam Hawf, Thomas Lambert, Colleston Morgan, Kathleen Padian), Louisiana Recovery School District (Kunjan Narechania, Jill Zimmerman, Gabriela Fighetti, Ray Cwiertniewicz), Louisiana Association of Public Charter Schools (Caroline Roemer), New Orleans Parents' Guide (Ayesha Rasheed), New Schools for New Orleans (Neerav Kingsland, Patrick Dobard, Michael Stone, Maggie Runyan-Shefa), and Urban League of Greater New Orleans (Erika McConduit, Dana Henry).

OTHER LOCAL EDUCATORS AND COMMUNITY MEMBERS. Flozell Daniels, Rose Drill Peterson, Ken Ducote, Lona Hankins, Karen Harper Royale, and Andre Perry were active participants in our conferences and public events. Dozens of others served on panels we organized. Hundreds attended our lunches and release events and provided valuable input in the process.

LOUISIANA DEPARTMENT OF EDUCATION. John White, Jessica Baghian, Laura Boudreaux, and Kim Nesmith were instrumental in facilitating data access.

OTHERS INVOLVED IN SURVEY DATA COLLECTION. For their assistance, I thank the Louisiana Public Health Institute (Lisanne Brown) and the University of Wisconsin Survey Center (John Stevenson).

TULANE UNIVERSITY. I am especially indebted to Scott Cowen, James Alm, and Steven Sheffrin for bringing me to Tulane to lead this work. John Ayers, Michael Bernstein, Brian Edwards, and Carole Haber also provided invaluable funding, support, and advice.

OTHER SCHOLARS. Joshua Angrist, David Figlio, Frederick Hess, Paul Hill, Gloria Ladson-Billings, Henry Levin, Helen (Sunny) Ladd, David Plank, and David Tyack have had particular influence on my thinking on these topics. I also thank the anonymous reviewers who provided extensive feedback.

FUNDERS. I gratefully acknowledge the support of the Laura and John Arnold Foundation, Tulane University (especially the Murphy Institute), William T. Grant Foundation, Spencer Foundation, and US Department of Education Institute of Education Sciences.

Background Data on New Orleans Demographics, Schools, and Socioeconomics

The main potential challenge to interpreting the results in chapter 4 as effects of the reforms is that the population may have changed in ways that increased student outcomes, separate from the reforms. As noted in the text, this was initially plausible, given the heavier flooding in low-income neighborhoods. For these reasons, the topic warrants its own appendix. Below is a summary from Harris and Larsen, "The Effects of the New Orleans School Reforms on Student Achievement, High School Graduation, and College Outcomes," which is available on the website of the Education Research Alliance for New Orleans and which I refer to as "the technical report" in what follows.

Since family income is generally a strong predictor of student educational outcomes, we started by analyzing students' eligibility for the federal free and reduced-price lunch (FRL) program. We show that the FRL percentage increased in New Orleans relative to the comparison group by one percentage point. However, FRL has two main problems: (a) it is set at a threshold and does not distinguish students in poverty from those in deep poverty, and (b) the administration of the FRL program, including eligibility, is determined at the school level and might therefore have been affected by the reforms. Nevertheless, it is noteworthy that the percentage of FRL-eligible students changed very little.

Given the problems with FRL, we commissioned the US Census Bureau to provide detailed demographics for households with students attending public schools in New Orleans and other districts in the state.[1] Some of the socioeconomic changes favored New Orleans, and others favored the remaining hurricane-affected districts. For example, median household income dropped by $736 in New Orleans but increased in the comparison districts by $1,750, for a simple difference-in-differences of −$2,486 (2012 dollars), meaning that the socioeconomic status of the comparison group improved relative to New Orleans. The difference-in-differences for the percentage of the population with a BA or higher, however, is 2 percentage points, this time favoring New Orleans.

The simple changes in New Orleans (without the comparison group) are shown in table A.1. Other researchers have also examined this issue. One concluded, consistent with the above analysis, that "the population has become if anything slightly more economically disadvantaged."[2] Another researcher concluded that the change in deep poverty was "similar" in New Orleans and in the rest of the metropolitan area.[3]

We also simulated the effects of the above demographic changes on student outcomes using a separate data set, the federal Early Childhood Longitudinal Survey, which includes both the US Census Bureau measures and test scores. We found that the potential bias on the test score effects, for example, ranges from −0.012 student-level standard deviations (s.d.), favoring the comparison districts, to 0.044 s.d., favoring New Orleans.

Finally, the technical report provides data on pre-reform third graders for New Orleans and other hurricane-affected districts, with figures for all pre-reform students and for only those students who returned (returnees). If the students who returned were higher-performing than those who did not return, and therefore inflated student scores post-reform, we would see it by comparing the pre-reform scores of returnees and non-returnees. Again, there is no evidence of such an advantage. By 2010 New Orleans returnees had somewhat *lower* pre-reform scores than the overall pre-reform New Orleans population while in the other districts, the returnee scores were higher than the overall pre-reform population. Once again, the difference-in-differences favors the comparison districts by 0.043 s.d.

The patterns in our results are inconsistent with population change as an explanation in other ways as well. If the most disadvantaged students returned more slowly, then we would have expected a large initial achievement effect followed by a flat or declining effect trend. This is

TABLE A.1. Background of students attending New Orleans publicly funded schools

City characteristic	Before Katrina (2000–2005)	After Katrina (2013–2015)
Student demographics (LDOE)		
Black	93.5%	87.7%
White	3.3%	5.9%
Hispanic	1.2%	3.8%
Other	2.0%	2.6%
Free/reduced price lunch eligible	83.2%	87.5%
Special education	11.3%	7.0%
English language learner	1.8%	2.6%
Other demographics (census)		
Household income (2013$)	$43,189	$42,453
Child poverty	57%	58%
% Public school parents w/ HS degree	33%	20%
% Public school parents w/ BA degree	10%	15%
School information		
# Schools operated by local/state agency	128	5
# Charter schools	5	77
Spending per pupil (2015$)	$9,689	$13,278
Citywide demographic information		
Population	454,845	390,711
School enrollment	64,920	45,608

Sources: Student and other demographic data: analysis of Louisiana Department of Education and US Census data, as analyzed and reported in Douglas N. Harris and Matthew Larsen, "The Effects of the New Orleans School Reforms on Student Test Scores, High School Graduation, and College Outcomes." School enrollment and funding: National Center for Education Statistics, "Revenues and Expenditures by Public School Districts." Post-Katrina spending: Christian Buerger and Douglas N. Harris, "How Did the New Orleans School Reforms Influence School Spending?" Number of schools for the 2014–2015 school year: Cowen Institute, "Public Schools in New Orleans, 2014–15 School Year."

Notes: Census data pertain to families with children attending publicly funded schools. In the top section, pre-Katrina demographic data is from the 2004–2005 school year, and post-Katrina data from 2014–2015. For demographic data from the census, the years are 2000 and 2013 (the latter averaged across samples of the American Community Survey with 2013 as the midpoint).

almost the opposite of the actual trend in the figures. In short, the likelihood that the results in chapter 4 are due to population change is very low. Our analyses of FRL data, US Census Bureau data, and the prereform test scores of returnees, as well as analyses by other researchers and the misalignment between the timing of such effects and the outcome improvement, all reinforce this conclusion.

Supplement to Chapter 4 on Student Outcome Data and Difference-in-Differences Estimates of Reform Effects

The discussion in chapter 4 of research methods and results regarding effects on student outcomes is brief and likely to leave researchers with a lot of questions. This technical appendix provides more detail on figures 4.1–4.4, including the difference-in-differences method used to estimate the main effects. I also elaborate on the measures of student outcomes, the process of creating the matched comparison groups, other aspects of the difference-in-differences method (especially the calculation of standard errors), and other evidence about threats to identification.

Still more detail, on this as well as appendix A, can be found in Harris and Larsen, "The Effects of the New Orleans School Reforms on Student Achievement, High School Graduation, and College Outcomes," which is available on the website of the Education Research Alliance for New Orleans and which I refer to this as "the technical report" in what follows.

City Rankings

Figure 4.1 provides descriptive evidence about New Orleans school improvement, in terms of statewide rankings of school districts. My research team and I calculated the values in two different ways: first, using publicly available district-average data and, second, using student-level data, both from the Louisiana Department of Education (LDOE). Most of the data reported in figure 4.1 are from the version using district-level data. However, statewide rankings for high school test scores and graduation rates were not publicly available in 2005, so the figure reports the rankings based on the student-level analysis.

We used both sources as a check on data validity. In general, they yield very similar results. The only exception is that our calculations for the 2005 New Orleans college entry rate are 5 percentage points higher than the publicly reported rate shown in figure 4.1 (the 2015 results are identical). This discrepancy is not especially surprising given the large number of decisions that go into these calculations (e.g., the pool of potential college attendees and the types of attendance counted).

Figure 4.1 is the only part of the analysis where I report results for high school test scores (ACT scores). I also omit the Louisiana state standardized high school test scores throughout the book for several reasons. First, the high school testing regime changed from graduation exams to end-of-course exams (EOCs) after Katrina; this means, for example, that schools were still adjusting to the test content in 2015 and that the scales and performance thresholds cannot be compared to pre-Katrina scores. Second, the age/grade at which students take the EOCs varies across students and districts, which can influence scores (student performance increases with age, other things being equal). Third, the increase in the high school graduation rate in New Orleans (see below) changed the composition of the group of test-takers, and likely reduced the city's average scores (this also affects the ACT scores). These factors make it difficult to identify effects on any high school scores. For this reason, I focus on the scores in elementary and middle school grades instead.

Student Outcome Data

TEST SCORE DATA. The test score data in figures 4.1 and 4.2 cover grades 3–8. Following common research practice, we standardized the data to a statewide mean of zero and standard deviation of one by grade, year, and subject (sometimes called z-scores). In what I report here, the results are averaged across subjects (math, English language arts, science, and social studies), though the results are similar in each subject.

HIGH SCHOOL GRADUATION DATA. The rankings in figure 4.1 report graduation rates using the standard approach of ninth-grade co-horts. Due to limitations in our data, figure 4.3 focuses on cohorts *of tenth graders*, so that we have enough years of data prior to the reforms to carry out the most rigorous types of analysis (see below). The effects in figure 4.3 look similar, but somewhat smaller, for ninth-grade cohorts.

High school graduation rates are calculated from the "exit codes" schools collect. Some critics of the reforms have argued that the gradua-tion rates might be distorted by schools misreporting these codes in order to raise their graduation rates, look better in the state account-ability system, and reduce their chances for takeover by the state RSD. We identified three exit codes, in particular, that were difficult for the state to verify: transfer to private schools, transfer to out-of-state pub-lic schools, and transfer to homeschooling. Coding a student with any of these transfers removes the student from the graduation rate calcula-tion. So a student who actually drops out, but is listed as transferring to a private school, for example, will not show up as a dropout, inflating the graduation rate.

A second potential problem is that charter schools in New Orleans might have simply made it easier for students to graduate, pushing stu-dents into GED courses (which counted toward the school ratings in the state accountability system) or online "credit recovery courses," which are widely considered less rigorous. To address these problems, we calcu-lated three different high school graduation rates: one that mirrored the state definition, one that counted all the hard-to-verify exits as dropouts, and another that counted nonregular diplomas as dropouts. The results are very similar among these three methods. The increase in test scores, too, suggests that the increase in graduation rates was not due to weak-ening standards.

In all of the figures, there is at least a one-year gap in the data when Hurricane Katrina struck. That year is uninformative about the reform's effects because of the long hurricane evacuation and the fact that the re-forms were still being put in place. Figure 4.3 includes an even larger gap because three to five years of data are required to calculate a single graduation rate. Also, note that the years reported on the x-axis are the years the students are in tenth grade, not the year of on-time graduation.

COLLEGE DATA. The college data underlying the analyses in figures 4.1 and 4.4 come from both the state Board of Regents (BOR) and the National Student Clearinghouse (NSC). As in other states, these are only available for Louisiana public high school graduates. BOR data are available for 2001–2011, while NSC data are available for 2004–2015; therefore, neither alone is sufficient to cover the full span of time.

Following convention, the denominator of the college entry data in figure 4.1 is the number of students who graduated high school (by city/district). As with high school graduation, however, we reported the effects on college entry differently to ensure validity. Specifically, the effects reported in figure 4.4 are based on the percentage of students who were *in twelfth grade*. The reason for this approach is that charter schools nationally have been accused of manipulating their college numbers by pushing out low-performing students prior to graduation (which removes them from the graduation-rate denominators).

The two data sources, BOR and NSC, have different strengths and weaknesses. The BOR data include only on-time attendance and only for in-state colleges, while the NSC data include attendance and graduation from all types of colleges. The accuracy of the NSC data also varies across colleges and variables. In both data sources, there are exceptions to the rule, as some colleges do not provide data.[1]

One additional potential concern is that the reforms might have led students to attend colleges with differing degrees of data validity, e.g., the reforms might have shifted student enrollments more toward in-state private colleges or out-of-state colleges, whose enrollments are poorly measured in the BOR data, or to two-year colleges, where enrollment and graduation is more poorly measured in the NSC data. We carried out a variety of tests for this problem. Perhaps the simplest and most convincing step was to reestimate the effects using each data set separately (for the available years). The results in this additional analysis are very similar to those shown in figure 4.4.

Difference-in-Differences Analysis

Difference-in-differences analysis involves comparing treatment groups (in this case, just New Orleans) with multiple comparison groups before and after a program or policy begins. Below, I discuss the important choice of comparison group, followed by a more detailed discussion of the estimation strategy.

In figures 4.2–4.4, the comparison group is limited to hurricane-affected school districts within Louisiana. Within these districts, a small number of schools are dropped and the remaining schools matched to pre-Katrina New Orleans schools, school by school (with replacement). To identify the comparison group for New Orleans, we used the following matching process: (a) restrict to hurricane-affected districts; (b) identify potential match schools, i.e., those that exist in all available pre- and post-reform years covered by our data, and have at least ten students in each tested subject and grade; (c) drop districts that have fewer than three to four potential school matches (depending on the outcome measure); and (d) among remaining schools, Mahalanobis match New Orleans schools to the comparison group based on pre-reform outcome levels. The entire matching process is carried out separately by district, so the set of schools in each district approximates the distribution of New Orleans. The matching variable is always the pre-reform value of the outcome measure of interest; for example, when we are studying test scores, we match on pre-Katrina test scores. A partial exception is that we have too few years to match on college graduation in the pre-Katrina years, so in that case, we only match on college entry (using the BOR data).

The above matching process applies to pooled estimates (e.g., comparing the results for students in fourth grade in 2005 with the fourth graders in 2015), which is the only real option with high school graduation and college outcomes. With test scores, we can also carry out panel analysis, that is, identifying students who returned to their home districts and tracking their individual trajectories before and after the reforms. Our preferred matching method, in this case, is similar in spirit to the one above, but involves matching specific students rather than whole schools. Specifically, we (a) restricted to hurricane-affected school districts; (b) dropped individual students who never returned to their pre-hurricane district; and (c) among the returning students in hurricane-affected districts, used Mahalanobis matching to identify comparison students with similar composite test score levels in both of the two most recent pre-reform years (2004 and 2005), stratifying by year of return and grade retention. This approach cannot be used with high school graduation and college outcomes because these are observed only once per student.

Our difference-in-differences estimates are based on a comparison of New Orleans with the matched comparison groups. Specifically, we estimated the following:

$$A_{ijt} = \gamma_j + X_{ijt}\beta + \lambda d_t + \delta(NOLA_j \cdot d_t) + \varepsilon_{ijt}$$

where A_{ijt} is the outcome of student i in school district j at time t, γ_j is a vector of school district fixed effects, X_{ijt} is a vector of student covariates,[2] d_t indicates whether the outcomes pertain to one pre-reform period or a single post-reform period, and $NOLA_j$ is an indicator set to one for New Orleans students and zero for students in the comparison districts. No other district in Louisiana experienced the reforms, so these districts represent a useful counterfactual.

Under certain assumptions discussed below, especially that student outcomes would have moved in parallel absent the treatment, ordinary least squares (OLS) estimation of δ provides an unbiased estimate of the average treatment effect. We test the parallel-trends assumption separately for each estimate, and almost all pass the test. We also estimate essentially the same model using the pooled and panel samples.

STANDARD ERRORS. We cluster the errors by district. Almost all of the effects reported in the main text are statistically significant at the usual standards of significance. This is especially true when we use the entire state as the comparison group, as opposed to just the hurricane-affected districts, where the estimates are insignificant in some years.

Analyses of Spending, Discipline, Segregation, and More

Throughout the book, I have reported the results of similar difference-in-differences analyses to estimate the effects on school spending, disciplinary incidents, segregation, and more. We followed the same general strategy in all of these cases: restricting the comparison group to hurricane-affected districts, finding schools in these districts that matched New Orleans schools on the measure of interest for the pre-reform period, testing whether New Orleans was on a parallel trend with these other schools pre-Katrina, and so on. (In some cases, we used a similar method called synthetic control, which is fundamentally similar to difference-in-differences.)

Since there are so many studies, each with its own complications, I recommend that interested readers turn to the technical reports cited in the endnotes to chapters 4–9.

NOTES

CHAPTER 1

1. Ashana Bigard, interviewed by author, February 8, 2019.

2. Patrick Dobard, interviewed by author, July 19, 2018.

3. See chapter 4.

4. Steve Ritea, "Police Are Ready for Start of School—They'll Enforce Curfew, Truancy, Speed Laws," *New Orleans Times-Picayune*, August 18, 2005.

5. "Number of Public School Districts and Public and Private Elementary and Secondary Schools: Selected Years, 1869–70 through 2010–11," National Center for Education Statistics, November 2012, table 98.

6. Douglas N. Harris, "High-Flying Schools, Student Disadvantage and the Logic of NCLB," *American Journal of Education* 113, no. 3 (May 2007): 367–94.

7. "Population of the 100 Largest Urban Places: 1960," US Bureau of the Census, June 15, 1998, table 19; Michelle Krupa, "Census Estimate Shows Strong Population Growth in Orleans, St. Bernard Parishes," *New Orleans Times-Picayune*, February 22, 2011, fig. 1.

8. Cindy Chang, "Louisiana Is the World's Prison Capital," *New Orleans Times-Picayune*, May 13, 2012.

9. Gregor Aisch et al., "The Best and Worst Places to Grow Up," *New York Times*, May 4, 2015. This online database is based on analysis by Raj Chetty and Nathaniel Hendren, "The Effects of Neighborhoods on Intergenerational Mobility I: Childhood Exposure Effects," *Quarterly Journal of Economics* 133, no. 3 (2018): 1107–62; Raj Chetty et al., "The Opportunity Atlas: Mapping the Childhood Roots of Social Mobility," Working Papers 18-42 (Center for Economic Studies, US Census Bureau, 2018).

10. Andre Perry, Douglas N. Harris, Christian Buerger, and Vicki Mack, *The Transformation of New Orleans Public Schools: Addressing System-Level Problems without a System* (New Orleans: Data Center, 2015).

11. Brian Thevenot, "Schools Sweep Indicts 11 More," *New Orleans Times-Picayune*, December 17, 2004.

12. Brian Thevenot, "Orleans Schools Scramble for 1st Day: Officials Race Clock and Shovel Trash," *New Orleans Times-Picayune*, August 14, 2005.

13. Rebecca Solnit and Rebecca Snedeker, *Unfathomable City: A New Orleans Atlas* (Berkeley: University of California Press, 2013).

14. David B. Tyack, *The One Best System: A History of American Urban Education* (Cambridge, MA: Harvard University Press, 1974).

15. The role of teacher unions and state laws on tenure and certification are the key areas where my definition of the System is broader than Tyack's *One Best System.*

16. Economists define the term "public goods"somewhat narrowly. I will use the term in a way that is more in line with colloquial use, i.e., goods that have value beyond what they provide to any individual.

17. The Founding Fathers did not place education in the US Constitution, but federal laws passed to facilitate the settlement of expanding federal lands and the creation of new states encouraged state leaders to include education in their state constitutions and to ensure that everyone was in reach of a publicly supported school. This gave rise to school districts. See William Fischel, *Making the Grade: The Economic Evolution of American School Districts* (Chicago: University of Chicago Press, 2009).

18. Charles M. Payne, *So Much Reform, So Little Change* (Cambridge, MA: Harvard Education Press, 2008); Frederick M. Hess, *The Same Thing Over and Over: How School Reformers Get Stuck in Yesterday's Ideas* (Cambridge, MA: Harvard Education Press, 2010).

19. Terry M. Moe, *Special Interest: Teachers Unions and America's Public Schools* (Washington, DC: Brookings Institution Press, 2011).

20. "Number of Public School Districts" (National Center for Education Statistics).

21. Karl E. Weick, "Educational Organizations as Loosely Coupled Systems," *Administrative Science Quarterly* 21, no. 1 (March 1976): 1-19.

22. Alan I. Abramowitz and Kyle L. Saunders, "Is Polarization a Myth?" *Journal of Politics* 70, no. 2 (April 2008): 542-55; Christopher Hare and Keith T. Poole, "The Polarization of Contemporary American Politics," *Polity* 46, no. 3 (July 2014): 411-29.

23. Poppy Markwell and Raoult Ratard, *Deaths Directly Caused by Hurricane Katrina* (Baton Rouge: State of Louisiana, Department of Health and Hospitals, 2008); "Hurricane Costs," National Oceanic and Atmospheric Administration, Office for Coastal Management, December 20, 2018.

24. Diane Ravitch, *Reign of Error: The Hoax of the Privatization Movement and the Danger to America's Public Schools* (New York: Vintage, 2013).

25. Stephen P. Klein, Laura Hamilton, Daniel F. McCaffrey, and Brian Stecher, "What Do Test Scores in Texas Tell Us?" *Education Policy Analysis Archives* 8, no. 49 (October 2000).

26. The statement is based on Center for Research on Educational Outcomes, *Multiple Choice: Charter School Performance in 16 States* (Palo Alto, CA: CREDO, Stanford University, 2009). This report is based on data from the preceding years, including the time Katrina made landfall. (More recent reports from CREDO are discussed in chapter 10.)

27. Douglas N. Harris, "How Everyone Is Getting It Wrong on New Orleans School Reform," *Washington Post*, August 31, 2015.

28. The word "miracle" was used many times in the media. John White, "A Fresh Turn in the New Orleans Charter School Miracle," *Wall Street Journal*, May 27, 2016; Brigitte Nieland, "The Education Miracle 10 Years after Hurricane Katrina," US Chamber of Commerce Foundation, August 25, 2015.

CHAPTER 2

1. Some would say that political action is the pursuit of one's interests and beliefs in collective decisions made by or within governments. As education is central to the formation of beliefs, others argue that educational decisions are political even when pursuing interests out-

side the auspices of government, though these distinctions are not central to the discussion in the text. See, for example, Lawrence A. Cremin, *Popular Education and Its Discontents* (New York: HarperCollins, 1989); Michael W. Apple, *Educating the Right Way: Markets, Standards, God, and Inequality* (New York: Routledge, 2013).

2. For a detailed analysis of bureaucracy as it is applied in government, see James Q. Wilson, *Bureaucracy: What Government Agencies Do and Why They Do It* (New York: Basic Books, 1989). Some of the earliest writing on the topic dates to the early 1900s and Max Weber.

3. Friedman first outlined his free-market ideas on schooling in 1955 in the wake of the *Brown v. Board* decision. See Milton Friedman, "The Role of Government in Education," in *Economics and the Public Interest*, ed. Robert A. Solo (New Brunswick, NJ: Rutgers University Press, 1955); Milton Friedman, *Capitalism and Freedom* (Chicago: University of Chicago Press, 1962).

4. See, for example, Valerie E. Lee and Julia B. Smith, "Collective Responsibility for Learning and Its Effects on Gains in Achievement for Secondary School Students," *American Journal of Education* 104 (1996): 103–47; Richard M. Ingersoll, "Short on Power, Long on Responsibility," *Educational Leadership* 65, no. 1 (2007): 20–25.

5. William A. Fischel, *Making the Grade: The Economic Evolution of American School Districts* (University of Chicago Press, 2009).

6. The most widely cited article regarding the combination of rising costs and stagnant outcomes is National Commission on Excellence in Education, *A Nation at Risk: The Imperative for Educational Reform* (Washington, DC: US Department of Education, NCEE, 1983). More recent articles have made the same arguments in terms of school productivity. See, for example, Eric A. Hanushek and Steven G. Rivkin, "Understanding the 20th Century Growth in School Spending," *Journal of Human Resources* 32, no. 1 (Winter 1997): 35–68; Caroline M. Hoxby, "Productivity in Education: The Quintessential Upstream Industry," *Southern Economic Journal* 71, no. 2 (2004): 208–32. One problem with this type of argument is the assumption that additional improvements in educational outcomes should require the same additional resources (what economists call constant returns to scale), which is unrealistic. Some productivity analyses also inadequately account for the so-called cost disease that makes productivity gains especially difficult in education. For a discussion of these issues and a rebuttal of *A Nation at Risk*, see Douglas N. Harris, Michael Handel, and Lawrence Mishel, "Education and the Economy Revisited: How Schools Matter," *Peabody Journal of Education* 79, no. 1 (2004): 36–63.

7. Perhaps the clearest articulation of these concerns comes from two books: John E. Chubb and Terry M. Moe, *Politics, Markets & America's Schools* (Washington, DC: Brookings Institution, 1990); Paul T. Hill, Lawrence C. Pierce, and James Guthrie, *Reinventing Public Education: How Contracting Can Transform America's Schools* (Chicago: University of Chicago Press, 1997).

8. For evidence on achievement gaps, see Sean F. Reardon, "The Widening Academic Achievement Gap between the Rich and the Poor: New Evidence and Possible Explanations," in *Whither Opportunity? Rising Inequality, Schools, and Children's Life Chances*, ed. Greg J. Duncan and Richard J. Murnane (New York: Russell Sage Foundation, 2011), 91–115. For discussion of the possible relation between achievement gaps and education policy, see Douglas N. Harris and Carolyn D. Herrington, "Accountability, Standards, and the Growing Achievement Gap: Lessons from the Past Half-Century," *American Journal of Education* 112, no. 2 (February 2006): 209–38.

9. Reardon, "Widening Academic Achievement Gap." For evidence on funding gaps, see

Bruce Baker, *Educational Inequality and School Finance: Why Money Matters for America's Students* (Cambridge, MA: Harvard Education Press, 2018).

10. Poul A. Nielsen and Donald P. Moynihan, "How Do Politicians Attribute Bureaucratic Responsibility for Performance? Negativity Bias and Interest Group Advocacy," *Journal of Public Administration Theory and Research* 27, no. 2 (April 2017): 269-83.

11. Given the temporary nature of their positions, there is an incentive for elected officials to create laws and rules that will last beyond their tenure. Frederick M. Hess, *Revolution at the Margins: The Impact of Competition on Urban School Systems* (Washington, DC: Brookings Institution Press, 2004), 57.

12. Hess, *Revolution at the Margins*, 17.

13. David K. Cohen and James P. Spillane, "Policy and Practice: The Relations between Governance and Instruction," *Review of Research in Education* 18, no. 1 (January 1992): 3-49.

14. Though it has a long history of study in political science and organizational theory, the compliance mentality is difficult to study and I could not find what I considered to be convincing evidence about it in schools. However, the notion that people are rule-followers by nature is a core tenet of social psychology. See, for example, Rom Harre and Paul F. Secord. *The Explanation of Social Behaviour* (Lanham, MD: Rowman & Littlefield, 1972).

15. Katharine O. Strunk et al., "It Is in the Contract: How the Policies Set in Teachers' Unions' Collective Bargaining Agreements Vary across States and Districts," *Educational Policy* 32, no. 2 (November 2018): 280-312.

16. Eileen Lai Horng, Daniel Klasik, and Susanna Loeb, "Principals' Time Use and School Effectiveness," *American Journal of Education* 116, no. 4 (August 2010): 491-523.

17. Michael F. Lovenheim and Alexander Willén, "The Long-Run Effects of Teacher Collective Bargaining," CESifo Working Paper 5977 (Ithaca, NY: Cornell University, 2016).

18. Randi Weingarten, "A New Path Forward: Four Approaches to Quality Teaching and Better Schools," *American Educator* 34, no. 1 (Spring 2010). In addition to union contracts, one reason teachers receive little feedback is the loose coupling of teaching. See Valerie E. Lee, Robert F. Dedrick, and Julia B. Smith, "The Effect of the Social Organization of Schools on Teachers' Efficacy and Satisfaction, *Sociology of Education* 64, no. 3 (July 1991): 190-208.

19. The following article drew considerable attention to this issue: Daniel Weisberg et al., *The Widget Effect: Our National Failure to Acknowledge and Act on Differences in Teacher Effectiveness* (Brooklyn, NY: New Teacher Project, 2009). For a more recent, academic treatment of the topic, see Matthew A. Kraft and Allison F. Gilmour, "Revisiting the *Widget Effect*: Teacher Evaluation Reforms and the Distribution of Teacher Effectiveness," *Educational Researcher* 46, no. 5 (July 2017): 234-49.

20. Public Agenda, *Teaching for a Living: How Teachers See the Profession Today*, November 2012.

21. Lee, Dedrick, and Smith, "Effect of the Social Organization of Schools," 192.

22. Mary M. Kennedy, "Recognizing Good Teaching When We See It," in *Handbook of Teacher Assessment and Teacher Quality*, ed. Mary M. Kennedy (San Francisco: Jossey Bass: 2010).

23. Ann Allen and David N. Plank, "School Board Election Structure and Democratic Representation," *Educational Policy* 19, no. 3 (July 2005).

24. The power of unions varies considerably across states, but two-thirds of teachers work under collective bargaining and another 8 percent work under other types of agreements. Some contracts come about because schools are legally required to bargain in good faith (i.e., collective bargaining). In six states, however, collective bargaining is banned; in

eleven others, collective bargaining is allowed but the "agency fees" collected by unions are not. Teachers can still join unions even when there is no collective bargaining, and some school districts voluntarily develop agreements with teachers that do not fall under collective bargaining (called "meet and confer"). See Richard B. Freeman and Eunice S. Han, "Public Sector Unionism without Collective Bargaining," paper presented at AEA Annual Meeting, San Diego, CA, January 6, 2013. Also, see Moe, *Special Interest.*

25. Jacqueline P. Danzberger, "Governing the Nation's Schools," *Phi Delta Kappan* 75, no. 5 (January 1994): 67–73; Council of Great City Schools, *Urban School Superintendents: Characteristics, Tenure, and Salary Eighth Survey and Report,* Fall 2014.

26. Anthony S. Bryk et al. "The State of Chicago School Reform," *Phi Delta Kappan* 76, no. 1 (September 1994): 74–74.

27. Weick, "Educational Organizations as Loosely Coupled Systems."

28. Cohen and Spillane, "Policy and Practice," 12.

29. Cohen and Spillane provide evidence that instruction varies more in the United States than in other countries. They also show that countries with more centralized control over the key drivers of teaching and learning—curriculum frameworks, curricular materials, and lesson plans—also have more uniform content. Cohen and Spillane, "Policy and Practice."

30. Cohen, Spillane, and Peurach note that, in theory, districts, states, or professional associations could create an "educational infrastructure" around curriculum and instruction that would homogenize, and perhaps increase, the quality of teaching; they argue, however, that such infrastructure is largely absent and the result is incoherence. David K. Cohen, James P. Spillane, and Donald J. Peurach, "The Dilemmas of Educational Reform," *Educational Researcher* 47, no. 3 (2018): 204–212.

31. Economists call this horizontal (i.e., type) differentiation and contrast it with vertical (i.e., quality) differentiation.

32. Adam Smith, *The Wealth of Nations* (London: W. Strahan and T. Cadell, 1776).

33. I am ignoring one assumption that economists usually start with: the idea that consumers are rational actors with fixed preferences. Since these assumptions undergird much of the logic behind political bureaucracy as well, I omit it here.

34. Barbara L. Wolfe and Robert H. Haveman, "Social and Nonmarket Benefits from Education in an Advanced Economy," in Conference Series no. 47 (Federal Reserve Bank of Boston, 2002), 97–131.

35. Subsidies can also have a side effect, however. If governments fully fund schools, and do not allow "copays" from families, then the price is zero for everyone. This means that the market power of the price mechanism is lost. Of course, copays make it more difficult for low-income families to gain access, so there is a trade-off.

36. For a review of the research, see Bruce Sacerdote, "Peer Effects in Education: How Might They Work, How Big Are They and How Much Do We Know Thus Far?" In *Handbook of the Economics of Education,* ed. Eric A. Hanushek, Stephen Machin, and Ludger Woessmann (Amsterdam: North Holland, 2010). For further discussion of the reasons that peers matter, see Douglas N. Harris, "How Do School Peers Influence Student Educational Outcomes? Theory and Evidence from Economics and Other Social Sciences," *Teachers College Record* 112, no. 4 (January 2010): 1163–1197.

37. Richard M. Ingersoll and Thomas M. Smith, "Keeping Good Teachers Is the Wrong Solution to the Teacher Shortage," *Educational Leadership* 60, no. 8 (May 2003): 30–33.

38. Students' family income predicts teacher turnover even after controlling for salaries,

overall school funding, leadership, and other relevant factors. Susanna Loeb, Linda Darling-Hammond, and John Luczak, "How Teaching Conditions Predict Teacher Turnover in California Schools," *Peabody Journal of Education* 80, no. 3 (2005): 44–70. Also, see Eric Hanushek, John Kain, and Steven Rivkin, "Why Public Schools Lose Teachers," *Journal of Human Resources* 39, no. 2 (2004): 326–54. For evidence that schools and teachers serving low-income students are also lower-performing on average, see, for example, Tim R. Sass et al. "Value Added of Teachers in High-Poverty Schools and Lower Poverty Schools." *Journal of Urban Economics* 72, nos. 2–3 (2012): 104–22.

39. There are even different ways of thinking about good citizenship. Westheimer and Kahne distinguish "personally responsible citizens," "participatory citizens," and "justice-oriented citizens." Joel Westheimer and Joseph Kahne. "What Kind of Citizen? The Politics of Educating for Democracy," *American Educational Research Journal* 41, no. 2 (January 2004): 237–69. Sondel discusses these conceptions in the context of charter schools. Beth Sondel, "Raising Citizens or Raising Test Scores? Teach for America, 'No Excuses' Charters, and the Development of the Neoliberal Citizen," *Theory & Research in Social Education* 43, no. 3 (August 2015): 289–313.

40. The objective of student growth or value-added measures is to identify the contribution of schools to student learning. This is challenging because some schools have students who start off at lower achievement levels than other schools (selection bias). Student growth measures account for these differences by focusing on how individual students improve over time; that is, accounting, as closely as possible, for where students start at the beginning of the school year. For more discussion on how value-added is calculated, see Douglas N. Harris, *Value-Added Measures in Education: What Every Educator Needs to Know* (Cambridge, MA: Harvard Education Press, 2011). For more on the implications of using test levels for measuring school performance, see Douglas N. Harris and Lihan Liu, *What Gets Measured Gets Done: Multiple Measures, Value-Added and the Next Generation of School Performance Measures under ESSA* (New Orleans: Education Research Alliance for New Orleans, Tulane University, 2018).

41. Hess makes a similar point when he writes that education has "exceptionally ambiguous output." Hess, *Revolution at the Margins*, 11.

42. Douglas N. Harris, "Class Size and School Size: Taking the Trade-Offs Seriously," *Brookings Papers on Education Policy*, no. 9 (2006–2007), 137–61.

43. One recent study of school closure, for example, found that students had trouble making friends at new schools when their prior schools were forced to close. Ben Kirshner, Matthew Gaertner, and Kristen Pozzoboni, "Tracing Transition: The Effect of High School Closure on Displaced Students," *Educational Evaluation and Policy Analysis* 32, no. 3 (September 2010): 407–29.

44. Harris, "Class Size and School Size."

45. The median wealth of African Americans increased by $120,000 from 1963 to 2016, while that of white households increased by $778,000 (real 2016 dollars). "9 Charts on Wealth Inequality in America," Urban Institute, fig. 3.

46. There is debate about the degree to which people self-segregate versus being pushed into segregated settings by norms, laws, and other government policies. Research seems to suggest that segregation is caused by both. The saying "birds of a feather flock together"—more formally called homophily—is one of the most widely accepted research findings in psychology and the social sciences. Like all such findings, it does not apply to everyone. Some families deliberately try to place their students in schools with racial, ethnic, and income diversity, but they are too few in number to create actually diverse schools. See Miller

McPherson, Lynn Smith-Lovin, and James M. Cook, "Birds of a Feather: Homophily in Social Networks," *Annual Review of Sociology* 27(2001): 415–44.

47. See, for example, Richard Rothstein, *The Color of Law: A Forgotten History of How Our Government Segregated America* (New York: Liveright, 2018).

48. The economist Thomas Schelling explained this using a thought experiment similar to the following: Suppose that most people are only happy when at least, say, 50 percent of their children's classmates are like themselves (e.g., same race and income). This suggests a fair degree of openness to people of other races, but still a preference for being in the majority. In this situation, families whose children are in schools with less than 50 percent like-classmates will switch to schools with more students like themselves. This single move makes both the old school and the new one more racially or economically insular; moreover, this is likely to induce families with a threshold of 49 percent to also move as well, and so on. See Thomas C. Schelling, "Dynamic Models of Segregation," *Journal of Mathematical Sociology* 1 (1971): 143–186.

49. Some research suggests that racial segregation has long-term consequences in the form of diminished quality of life when students become adults. Steven G. Rivkin, "School Desegregation, Academic Attainment, and Earnings," *Journal of Human Resources* 35, no. 2 (Spring 2000): 333–46; Rucker C. Johnson, "Long-Run Impacts of School Desegregation & School Quality on Adult Attainments," NBER Working Paper No. 16664 (Cambridge, MA: National Bureau of Economic Research, 2015).

50. Wolfe and Haveman, "Social and Nonmarket Benefits."

51. See Hess, *Revolution at the Margins*, 5. Hess's book covers some of the same general ground as the current chapter but is focused more on how traditional public schools respond to the introduction of vouchers.

52. In addition to wanting their children to be well-rounded, parents might be conservative because they are uncertain about their young children's aptitudes and interests. The best course is often to provide families a wide variety of educational interests, so they can learn over time what best suits their children. See Byron W. Brown, "Why Governments Run Schools," *Economics of Education Review* 11, no. 4 (December 1992): 287–300.

53. Hess discusses why urban school districts often do not respond to competition the way we might expect. Hess, *Revolution at the Margins*. Labaree takes a sociological approach, arguing that the public and private goals are largely incompatible. David F. Labaree, "Public Goods, Private Goods: The American Struggle over Educational Goals," *American Education Research Journal* 34, no. 1 (Spring 1997): 39–81. Levin focuses especially on the roles played by economies of scale, transaction costs, and externalities. Henry M. Levin, "Some Economic Guidelines for Design of a Charter School District," *Economics of Education Review* 31 (2012): 331–43. While my discussion of these is largely consistent with his, I add to this by showing (a) the importance of switching costs and fixed demand, (b) how economies of scale combine with geography to limit options, and (c) how this extended set of assumptions is more severely violated for disadvantaged students (e.g., because classmate effects yield different tiers of quality). Perhaps the most important contribution of this section, however, is showing how all the unusual features of schooling are connected and compound one another. See also Julian R. Betts and Tom Loveless, *Getting Choice Right: Ensuring Equity and Efficiency in Education Policy* (Washington, DC: Brookings Institution, 2005).

CHAPTER 3

1. Dawn Ruth, "Leslie Jacobs," *New Orleans Magazine*, December 2008.

2. April Capochino, "Orleans Parish Struggles to Assign Classrooms," *New Orleans City Business*, August 1, 2015.

3. Boston Consulting Group, "The State of Public Education in New Orleans."

4. Brian Thevenot, "Audit Probes Millions Paid to Ex-Employees: Thousands Got Checks in Past 4 Years," *New Orleans Times-Picayune*, November 6, 2003.

5. Peter F. Burns and Matthew O. Thomas, "Teaching in the Storm's Wake: Post-Katrina Public Education Reform in New Orleans," paper presented at American Political Science Association annual meeting, Toronto, Ontario, September 2009.

6. Brian Thevenot, "School Board Searches Soul for $30,000," *New Orleans Times-Picayune*, September 3, 2000; Brian Thevenot, "'It's Time: Schools Chief Davis to Leave," *New Orleans Times-Picayune*, June 14, 2002.

7. Leslie Jacobs, interviewed by author, March 27, 2018.

8. In addition to three governor-appointed seats, one BESE member is elected from each of the state's eight congressional districts, for a total of eleven members.

9. Sarah Usdin, interviewed by author, August 22, 2018.

10. Greg Richmond, interviewed by author, July 18, 2018.

11. Leslie Jacobs, interviewed by author, March 27, 2018.

12. Bill Walsh, "House Speaker: Rebuilding N.O. Doesn't Make Sense," *New Orleans Times-Picayune*, July 28, 2010.

13. Paul T. Hill, "Re-Creating Public Education in New Orleans," *Education Week* 25, no. 4 (September 21, 2005): 48.

14. The portfolio analogy is problematic. The value of financial portfolios is easier to judge than the quality of schools and does not involve the same equity considerations. Also, a school portfolio manager cannot open and close schools nearly as readily one can buy and sell stocks. Hill did not use this "portfolio" language until after the New Orleans reforms, though he had discussed similar ideas before. He first used the term in Paul T. Hill, "Putting Learning First: A Portfolio Approach to Public Schools" (Washington, DC: Progressive Policy Institute, 2006).

15. Milton Friedman, "The Promise of Vouchers" *Wall Street Journal*, December 5, 2005.

16. Friedman's prior writings made brief references to regulation, but these were so vague that they seemed aimed at appeasing critics rather than indicating a genuine belief that regulation would make the market work more effectively.

17. Kenneth K. Wong, Francis X. Shen, Dorothea Anagnostopolous, and Stacey Rutledge, *The Education Mayor: Improving America's Schools* (Washington, DC: Georgetown University Press, 2007). For evidence on vouchers, see chapter 10.

18. Leslie Jacobs, interviewed by author, March 27, 2018.

19. Terry Moe, *The Politics of Institutional Reform: Katrina Education and the Second Face of Power* (Cambridge: Cambridge University Press, 2019).

20. Liva Baker, *Second Battle of New Orleans: The Hundred-Year Struggle to Integrate the Schools* (New York: HarperCollins, 1996).

21. Scott Cowen (president emeritus, Tulane University), interviewed by author, April 9, 2018. Most of the discussion in this paragraph is based on this interview.

22. Bring New Orleans Back Committee, "Rebuilding and Transforming: A Plan for World-Class Public Education in New Orleans" (January 17, 2006).

23. Designed to address Jim Crow laws that inhibited voting, especially among blacks in

the South, the Voting Rights Act of 1965, as amended in later years, prohibited laws and rules that had the intent or effect of limiting voting opportunities for racial minorities. Eliminating the Orleans Parish School Board or shifting all control to other agencies, especially non-elected or nonlocal agencies, probably would have been a violation because it would have limited the opportunity for black residents to vote for leaders of their local schools. By allowing the district and its board to continue operating, the reforms apparently avoided this legal problem. (A US Supreme Court decision subsequently changed the interpretation of the Voting Rights Act, but this was well after the reform decisions were being made.)

24. Mary Landrieu had been impressed with Vallas's testimony at a US Senate hearing some years earlier and recommended him for the RSD job. Vallas had been appointed school superintendent in Chicago, and held a similar position in Philadelphia at the time the RSD position came open. Philadelphia happened to be one of the cities Cowen and Pastorek had both looked to as a potential reform model for New Orleans in the immediate post-Katrina aftermath. Some Philadelphia schools had been turned over to charter management organizations or otherwise contracted out. Other schools were still run by the district, still with a strong central office, a single curriculum, and strong school-level accountability. In this respect, Vallas was an awkward fit. While he had some experience with charters, he was mainly known for a top-down approach, requiring schools to adopt what he considered to be best practices and centrally managed instruction.

25. Terry M. Moe, "Teachers Unions in the United States: The Politics of Blocking," in *The Comparative Politics of Education: Teacher Unions and Education Systems around the World*, ed. Terry M. Moe and Susanne Wiborg (New York: Cambridge University Press, 2017).

26. Brian Thevenot, "Final Antics of School Board Laid Bare—Mose Jefferson Trial Charts End of an Era," *New Orleans Times-Picayune*, August 23, 2009, 1.

27. Laura Maggi, "State to Run Orleans Schools: Local Board Loses Authority over 102," *New Orleans Times-Picayune*, November 23, 2005.

28. Steve Ritea, "BESE Approves Operating Plan for N.O. Schools: Takeover Draws Audience Barbs and Some Official Olive Branches," *New Orleans Times-Picayune*, June 13, 2006.

29. Matthew Candler, interviewed by author, April 20, 2018.

30. This and other references draw from the contract itself: "Agreement between United Teachers of New Orleans and Orleans Parish School Board Teacher Bargaining Agreement: July 1, 2003–June 30, 2006."

31. The contract stated that a minimum of ten days had to pass between classroom observations. Also, teachers could remove of any negative evaluation from their personnel files after a period of three years.

32. Eventually, the state eliminated tenure for teachers in traditional public schools as well. See Nathan Barrett, Katharine O. Strunk, and Jane Arnold Lincove, "When Tenure Ends: The Short-Run Effects of the Elimination of Louisiana's Teacher Employment Protections on Teacher Exit and Retirement" (New Orleans: Education Research Alliance for New Orleans, Tulane University, 2017).

33. Some additional details about the funding are worth noting. Funding for the OPSB schools flowed through the district and was generally distributed to schools on an equal per-student basis. Later, the OPSB and RSD agreed on a differentiated funding formula across essentially all of the city's publicly funded schools that gave more funding to schools with more special education and free-lunch students.

34. The original aim of NSNO, according to Usdin, was to help schools obtain back office

support, such as accounting and contracting for services, but that quickly changed as they came to believe the cost savings were small and as school leaders indicated they could handle such matters on their own. They believed that recruiting teachers and schools was a more useful role.

35. Meredith I. Honig, "The New Middle Management: Intermediary Organizations in Education Policy Implementation." *Educational Evaluation and Policy Analysis* 26, no. 1 (March 2004): 65–87.

36. In addition to those mentioned so far, Kati Haycock, founder and CEO of the Education Trust, and Michelle Rhee, then chancellor of the District of Columbia Public Schools, attended some of the meetings, according to Jacobs.

37. Walter Isaacson, interviewed by author, August 29, 2018.

38. "Greater New Orleans Area," Teach for America.

39. Scott Cowen, interviewed by author, April 9, 2018.

40. Douglas N. Harris and Matthew F. Larsen, *What Effect Did the New Orleans School Reforms Have on Student Achievement, High School Graduation, and College Outcomes?* (New Orleans: Education Research Alliance for New Orleans, Tulane University, 2018).

41. Nathan Barrett and Douglas N. Harris, *Significant Changes in the New Orleans Teacher Workforce* (New Orleans: Education Research Alliance for New Orleans, Tulane University, 2015).

42. Aesha Rasheed, the founder of the Parents' Guide, was African American, though the role of that organization was arguably smaller than most of the others listed, such as NSNO and the Cowen Institute. Kira Orange-Jones was a third prominent African American leader who eventually became CEO of the Louisiana branch of Teach for America and an elected member of the state board.

43. Howard Fuller, quoted in John Thompson, "Why It's Time to Throw Out Punitive Ed Policy in NOLA," *Hechinger Report*, June 23, 2005.

44. David B. Tyack, *The One Best System: A History of American Urban Education* (Cambridge, MA: Harvard University Press, 1974), 148, 156. Tyack also argued that one of the goals of those building the One Best System was to "improve the class origins of teacher and board members" (128).

45. See, for example, Jeffrey Henig, "Portfolio Management Models and the Political Economy of Contracting Regimes," in *Between Public and Private: Politics, Governance, and the New Portfolio Models for Urban School Reform*, ed. Katrina E. Bulkley, Henry M. Levin, and Jeffrey Henig, 27–52 (Cambridge, MA: Harvard Education Press, 2010).

CHAPTER 4

1. Center for Research on Educational Outcomes, *Multiple Choice: Charter School Performance in 16 States* (Palo Alto, CA: CREDO, Stanford University, 2009).

2. Those arguing that test- and market-based reforms may not have gone far enough include Paul Hill and Robin Lake, *Charter Schools and Accountability in Public Education* (Washington, DC: Brookings Institution Press, 2004); Paul Peterson, "Holding Students to Account," in *What Lies Ahead for America's Children and Their Schools*, ed. Chester E. Finn and Richard Sousa (Stanford, CA: Hoover Institution Press, 2014).

3. Douglas N. Harris, "High-Flying Schools, Student Disadvantage, and the Logic of NCLB," *American Journal of Education* 113, no. 3 (May 2007): 367–94.

4. The state began requiring students to take the ACT to graduate in 2013, which changes the pool of test-takers and makes it difficult to compare trends in average ACT score. While

this policy affected the rest of the state as well, it may have affected the rankings unevenly across districts. For this reason, I do not examine ACT scores further.

5. See appendix B and the full technical report for this study: Douglas N. Harris and Matthew F. Larsen, *The Effects of the New Orleans School Reforms on Student Achievement, High School Graduation, and College Outcomes?* (New Orleans: Education Research Alliance for New Orleans, Tulane University, 2018).

6. Emily Badger and Kevin Quealy, "How Effective Is Your School District? A New Measure Shows Where Students Learn the Most," *New York Times*, December 5, 2017. The article is based on work by Sean Reardon, *Educational Opportunity in Early and Middle Childhood: Variation by Place and Age* (Palo Alto, CA: Stanford University, Center for Education Policy Analysis, 2018).

7. Center for Research on Education Outcomes, "Urban Charter School Study: Report on 41 Regions" (Palo Alto, CA: CREDO, Stanford University, 2015), 9.

8. Figure 4.3 shows that the effects on high school graduation are not significant in all years. However, the average effect across years (not shown) is statistically significant.

9. Ashana Bigard, interviewed by author, February 8, 2019.

10. For evidence that teacher effectiveness varies across measures, see C. Kirabo, "What Do Test Scores Miss? The Importance of Teacher Effects on Non-Test Score Outcomes," *Journal of Political Economy* 126 no. 5 (2008): 2072–2107. For evidence regarding inconsistency in school performance across measures, see Michael Q. McShane, Patrick J. Wolf, and Collin Hitt, *Do Impacts on Test Scores Even Matter? Lessons from Long-Run Outcomes in School Choice Research Attainment versus Achievement Impacts and Rethinking How to Evaluate School Choice Programs* (Washington, DC: American Enterprise Institute, 2018).

11. This is based on unpublished analyses carried out in collaboration with Siyu Quan, a research associate of ERA–New Orleans.

12. Donald T. Campbell, "Assessing the Impact of Planned Social Change," *Evaluation and Program Planning* 2, no. 1 (1979): 85.

13. There are two main counterarguments on this point: First, some agree that teaching to the test does not help students learn, but note that test scores are a prerequisite to college and therefore later life success. Second, others argue that frequent testing constitutes useful practice as it provides performance feedback. This is probably true if someone explains what the correct answer was and why, though students usually receive little such feedback on standardized tests.

14. Daniel Koretz, *Measuring Up: What Educational Testing Really Tells Us* (Cambridge, MA: Harvard University Press, 2009); Daniel Koretz, *The Testing Charade: Pretending to Make Schools Better* (Chicago: University of Chicago Press, 2017).

15. One study shows that students who evacuated from New Orleans experienced greater improvements in school quality than students who evacuated from other districts. Bruce Sacerdote, "When the Saints Come Marching In: Effects of Katrina Evacuees on Schools, Student Performance and Crime," *American Economic Journal: Applied Economics* 4, no. 1 (2012): 109–35.

16. Brian A. Jacob, Lars Lefgren, and David P. Sims, "The Persistence of Teacher-Induced Learning," *Journal of Human Resources* 45, no. 4 (2010): 915–43.

17. Some critics of the reforms have gone further and questioned whether the effects on test scores were real by pointing to the performance of Louisiana charter schools on the US Department of Education's National Assessment of Educational Progress (NAEP). However, the NAEP test is given in only a small random sample of schools; this includes only three to

five charter schools in the entire state of Louisiana, with no distinction made between those in New Orleans and those in other parts of the state.

18. I made this conversion using Louisiana's performance on the NAEP. I determined, first, how far Louisiana was below the national average (in standard deviation units), then how far New Orleans was from the state average (at baseline). This is where the 22nd percentile figure comes from. Next, I added the reform effect size (again, in standard deviation units) to obtain the shift to the 37th percentile. I describe this as a "rough" estimate because it requires assumptions, such as that New Orleans was just as far below the state average on NAEP as on the state test.

19. In 2005 New Orleans schools were spending $9,689 per pupil. The difference-in-differences effect was $1,359 per pupil. These figures are adjusted for inflation (2015 dollars) and based on the same type of difference-in-differences analyses described for figure 4.1. In this case, the matched comparison group had similar spending patterns prior to the reforms. This analysis focuses on operating funds and excludes the large investment in facilities. However, for most of this period, especially the early years, the buildings were arguably in worse shape than before the reforms. Funding for school reconstruction from the Federal Emergency Management Agency (FEMA) was not made available until 2010, and only sixteen projects had been completed as of 2013. By that point, most of the effects reported in the main text had already occurred. These spending figures come from Christian Buerger and Douglas N. Harris, *How Did the New Orleans School Reforms Influence School Spending?* (New Orleans: Education Research Alliance for New Orleans, Tulane University, 2017).

20. For recent evidence that school spending improves student outcomes, see C. Kirabo Jackson, Rucker C. Johnson, and Claudia Persico, "The Effects of School Spending on Educational and Economic Outcomes: Evidence from School Finance Reforms," *Quarterly Journal of Economics* 131, no. 1 (February 2016): 157–218. For a contrary interpretation of prior evidence, see Eric A. Hanushek, "Spending on Schools," in *A Primer on American Education*, ed. Terry Moe (Stanford, CA: Hoover Press, 2001): 69–88.

21. The most recent operating millage election just prior to Katrina received 65 percent support. In 2008, just after the reforms, this increased to 87 percent. In 2017 support dropped back to 67 percent. The tax rate was the same in all three cases. This increased support cannot be directly or completely attributed to reforms because voting might have been affected by, for example, whether the city had recently had millage elections for other services such as jails, police, fire, and parks. The fact that polls suggest voter support for the reforms, however, reinforces the idea that the reforms helped build local support.

22. Formally, we can we can think of two counterfactual scenarios that might be of interest: reform without funding and funding without reform. We are primarily interested in the former, though a key point of this section is that the inefficiency of the district likely would have meant that funding alone had little effect.

23. See chapter 7.

24. Cowen Institute, *State of Public Education in New Orleans* (2010), 13.

25. Cowen Institute, *Perceptions of Public Education* (2017), 7, 9.

26. Cowen Institute, *Research Brief: K–12 Education through the Public Eye: Parents' Perceptions of School Choice* (2011). There is a related question in the 2017 report, which focuses on whether "public charter schools" had improved education in the city, as opposed to whether the schools were better after the reforms. The figures are broken down separately for public (71%) and private school parents (62%), with no overall figures. Based on the population percentages of students in private schools, the weighted average would be 69 percent,

which suggests a continuous, positive trend in perceptions. Cowen Institute, *Perceptions of Public Education in New Orleans* (2017), 4.

27. Cowen Institute, *Research Brief* (2011), 10.

28. Cowen Institute, *K–12 Public Education through the Public's Eye: Parents' and Adults' Perception of Public Education in New Orleans* (2015), 3.

29. Cowen Institute, *K–12 Public Education through the Public's Eye: Voters' Perception of Public Education* (New Orleans: Cowen Institute, Tulane University, 2013), 7.

30. Michael H. Birnbaum and Yass Sotoodeh, "Measure of Stress: Scaling the Magnitudes of Life Changes," *Psychological Science* 2, no. 4 (July 1991): 236–43.

31. Karen B. DeSalvo et al., "Symptoms of Posttraumatic Stress Disorder in a New Orleans Workforce following Hurricane Katrina," *Journal of Urban Health* 84, no. 2 (March 2007): 142–52.

32. For a review, see John F. Pane et al., "Effects of Student Displacement in Louisiana during the First Academic Year after the Hurricanes of 2005," *Journal of Education for Students Placed at Risk* 13, nos. 2–3 (October 2008): 168–211.

33. Eric A. Hanushek, John F. Kain, and Steven G. Rivkin, "Disruption versus Tiebout Improvement: The Costs and Benefits of Switching Schools," *Journal of Public Economics* 88, nos. 9–10 (2004): 1721–46.

34. Lindsay Bell Weixler, Douglas N. Harris, and Nathan Barrett, "Teachers' Perspectives on the Learning and Work Environments under the New Orleans School Reforms," *Educational Researcher* 47, no. 8 (2018): 502–15. Also, see chapter 7 for more discussion of this survey.

CHAPTER 5

1. This point reiterates the earlier references to Frederick Hess and Charles Payne. Charles M. Payne, *So Much Reform, So Little Change* (Cambridge, MA: Harvard Education Press, 2008); Frederick M. Hess, *The Same Thing Over and Over: How School Reformers Get Stuck in Yesterday's Ideas* (Cambridge, MA: Harvard Education Press, 2010). For evidence on the factors affecting policy implementation, see, for example, Susan Fuhrman, William Clune, and Richard Elmore, "Research on Education Reform: Lessons on the Implementation of Policy," in *Education Policy Implementation*, ed. Allan Odden (Albany: State University of New York Press, 1991).

2. For a general discussion of buffering as applied to schooling, see Meredith I. Honig and Thomas C. Hatch, "Crafting Coherence: How Schools Strategically Manage Multiple, External Demands," *Educational Researcher* 33, no. 8 (2004):16–30. For an analysis specifically focused on the school human resource–related issues that are the subject of this chapter, see Stacey A. Rutledge et al., "Certify, Blink, Hire: An Examination of the Process and Tools of Teacher Screening and Selection," *Leadership and Policy in Schools* 7, no. 3 (June 2008): 237–63.

3. Hess uses "businesslike" in his book *Revolution at the Margins: The Impact of Competition on Urban School Systems* (Washington, DC: Brookings Institution Press, 2004). He writes that "advocates of education competition are likely mistaken when they interpret the distribution of videos and T-shirts and the launching of innovative programs as harbingers of a 'businesslike' transformation that will enhance systemwide productivity and efficiency" (5).

4. This and all subsequent analyses of school spending come from Christian Buerger and Douglas N. Harris, *How Did the New Orleans School Reforms Influence School Spending?* (New Orleans: Education Research Alliance for New Orleans, Tulane University, 2017).

5. The costs listed here are not entirely fixed. Accounting, IT, and other systems become somewhat more costly as more students and staff are involved. In this respect, the costs include a combination of fixed and variable costs.

6. David Arsen and Yongmei Ni, "Is Administration Leaner in Charter Schools? Resource Allocation in Charter and Traditional Public Schools," *Education Policy Analysis Archives* 20, no. 31 (October 2012): 1–24.

7. Huriya Jabbar, "Recruiting 'Talent': School Choice and Teacher Hiring in New Orleans," *Educational Administration Quarterly* 54, no. 1 (2018): 139.

8. Buerger and Harris, *How Did the New Orleans School Reforms Influence School Spending?*, 22.

9. Nationally, it is common for charter schools to opt out of pensions. See Amanda Olberg and Michael J. Podgursky, *Charting a New Course to Retirement: How Charter Schools Handle Teacher Pensions* (Washington, DC: Thomas B. Fordham Institute, June 2011). However, according to our research team member Nathan Barrett, 42 percent of New Orleans charter schools had voluntarily opted into the state pensions system as of 2016, apparently to serve the financial needs of more experienced teachers who had started teaching prior to Katrina. This percentage has declined over time as more new charter schools were opened. The figures in the text also ignore health benefits.

10. Douglas N. Harris and Tim R. Sass, "Teacher Training, Teacher Quality, and Student Achievement," *Journal of Public Economics* 95, nos. 7–8 (August 2011): 798–812.

11. One newspaper article noted that, before the 2008–2009 school year, "competition for TeachNOLA was just as fierce: About 2,450 people applied for just over 100 spots in a teacher training and recruiting program does not even guarantee them jobs in New Orleans schools." Colley Charpentier, "N.O. Has Abundance of Teacher Applicants," *New Orleans Times-Picayune*, July 29, 2008). Another article reported more than a thousand teacher applications through the state RSD website in a three-month span, which apparently far exceeded the number of openings then available. Steve Ritea, "Bell's About to Ring," *New Orleans Times-Picayune*, July 6, 2006. Another article reported that charter schools saying they had "more than enough qualified applicants." Steve Ritea, "Schools Could Be Short on Teachers—Pressed District Scraps 'Rigorous' Test Process," *New Orleans Times-Picayune*, July 13, 2006.

12. Douglas N. Harris and Scott Adams, "Understanding the Level and Causes of Teacher Turnover: A Comparison with Other Professions," *Economics of Education Review* 26, no. 3 (June 2007): 325–37; Donald Boyd, Hamilton Lankford, Susanna Loeb, and James Wyckoff, "The Draw of Home: How Teachers' Preferences for Proximity Disadvantage Urban Schools," *Journal of Policy Analysis and Management* 24, no. 1 (2005): 113–32.

13. David A. Stuit and Thomas M. Smith, "Explaining the Gap in Charter and Traditional Public School Teacher Turnover Rates," *Economics of Education Review* 31, no. 2 (April 2012): 268–79.

14. Jim Collins, *Good to Great: Why Some Companies Make the Leap . . . and Others Don't* (New York: HarperBusiness, 2011).

15. Paul Pastorek, like Jacobs, had first gotten involved in education through his business as a lawyer. Scott Cowen had been a management professor before becoming president of Tulane. Mary Landrieu had worked as a real estate agent prior to her political career. Many others either had MBAs before they came or, because so many had come out of TFA, left the education sector in New Orleans to get one.

16. Leslie Jacobs, interviewed by author, March 27, 2018.

17. Jabbar, "Recruiting 'Talent,'" 129.

18. Jabbar, "Recruiting 'Talent,'" 130.

19. See, for example, Thomas S. Dee, "A Teacher Like Me: Does Race, Ethnicity, or Gender Matter?" *American Economic Review* 95, no. 2 (May 2005): 158–65. While the match between the race of student and teacher clearly matters, the reasons are not entirely clear. It could be because black teachers have higher expectations for black students on average, or because teachers of the same race serve as role models. See also the later discussion of culturally relevant pedagogy.

20. Observable teacher characteristics explain 8.5 percent of the variation in teacher performance according to Dan D. Goldhaber, Dominic J. Brewer, and Deborah J. Anderson, "A Three-Way Error Components Analysis of Educational Productivity," *Education Economics* 7, no. 3 (1999): 199–208.

21. TeachNOLA was created in partnership with the New Teacher Project (TNTP). Both TNTP and TFA were founded by Wendy Kopp. TeachNOLA provided the brief induction program and other training for local TFA teachers.

22. There has been some debate about the role of teachers' academic background and general cognitive ability. For some of the most recent evidence, see Eric A. Hanushek, Marc Piopiunik, and Simon Wiederhold, "The Value of Smarter Teachers: International Evidence on Teacher Cognitive Skills and Student Performance," NBER Working Paper 20727 (Cambridge, MA: National Bureau of Economic Research, 2018).

23. The state produces an annual report on the value-added of teacher preparation programs. The latest report, consistent with earlier ones, shows that the New Teacher Project, which also trains Teach for America teachers, had value-added that was well above average in four of the five subject areas assessed. State of Louisiana, *Overview of 2011–2012 Annual Report for Teacher Preparation*, May 2013. The most rigorous evidence on the value-added of TFA teachers comes from Steven Glazerman, Daniel Mayer, and Paul Decker, "Alternative Routes to Teaching: The Impacts of Teach for America on Student Achievement and Other Outcomes," *Journal of Policy Analysis and Management* 25, no. 1 (Winter 2006): 75–96; Melissa A. Clark et al., *The Effectiveness of Secondary Math Teachers from Teach for America and the Teaching Fellows Programs* (Washington, DC: National Center for Education Evaluation and Regional Assistance, US Department of Education, 2013).

24. Jabbar, "School Choice and Teacher Hiring," 132.

25. Retrospective surveys, especially when the events are ten years in the past, can be unreliable. However, we designed the survey so that we could test validity by comparing the answers to some questions to other, more objective sources of data. We also attempted to corroborate the survey results in interviews with local leaders. The results reported in the text are all corroborated by these additional analyses. Another potential problem was that the perceptions of the returning teachers might not have been representative of all teachers in the post-reform period. Again, we tested for similarities between the returning and nonreturning teachers where possible. The discussion of these and other methodological issues, and the analysis in the text, is based on Lindsay Bell Weixler, Douglas N. Harris, and Nathan Barrett, "Teachers' Perspectives on the Learning and Work Environments under the New Orleans School Reforms," *Educational Researcher* 47, no. 8 (2018), 502–15.

26. A report by New Schools for New Orleans also documents fierce competition for the best teachers. Christen Holly et al., *Ten Years in New Orleans: Public School Resurgence and the Path Ahead* (New Orleans: New Schools for New Orleans, 2015), 37.

27. Unfortunately, it is not possible to go back to the pre-reform years in this analysis of teacher value-added because the data for those early years does not link students to teachers.

28. Betheny Gross and Michael DeArmond, "How Do Charter Schools Compete for Teachers? A Local Perspective," *Journal of School Choice* 4, no. 3 (September 2010): 254–77.

29. The finding of increased focus on academic and socio-emotional goals was statistically significant. The estimate for vocational goals was in the same direction but statistically insignificant.

30. Weixler, Harris, and Barrett, "Teachers' Perspectives." While this was part of a broader national trend, and the pressures of No Child Left Behind, we found that the increase in New Orleans seemed larger than what we saw when we looked at national data sets.

31. See Valerie E. Lee, Robert F. Dedrick, and Julia B. Smith, "The Effect of the Social Organization of Schools on Teachers' Efficacy and Satisfaction," *Sociology of Education* 64, no. 3 (July 1991): 193.

32. Carolyn Sattin-Bajjaj, *"It's Hard to Separate Choice from Transportation": Perspectives on Student Transportation Policy from Three Choice-Rich School Districts* (Washington, DC: Urban Institute, 2018).

33. We carried out extensive analyses to rule out alternative interpretations in the surveys. First, going into our analysis, we worried that returning pre-Katrina teachers—most of whom had several years of experience under the System and had been fired en masse by those who created the reforms—would report back negative impressions that were not representative of what was actually happening in schools post-reform. In the end, though, they reported a mix of positive and negative changes in the schooling environment that seems to provide a realistic account. Second, we considered whether some of the drop in job satisfaction could be due to remaining bitterness over the unfair process of school reform or other factors that may have made returning teachers different from new teachers. To address this, we asked both new and returning teachers to answer some questions about how they viewed the post-reform schools. The new and returning teachers gave similar responses on these other questions. Since returning teachers had more experience and a different racial composition, we adjusted the results to control for these differences. Both analyses suggested a real decline in teacher satisfaction independent of the mass firing. Weixler, Harris, and Barrett, "Teachers' Perspectives."

34. Harris and Adams, "Understanding the Level and Causes of Teacher Turnover."

35. Nathan Barrett, Katharine O. Strunk, and Jane Arnold Lincove, "When Tenure Ends: The Short-Run Effects of the Elimination of Louisiana's Teacher Employment Protections on Teacher Exit and Retirement," Working Paper, October 29, 2018.

36. I am not aware of published evidence on this topic, but I have carried out an unpublished analysis showing that 43 percent of public school teachers in Florida rated in the highest performance category worried "quite a bit" about their job security. Douglas N. Harris and Lihan Liu, "Perception versus Reality: Teacher Value-Added Measures in Florida," working paper, June 26, 2015.

37. Three kinds of studies suggest the importance of teacher autonomy. For research on how teachers value "faculty participation," see Richard Ingersoll, "Teacher Turnover and Teacher Shortages: An Organizational Analysis," *American Educational Research Journal* 38, no. 3 (2001): 499–534. Studies of the relation between school leadership and teacher satisfaction find that teachers prefer "transformational" over "transactional" and "autocratic" principals. See Ronit Bogler, "The Influence of Leadership Style on Teacher Job Satisfaction," *Educational Administration Quarterly* 37, no. 5 (December 2001): 662–83. Finally, autonomy is associated with higher levels of satisfaction and reduced stress. See L. Carolyn Pearson and William Moomaw, "The Relationship between Teacher Autonomy and Stress, Work Satisfac-

tion, Empowerment, and Professionalism," *Educational Research Quarterly* 29, no. 1 (2005): 37–53.

38. Of the results listed in this section, this is one of the only ones that was not statistically significant, which is why I express more caution in stating the conclusion.

39. Frederick Hess suggests a similar trade-off when he writes, "Teachers' autonomy conflicts with the preference of many teachers for a sharing and supportive school community." Hess, *Revolution at the Margins*, 69.

40. Abigail Thernstrom and Stephan Thernstrom, *No Excuses: Closing the Racial Achievement Gap* (New York: Simon and Schuster, 2003).

41. This is based on interviews with local education leaders familiar with all the schools. The range of estimates reflects that there was some inconsistency in how those interviewees identified no-excuses schools.

42. Adam Gamoran and Cristina M. Fernandez, "Do Charter Schools Strengthen Education in High-Poverty Urban School Districts?" in *Choosing Charters: Better Schools or More Segregation?* ed. Iris C. Rotberg and Joshua L. Glazer (New York: Teachers College Press, 2018), 133–52. The first entry in the effective-schools literature was a small study of eight schools in Michigan, as reported in Wilbur B. Brookover and Lawrence W. Lezotte, *Changes in School Characteristics Coincident with Changes in Student Achievement* (Washington, DC: National Institute of Education, Michigan State University, 1977). The idea was also popularized by Ronald Edmonds, "Effective Schools for the Urban Poor," *Educational Leadership* 37, no. 1 (1979): 15–24. For a more recent, comprehensive, and systematic review, see Michael A. Zigarelli, "An Empirical Test of Conclusions from Effective Schools Research," *Journal of Education Research* 90, no. 2 (December 1996): 103–10.

43. Nathan Barrett and Douglas N. Harris, *A Different Approach to Student Behavior: Addressing School Discipline and Socio-Emotional Learning through Positive Behavior Intervention Systems* (New Orleans: Education Research Alliance for New Orleans, Tulane University, 2018).

44. Edward L. Deci, Richard Koestner, and Richard M. Ryan, "Extrinsic Rewards and Intrinsic Motivation in Education: Reconsidered Once Again," *Review of Educational Research* 71, no. 1 (2001): 1–27.

45. Brian Thevenot, "Recovery School District Superintendent Paul Vallas Wants No Return to Old Ways," *New Orleans Times-Picayune*, July 24, 2009.

46. Ashana Bigard, interviewed by author, February 8, 2019.

47. Larry Cuban, "Why Is It So Hard to Get "Good" Schools?" in *Reconstructing the Common Good in Education*, ed. Larry Cuban and Dorothy Shipps (Palo Alto, CA: Stanford University Press, 2000), 148–69.

48. Victor Lavy, "Expanding School Resources and Increasing Time on Task: Effects of a Policy Experiment in Israel on Student Academic Achievement and Behavior," NBER Working Paper 18369 (Cambridge, MA: National Bureau of Economic Research, 2016).

49. This statement is based on ongoing research by Sarah Woodward, a research associate of the Education Research Alliance for New Orleans.

50. The latest edition of the book lists sixty-two techniques with such headings as "Setting High Academic Expectations," "Planning That Ensures Academic Achievement," "Structuring & Delivering Your Lessons," "Engaging Students in Your Lessons," "Creating a Strong Classroom Culture," "Setting & Maintaining High Behavioral Expectations," "Building Character and Trust," and "Improving Your Pacing," as well as "Challenging Students to Think Criti-

cally." Doug Lemov, *Teach Like a Champion: 62 Techniques That Put Students on the Path to College* (San Francisco: Jossey-Bass, 2015), 6.

51. Lemov, *Teach Like a Champion*, 6.

52. Gloria Ladson-Billings, "Toward a Theory of Culturally Relevant Pedagogy," *American Research Journal* 32, no. 3 (1995): 465–91. Also, see Gloria Ladson-Billings, *The Dreamkeepers: Successful Teachers of African American Children* (San Francisco: Jossey-Bass, 2009).

53. Leslie Jacobs, interviewed by author, March 27, 2018.

54. Margaret C. Wang, Geneva D. Haertel, and Herbert J. Walberg, "Toward a Knowledge Base for School Learning," *Review of Educational Research* 63, no. 3 (1993): 249–294.

55. Cuban, "Why Is It So Hard to Get 'Good' Schools?"

56. Edward L. Deci, Richard Koestner, and Richard M. Ryan, "A Meta-Analytic Review of Experiments Examining the Effects of Extrinsic Rewards on Intrinsic Motivation," *Psychological Bulletin* 125, no. 6 (1999): 627–68.

CHAPTER 6

1. Huriya Jabbar, *How Do School Leaders Respond to Competition?* (New Orleans: Education Research Alliance for New Orleans, Tulane University, 2015), 11.

2. Huriya Jabbar, "Competitive Networks and School Leaders' Perceptions: The Formation of an Education Marketplace in Post-Katrina New Orleans," *American Educational Research Journal* 52, no. 6 (December 2015): 1093–1131.

3. Douglas N. Harris, *Value-Added Measures: What Every Educator Needs to Know* (Cambridge, MA: Harvard Education Press, 2011).

4. For general evidence on how charter schools select students, see Jennifer Jennings, "School Choice or Schools' Choice? Managing in an Era of Accountability," *Sociology of Education* 83, no. 3 (2010): 227–247; Kevin Welner, *The Dirty Dozen: How Charter Schools Influence Student Enrollment* (Boulder, CO: National Education Policy Center, 2013); Isaac McFarlin and Peter Bergman, "Education for All? A Nationwide Audit Study of Schools of Choice," unpublished working paper (2018).

5. Most of the evidence on exclusion in New Orleans comes from two sources: Jabbar, *How Do School Leaders Respond to Competition?*; Huriya Jabbar, "Selling Schools: Marketing and Recruitment Strategies in New Orleans," *Peabody Journal of Education* 91, no. 1 (2016): 4–23.

6. Several situations exist that may require the district/authorizer to place students in schools midyear, outside the usual admissions process: families enter a school district in the middle of the school year, a school closes in the middle of the year, or a student might need to move for safety reasons or bullying. Midyear placements are difficult and disruptive especially for the receiving schools. The steps listed here allow schools to avoid these placements, even when, again, the students have to attend school somewhere.

7. I heard a handful of anecdotes about this form of exclusion, though the intent of the school is hard to establish. The most well known and convincing case of this nationally involves Success Prep Academies in New York City. School leaders there maintained "got to go" lists of students they wanted to induce to leave. Kate Taylor, "At a Success Academy Charter School, Singling Out Pupils Who Have 'Got to Go,'" *New York Times*, October 29, 2015, A1.

8. Jabbar, *How Do School Leaders Respond to Competition?*

9. Jabbar, *How Do School Leaders Respond to Competition?*, 21.

10. Jabbar, *How Do School Leaders Respond to Competition?*, 15.

11. Though research on general education teachers shows a weak relationship between

teacher credentials and school performance, the relation is stronger among special education teachers. See Tim Sass and Li Feng, "What Makes Special-Education Teachers Special? Teacher Training and Achievement of Students with Disabilities," *Economics of Education Review* 36 (October 2013):122–34.

12. See, for example, Christopher Lubienski, "School Choice as a Civil Right: District Responses to Competition and Equal Educational Opportunity," *Equity and Excellence in Education* 38, no. 4 (2005): 331–341; Jennings, "School Choice or Schools' Choice?," 227–247.

13. Much of the discussion in this section is based on Monica Hernandez, *Is There No Excuse? The Effects of the New Orleans School Reforms on School Discipline* (New Orleans: Education Research Alliance for New Orleans, Tulane University, 2018). Hernandez analyzed data using a method similar to difference-in-differences (see appendix B), called the synthetic control method.

14. Ralph Adamo, "NOLA's Failed Education Experiment: Privatization Runs Amok in the Post-Katrina New Orleans School System," *American Prospect*, August 15, 2007; Steve Ritea and Rob Nelson, "Problems Plague N.O. Schools Recovery," *New Orleans Times-Picayune*, October 9, 2006.

15. School discipline data are particularly difficult to interpret. Changes in suspensions and expulsions can reflect (a) changes in actual student behavior; (b) changes in the likelihood of punishment (strictness); and (c) changes in the accuracy of punishment reporting. Separating these factors is not just a problem in New Orleans or with charter schools.

16. This law applied to traditional public schools and to the charter schools authorized by the state RSD. However, it did not apply to charter schools authorized by the local OPSB. The laws and authorizer rules are also vague about exactly what kind of transportation needs to be provided; schools can meet the letter of the law but not the spirit by limiting the number and convenience of bus stops.

17. This quote and other aspects of the discussion in this section are from Carolyn Sattin-Bajaj, *"It's Hard to Separate Choice from Transportation": Perspectives on Student Transportation Policy from Three Choice-Rich School Districts* (Washington, DC: Urban Institute, 2018).

18. Douglas N. Harris and Matthew F. Larsen, *What Schools Do Families Want (and Why)?* (New Orleans: Education Research Alliance for New Orleans, Tulane University, 2015).

19. The discussion of transit times comes from Jane Arnold Lincove and Jon Valant, *New Orleans Students' Commute Times by Car, Public Transit, and School Bus* (Washington DC: Urban Institute, 2018). For the sample of schools studied, the authors could not determine the number of students at each bus stop. Most likely, those at the more extreme distances and times had fewer students.

20. Ashana Bigard, interviewed by author, February 8, 2019.

21. Harris and Larsen, *What Schools Do Families Want (and Why)?*

22. Giuseppe Curcio, Michele Ferrara, and Luigi De Gennaro, "Sleep Loss, Learning Capacity and Academic Performance," *Sleep Medicine Reviews* 10, no. 5 (October 2006): 323–37.

23. Sattin-Bajaj, *"It's Hard to Separate Choice from Transportation,"* 19.

24. Sattin-Bajaj, *"It's Hard to Separate Choice from Transportation,"* 19.

25. Specifically, we took the standard deviation of school value-added in New Orleans divided by the same figure for other districts in the state. Dividing by the average standard deviation in districts across the state helps account for the possibility that factors other than the reforms might have influenced the variation in quality across schools, in ways similar to the earlier difference-in-differences analyses.

26. I am using a pseudonym for the school because my point is not to single out any given school but to highlight the broader problem of tiers. However, it is difficult to explain the nature of the advantages that Saenger had without giving away details that preclude complete anonymity. All of the information reported here is publicly available.

27. The school board eventually voted to remove the boundaries, a change that went into effect in 2017.

28. An article in the *Wall Street Journal* reported a much higher ratio of 9:1; however, a school official indicated to me that the correct figure was probably more like 4:1. Stephanie Banchero, "Inside the Nation's Biggest Experiment in School Choice," *Wall Street Journal*, September 29, 2013.

29. As a matter of full disclosure, my younger daughter was admitted to, and attended, Saenger after I wrote this section.

30. Ken Ducote, "The Role of Communities in Schools," presented at "The Urban Education Future? Lessons from New Orleans 10 Years After Hurricane Katrina," New Orleans, June 29, 2015.

31. Ducote, "Role of Communities in Schools."

32. Lindsay Bell Weixler, Jane Arnold Lincove, and Alica Gerry, *The Provision of Public Pre-K in the Absence of Centralized Enrollment* (New Orleans: Education Research Alliance for New Orleans, Tulane University, 2017).

33. Daphna Bassok et al., "Within- and Between-Sector Quality Differences in Early Childhood Education and Care," *Child Development* 87, no. 5 (2016): 1627–45.

34. Had funding been sufficient to cover costs, the incentives would have flipped, and the number of pre-K seats probably would have increased. It was the combination of low funding and the performance-based contracts with charter schools that created the problem.

35. This is related to the economic notion of "club goods," which are "non-rival," meaning that consumption by each member does not take away from the consumption of others, up to the point of congestion (e.g., traffic congestion). What distinguishes the country club from other club goods is that the consumption value depends on the types of people admitted (again, see the discussion of classmate effects in chapter 2).

CHAPTER 7

1. John White, interviewed by author, May 10, 2018.

2. When my family applied to schools for my youngest daughter when we first arrived in New Orleans, the Saenger school had an application process so complex, with multiple pages describing just the process itself, that almost no one understood how it worked. This likely dissuaded some people from applying and disqualified others who persisted but misunderstood the forms and rules.

3. Huriya Jabbar, "Recruiting 'Talent': School Choice and Teacher Hiring in New Orleans," *Educational Administration Quarterly* 54, no. 1 (July 2017): 115–51. The problem lessened somewhat once schools and their grade configurations were well established because, at that point, most of the students in any given year were simply returning from the prior year. In the early years of the reforms, schools were being created from scratch, so most students were new and enrollment numbers less predictable. This highlights the differences between the start-up challenges and the long-term ones.

4. This section is based on Douglas N. Harris, Jon Valant, and Betheny Gross, "The New Orleans OneApp," *Education Next* 15, no. 4 (2015): 17–22.

5. The RSD's first step was forcing schools to use a common application form, which

shed the questions schools were not supposed to ask. But the form itself was only a small part of the problem. This still left all the key admission and enrollment decisions to the schools.

6. The priority categories included geography—specifically, whether families' homes were located within the broad geographic zones of the schools. While this might sound a bit like the old attendance-zone system, there were now only six zones in the entire city, averaging about twenty-eight square miles each, and living in these very large zones still did not guarantee admission to a school within the zone.

7. The process is somewhat more complicated than the text describes as there are many iterations of the "deferred acceptance" algorithm. Again, see Harris, Valant, and Gross, "New Orleans OneApp," 17–22.

8. There were multiple rounds to the OneApp process, so that families not happy with their first assignment could submit a new rank-ordered list and try again.

9. A key problem with centralized matching algorithms is that some designs, such as the one initially adopted in Boston, are not strategy-proof, i.e., they give parents incentives to misrepresent their true preferences in order to get what they actually want. This in turn reduces the efficiency (in the sense considered by economists). See Parag Pathak and Tayfun Sonmez, "Leveling the Playing Field: Sincere and Sophisticated Players in the Boston Mechanism," *American Economic Review* 98, no. 4 (September 2008): 1636–52.

10. John White, interviewed by author, May 10, 2018.

11. John White, interviewed by author, May 10, 2018.

12. Cowen Institute, *Spotlight on Choice* (New Orleans: Cowen Institute, Tulane University, 2013).

13. Cowen Institute, *K-12 Public Education through the Public's Eye: Parents' and Adults' Perception of Public Education in New Orleans* (New Orleans: Cowen Institute, Tulane University, 2015), 7.

14. Cowen Institute, *NOLA by the Numbers: 2014 School Performance Scores* (New Orleans: Cowen Institute, Tulane University, 2014), 4.

15. EnrollNOLA, *Annual Report November 2017* (New Orleans: EnrollNOLA, November 2017), 5. This figure includes only kindergarten and grade 9 because this is when parents are most actively choosing. The percentage getting their top choices is higher in other grades, in part because of the switching costs discussed in chapter 2, which lead families to avoid changing schools.

16. One study showed that there was, specifically, a "step down" in quality. Jane Arnold Lincove, Jon Valant, and Joshua M. Cowen, "You Can't Always Get What You Want: Capacity Constraints in a Choice-Based School System," *Economics of Education Review* 67 (2018): 94–109.

17. Center for Reinventing Public Education, *New Orleans: Citywide Education Progress Report* (Bothell: CRPE, University of Washington Bothell, 2017), 1.

18. The results for achievement were also corroborated in a separate analysis we conducted of student mobility. We found that when students did move, they moved to schools with higher average School Performance Scores. Spiro Maroulis, Robert Santillano, Douglas Harris, and Huriya Jabbar, *The Push and Pull of Student Performance: Evidence from Student Mobility in New Orleans* (New Orleans: Education Research Alliance for New Orleans, Tulane University, 2016).

19. Carolyn Sattin-Bajaj, *"It's Hard to Separate Choice from Transportation": Perspectives on Student Transportation Policy from Three Choice-Rich School Districts* (Washington, DC: Urban Institute, 2018).

20. Douglas N. Harris and Matthew F. Larsen, *What Schools Do Families Want (and Why)?* (New Orleans: Education Research Alliance for New Orleans, Tulane University, 2015).

21. Cowen Institute, *Perceptions of Public Education*, 9.

22. Harris and Larsen, *What Schools Do Families Want (and Why)?* 3.

23. Parent surveys are likely to be distorted because people are often not conscious of the ways they make choices and are subject to various unconscious biases. The factors that families consider in choosing schools can be sensitive topics, especially given the importance of classmates. Parents might not want to say that they considered student race, religion, or other background characteristics, for fear they would sound discriminatory. For evidence on the problems with survey responses, see Delroy L. Paulhus, "Socially Desirable Responding: The Evolution of a Construct," in *The Role of Constructs in Psychological and Educational Measurement*, ed. Henry I. Braun, Douglas N. Jackson, and David E. Wiley (Mahwah, NJ: Erlbaum, 1991), 49–69. School enrollment levels and transfer rates are potential alternative measures of demand, but both are poor indicators, as they conflate actual demand and school quality with family constraints and other factors. OneApp, in contrast, is set up to ensure that families' rankings of schools reflect their true preferences.

24. Cowen Institute, *Research Brief: K–12 Education through the Public Eye: Parents' Perceptions of School Choice* (New Orleans: Cowen Institute, Tulane University, 2011), 1.

25. Ashana Bigard, interviewed by author, February 8, 2019.

26. Marta Jewson, "Trauma Is the Norm for Many New Orleans Kids: This School Was Made For Them," *The Lens*, December 29, 2018.

27. The other cities in the analysis were Atlanta (Georgia), Baton Rouge (Louisiana), and Jackson (Mississippi). The conclusion that cities with more charter schools have more variety is based both on descriptive statistics and cluster analysis that allowed us to statistically test whether schools tended to coalesce around some typical school, considering all school characteristics simultaneously. Paula Arce-Trigatti, Douglas N. Harris, Huriya Jabbar, and Jane Arnold Lincove. "Many Options in New Orleans Choice System," *Education Next* 15, no. 4 (2015): 25–33.

28. Harris and Larsen, *What Schools Do Parents Want (and Why)?*

29. This based on the General Social Survey as reported by Harry Enten, "Americans' Opinions on Spanking," *FiveThirtyEight*, September 15, 2014.

30. John Yun and Sean Reardon, "Private School Racial Enrollments and Segregation," in *School Choice and Diversity: What the Evidence Says*, ed. Janelle Scott (New York: Teachers College Press, 2005), 51.

31. We calculated that, in the pre-Katrina period, schools zoned for the highest-income neighborhoods were 1.3 letter grades higher than schools zoned for low-income neighborhoods. That disparity lessened under the reforms but still remained.

32. The analysis discussed in this section is based on Lindsay Bell Weixler, Nathan Barrett, Douglas N. Harris, and Jennifer Jennings, *Changes in New Orleans School Segregation after Hurricane Katrina* (New Orleans: Education Research Alliance for New Orleans, Tulane University, 2017).

33. By one measure, called dissimilarity, a perfectly integrated system is one where the student population is evenly dispersed across schools. The problem with this measure is that it does not take into account segregation across districts or between the public and private sectors. By this measure, New Orleans schools could be perfectly "integrated" and still have every school with 80 percent minority and low-income students, reflecting the district as a whole. We therefore used the isolation index as a second measure to account for segregation both

within and between districts and sectors. Partly because the demographics of the city did not change very much, the results are similar—similarly unchanged—in both measures.

34. This analysis focused only on kindergarten and grade 9 because those are the most common transition grades. We would expect segregation to change more slowly in other grades because students tend to stay in the same school from year to year. Segregation in these two transition grades therefore should be most sensitive to changes in policies.

35. The increases in segregation were reinforced by our analysis of student transfers. When low-income students transferred, they were less likely than higher-income counterparts to move to higher-performing schools. See Spiro Maroulis, Robert Santillano, Douglas N. Harris, and Huriya Jabbar, *What Happened to Student Mobility after the New Orleans' Market-Based School Reforms?* (New Orleans: Education Research Alliance for New Orleans, Tulane University, 2016).

36. Much of the segregation was between the public and private sectors. A quarter of all school-age children and the vast majority of the middle-class children (especially whites but to some degree blacks) attended private schools or had left for suburban public schools. In contrast, 80 percent of the students remaining in public schools were poor and/or black, with the remaining 20 percent heavily concentrated in the top-tier selective public schools.

37. Cowen Institute, *Parents' Perceptions of School Choice*, 1.

CHAPTER 8

1. Ken Ducote, interviewed by author, January 11, 2018.

2. Patrick Sims, *Charter Management Organizations in New Orleans* (New Orleans: Cowen Institute, Tulane University, 2015).

3. Huriya Jabbar, "Recruiting 'Talent': School Choice and Teacher Hiring in New Orleans," *Educational Administration Quarterly* 54, no. 1 (2018): 138.

4. The figure leaves out portions of the organizational chart, for example, the area superintendents who worked under the district superintendent and had more direct interaction with schools. I have also left out that traditional public schools had some voluntary relationships with other organizations, especially local neighborhood associations. These details do not change the fundamental point that the structure itself was fundamentally different under OPSB relative to the reforms.

5. This list of conditions, and the section generally, draws on the work of Barbara Gray, who also emphasizes that the various actors need to perceive that they are interdependent and that the stakes are high. I have downplayed the role of interdependence because this is usually self-evident in the case of schooling. Barbara Gray, "Conditions Facilitating Interorganizational Collaboration." *Human Relations* 38, no. 10 (1985): 911–36. Also, note that the general conditions for cooperation are not completely separable from the conditions necessary to solve particular problems because, for example, the degree of trust depends on which actors need to be involved.

6. Rodney Clark et al., "Racism as a Stressor for African Americans: A Biopsychosocial Model," *American Psychologist* 54, no. 10 (October 1999): 805–16.

7. Karen B. DeSalvo et al., "Symptoms of Posttraumatic Stress Disorder in a New Orleans Workforce Following Hurricane Katrina," *Journal of Urban Health* 84, no. 2 (March 2007): 142–52; John F. Pane et al., "Effects of Student Displacement in Louisiana during the First Academic Year after the Hurricanes of 2005," *Journal of Education for Students Placed at Risk* 13, nos. 2–3 (October 2008): 168–211.

8. As White put it: "[There was] this ethos within the department [New York City

Department of Education] that the way you lead a school system is with the consent of the principals, and I knew that we [in the RSD] would never move this system toward any lasting change unless you helped the principals, or in some case the CMO leaders, understand and believe that the policy changes were theirs, because the truth of it is the money was with them. The hiring power was with them. The political power was with them." John White, interviewed by author, May 10, 2018.

9. The Master Plan Oversight Committee (MPOC) for facilities was tasked with periodic reviews of the budget, analysis of demographic trends affecting school construction, ensuring the use of cost controls, and checking progress made by RSD and OPSB on their respective responsibilities. Later, a Peer Review Committee of school leaders was created by the state superintendent to ensure that the buildings being designed to meet school needs. The MPOC included five members, who had to be approved by OPSB and BESE, and held public meetings on building construction throughout the city; more than a thousand citizens attended them.

10. Regarding school discipline, the Center for Restorative Approaches was created to support the use of an approach called restorative justice. Rather than suspending and expelling students, the organization would bring students involved in altercations, and their families, together to resolve their differences and use these "discipline problems" as an opportunity to teach conflict resolution and mediation skills.

11. Matthew Candler, interviewed by author, December 12, 2018.

12. Danielle Dreilinger, "$310,000 in for Sleepy Orleans Parish School Board Race," *New Orleans Times-Picayune*, 2016; Sarah Reckhow et al., "'Outsiders with Deep Pockets': The Nationalization of Local School Board Elections," *Urban Affairs Review* 53 no. 5 (2017): 783–811.

13. Reckhow et al., "Outsiders with Deep Pockets," 794.

14. I explained earlier that schools were funded on a per-student basis. In the early years, this was done with minimal adjustments for the cost of services. Weighted student funding meant that students with disabilities and low-income students would receive more money. Schools that served few of these students, including Saenger, protested but to no avail.

CHAPTER 9

1. Whitney Bross and Douglas N. Harris, *How (and How Well) Do Charter Authorizers Choose Schools? Evidence from the Recovery School District in New Orleans* (New Orleans: Education Research Alliance for New Orleans, Tulane University, 2016).

2. The economist Max Sawicky has a useful economics-based critique of contracting that influenced my early thinking on this. His work also describes school contracting efforts during the 1980s, before the charter school movement. Max Sawicky, "Contracting and Economic Efficiency," in *Risky Business: Private Management of Public Schools*, ed. Craig E. Richards, Rima Shore, and Max Sawicky (Washington, DC: Economic Policy Institute, 1996), 127–76.

3. The analysis in this section is based on all the charter applications we could obtain from the period 2007–2014. After extensive searches of public records and newspaper reports, we found fifteen applications in 2005–2006; however, based on conversation with various state and local officials, we have reason to believe some applications are missing from this count. See Bross and Harris, *How (and How Well) Do Charter Authorizers Choose Schools?*

4. The RSD later switched from NACSA to another third-party organization to review and make recommendations on charter applications.

5. The state approval involved the following steps: the RSD superintendent made recom-

mendations to the state superintendent; the state superintendent made recommendations to the state board; and the state board voted the applications up or down. The OPSB also chartered almost all of its schools, but through a different process, with most schools being turned over to the teachers and leaders who had run them before Katrina and the reforms. Given how few OPSB charter schools there were, I do not discuss the OPSB chartering process in this book.

6. The NACSA measures did predict future renewal in a way that was statistically significant. The NACSA measures were also positively correlated with school value-added, but this was statistically insignificant at least in part due to there being little variance in NACSA ratings among accepted applications and to the imprecision of growth measures. Also, note that the rules for state authorization required progressively higher standard for re-renewals.

7. We found that larger CMOs had higher value-added, as measured by Center for Research on Education Outcomes, *Charter Management Organizations 2017* (Palo Alto, CA: CREDO, Stanford University, 2017).

8. Ashana Bigard, interviewed by author, February 8, 2019.

9. Whitney Bross, Douglas N. Harris, and Lihan Liu, *The Effects of Performance-Based School Closure on Student Performance* (New Orleans: Education Research Alliance for New Orleans, Tulane University, 2016).

10. Bross, Harris, and Liu, *Effects of Performance-Based School Closure.*

11. "Closure" usually refers to situations where the building is no longer used as a school. With takeovers, management is turned over to a different organization. The actions taken in New Orleans were essentially all takeovers.

12. The method is similar to the difference-in-differences method described in chapter 4 for the effects of the reforms on student outcomes, except the best comparison involved matching schools taken over now to schools taken over in the future.

13. The estimated effects on high school test scores appeared positive, but were statistically insignificant and harder to interpret (which is why they are excluded from the main results in chapter 4).

14. High school closures and takeovers might be more disruptive for students because (a) students need to take specific courses in order to graduate, and these courses might either fill up or not be offered in the same grade in different schools; (b) students have fewer years to reacclimate before graduating; and (c) friendships are more firmly established in high school, making it more difficult to adjust socially.

15. Prior research shows that when students switch teachers, their achievement increases in ways we would predict based on past teacher performance. See Raj Chetty, John N. Friedman, and Jonah E. Rockoff, "Evaluating Bias in Teacher Value-Added Estimates," *American Economic Review* 104, no. 9 (September 2014): 2593–2632. Our analysis suggests that the same logic applies when students switch schools.

16. Bross, Harris, and Liu, *Effects of Performance-Based School Closure.*

17. We carried out the same type of analysis in Baton Rouge, just an hour down the road from New Orleans. It became clear that in Baton Rouge, where some of the takeover decisions were made by the school district, students were ending up in schools with lower student growth than the ones they had been forced out of. Again, looking across all the cities, the key to success is taking over the lowest-performing schools. This may sound self-evident, but it is surprisingly difficult for governments to do, given the political pressures they face. School districts simply do not normally make decisions based on performance. Charter school authorizers sometimes face some of the same pressures.

18. OPSB actually had limited power to authorize because the district did not control school buildings. Authorization without control of buildings (or a source of funding to rent them) curtailed its options. For part of the post-reform period, state law also allowed non-profit organizations to serve as authorizers, but no such authorizers emerged and therefore no charter schools were authorized by nonprofits. Finally, a few charter schools in New Orleans are written into state law—in effect, authorized directly by the Louisiana legislature.

19. There was one apparent case of authorizer shopping in New Orleans, even with just two authorizers. A school slated for takeover by the state RSD ended up moving instead under the control of the Orleans Parish School Board. Note that another way to avoid authorizer shopping is to ban schools from switching authorizers, but this would not stop schools from shopping for authorizers when they first open.

20. That correlation was especially high for elementary schools and especially at the low end of the SPS scale, where closure and takeover were most relevant. Douglas N. Harris and Lihan Liu, *What Gets Measured Gets Done: Multiple Measures, Value-Added and the Next Generation of School Performance Measures under ESSA* (New Orleans: Education Research Alliance for New Orleans, Tulane University, 2018).

21. For a review of research concluding that cost reduction and improvement on contracted outcomes are common, see William L. Megginson and Jeffry M. Netter, "From State to Market: A Survey of Empirical Studies on Privatization," *Journal of Economic Literature* 39, no. 2 (June 2001): 321–89.

22. My corollary assumes a particular form of contract, like those used with charter schools, in which the government pays a fixed amount (in total or per person) so long as they meet minimum quality standards. Other contacts involve, for example, cost-sharing, which diminishes the pressure to reduce costs.

23. This logic might not seem to apply in New Orleans because the state authorized only a handful of for-profit CMOs (and those few were closed or taken over quickly). However, nonprofit leaders can also benefit for higher revenues and lower costs in similar ways (e.g., higher salaries). Economists refer to this as "rent-seeking."

24. Bruce Baker and Gary Miron, *The Business of Charter Schooling: Understanding the Policies That Charter Operators Use for Financial Benefit* (Boulder: National Education Policy Center, University of Colorado, 2016).

25. Preston Green, Bruce D. Baker, and Joseph Oluwole, "Are Charter Schools the Second Coming of Enron? An Examination of the Gatekeepers That Protect against Dangerous Related-Party Transactions in the Charter School Sector," *Indiana Law Journal* 93, no. 4 (Winter 2018): 1121–60.

26. Matthew Candler, interviewed by the author, December 12, 2018.

27. Kevin Lawrence Henry and Adrienne D. Dixson, "'Locking the Door before We Got the Keys': Racial Realities of the Charter School Authorization Process in Post-Katrina New Orleans," *Educational Policy* 30, no. 1 (2016): 227. The quote, and surrounding text in the article, does not make clear exactly who "these people" were, but they would appear to be associated with reform organizations.

28. Henry and Dixson, "Locking the Door," 226.

29. Matthew Candler, interviewed by author, December 12, 2018.

30. Patrick Dobard, interviewed by author, July 19, 2018. Dobard's words echo those of Howard Fuller (see chapter 3).

31. Bross and Harris, *How (and How Well) Do Charter Authorizers Choose Schools?*

32. For additional evidence supporting this point, see Jane Arnold, Jon Valant, and

Joshua M. Cowen, "You Can't Always Get What You Want: Capacity Constraints in a Choice-Based School System," *Economics of Education Review* 67 (2018): 94–109.

CHAPTER 10

1. Center for Research on Educational Outcomes, *National Charter School Study* (Palo Alto, CA: CREDO, Stanford University, 2013).

2. The method used by CREDO has been called into question by the economist Caroline Hoxby (see the CREDO website for the back and forth). However, two articles comparing CREDO's method to other quasi-experimental methods and to randomized control trials find that the results have internal validity (i.e., limited bias). Devora H. Davis and Margaret E. Raymond, "Choices for Studying Choice: Assessing Charter School Effectiveness Using Two Quasi-Experimental Methods," *Economics of Education Review* 31, no. 2 (April 2012): 225–36; Kenneth Forston et al., "Using an Experimental Evaluation of Charter Schools to Test Whether Nonexperimental Comparison Group Methods Can Replicate Experimental Impact Estimates," NCEE 2012-4019 (Washington, DC: US Department of Education, 2012). Also, see the following study, which finds qualitatively similar results using different methods to study charter schools in Boston: Atila Abdulkadiroğlu et al., "Accountability and Flexibility in Public Schools: Evidence from Boston's Charters and Pilots," *Quarterly Journal of Economics* 126 (2011): 699–748.

3. In addition to the studies cited in the text, two studies examine charter improvements over time in North Carolina and Texas, respectively: Helen F. Ladd, Charles T. Clotfelter, and John B. Holbein, "The Growing Segmentation of the Charter School Sector in North Carolina," NBER Working Paper 21078 (Cambridge, MA: National Bureau of Economic Research, 2015); Patrick L. Baude et al., "The Evolution of Charter School Quality," NBER Working Paper 20645 (Cambridge, MA: National Bureau of Economic Research, 2014).

4. The estimated effects of charter schools in this case were negative but statistically insignificant. Melissa A Clark et al., "Do Charter Schools Improve Student Achievement?" *Educational Evaluation and Policy Analysis* 37, no. 4 (December 2015): 419–36.

5. CREDO, *National Charter School Study*.

6. Kevin Booker et al., "The Effects of Charter High Schools on Educational Attainment," *Journal of Labor Economics* 29, no. 2 (2011): 377–415; Will S. Dobbie and Roland G. Fryer Jr., "The Medium-Term Impacts of High-Achieving Charter Schools," *Journal of Political Economy* 123, no. 5 (September 2015): 985–1037.

7. Joshua D. Angrist, Sarah R. Cohodes, Susan M. Dynarski, Parag A. Pathak, and Christopher Walters, "Stand and Deliver: Effects of Boston's Charter High Schools on College Preparation, Entry, and Choice." *Journal of Labor Economics* 34 no. 2 (2016): 275–318.

8. One study found positive charter effects on earnings: Tim Sass et al., "Charter High Schools' Effects on Long-Term Attainment and Earnings," *Journal of Policy Analysis and Management* 35, no. 3 (2016): 683–706. Another study found negative effects: Will S. Dobbie and Roland G. Fryer Jr., "Charter Schools and Labor Market Outcomes," NBER Working Paper 22502 (Cambridge, MA: National Bureau of Economic Research, 2016).

9. The conclusion that charter schools generate a variety of options is echoed in the three-city comparison that included New Orleans discussed in chapter 6: Gross et al., *Are City Schools Becoming Monolithic?* In a second study by the National Association of Public Charter Schools, the prevalence of US charter schools reporting instructional and curricular specializations in the 2011–2012 school year was as follows: college-prep (40.5%), core knowledge (33.9%), child-centered (29.5%), project-based (28.9%), arts (28.0%), community service

(27.9%), inquiry-based (25.8%), technology (22.5%), math-science or STEM (21.3%), and service learning (19.1%). National Alliance of Public Charter Schools, *Instructional Delivery and Focus of Public Charter Schools: Results from the NAPCS National Charter School Survey, School Year 2011–2012* (Washington, DC: National Association of Public Charter Schools, 2013).

10. Jonathan N. Mills and Patrick J. Wolf, *How Has the Louisiana Scholarship Program Affected Students? A Comprehensive Summary of Effects after Three Years* (New Orleans: Education Research Alliance for New Orleans, Tulane University, 2017), 2. Low-income in this case meant below 250 percent of the poverty line. Students also had to be either starting kindergarten or attending a traditional public school with a grade of C, D, or F. A second study replicated these results with fewer years of data: Atila Abdulkadiroğlu, Parag A. Pathak, and Christopher R. Walters, "Free to Choose: Can School Choice Reduce Student Achievement?" *American Economic Journal: Applied Economics* 10, no. 1 (January 2018): 175–206.

11. Mills and Wolf, *Louisiana Scholarship Program*, 2. One might wonder whether the Louisiana voucher program led low-performing students to leave New Orleans charter schools, thus lifting the charter performance documented in chapter 4. This is implausible, however. Our analysis of US Census data suggests that the family incomes of students attending private schools *increased* relative to other districts (difference-in-differences). Also, leaders of publicly funded schools reported in interviews that they faced limited competition from voucher schools. Huriya Jabbar and Dongmei M. Li, "Multiple Choice: How Public School Leaders in New Orleans' Saturated Market View Private School Competitors, *Education Policy Analysis Archives* 24, no. 94 (September 2016): 12 (note).

12. Initially, the voucher effects were strongly negative. Students across the state who received and used vouchers saw an 8–12 percentile point *drop* in their scores, relative to students who had applied for but not received vouchers and who, instead, mostly attended public schools. The effects became less negative, but are not always statistically significant. See Mills and Wolf, *Louisiana Scholarship Program*.

13. Students who wished to use vouchers also applied through the centralized OneApp system, ranking public schools and private ones simultaneously in one list (see chapter 6 for more on the OneApp). Where there were more applicants than slots, students were randomly selected. See Mills and Wolf, *Louisiana Scholarship Program*.

14. Atila Abdulkadiroğlu, Parag A. Pathak, and Christopher R. Walters, "Free to Choose: Can School Choice Reduce Student Achievement?" *American Economic Journal: Applied Economics* 10, no. 1 (January 2018): 175–206.

15. David N. Figlio, *Evaluation of the Florida Tax Credit Scholarship Program Participation, Compliance and Test Scores in 2009–10*, August 2011; Mark Berends and R. Joseph Waddington, "School Choice in Indianapolis: Effects of Charter, Magnet, Private, and Traditional Public Schools," *Education Finance and Policy* 13, no. 2 (Spring 2018): 227–55; David Figlio and Krzysztof Karbownik, *Evaluation of Ohio's EdChoice Scholarship Program: Selection, Competition, and Performance Effects* (Columbus: Thomas B. Fordham Institute, 2016).

16. To be precise, this review suggests that the estimates are slightly positive but not statistically different from zero. For the review of studies, see M. Danish Shakeel, Kaitlin P. Anderson, and Patrick J. Wolf, *The Participant Effects of Private School Vouchers across the Globe: A Meta-Analytic and Systematic Review*, EDRE Working Paper (Fayetteville: Department of Education Reform, University of Arkansas, 2016).

17. The effects by length of participation are subject to selection bias. In general, those

who remain enrolled in the same school will look better than those who are mobile, regardless of the type of school. This problem remains even in randomized control trials because students are randomly assigned to admission, not whether they stay. Researchers can address this using an approach called instrumental variables, though the assumptions required for such analyses do not hold in this case. Also, even if the estimates were valid, such effects apply only to a small fraction of students (i.e., those who stay), when we are really interested in the net effect on everyone who participates.

18. Heidi H. Erickson, Jonathan N. Mills, and Patrick J. Wolf, *The Effect of the Louisiana Scholarship Program on College Entrance* (Fayetteville: University of Arkansas, Department of Education Reform, 2019).

19. Matthew M. Chingos and Paul Peterson, "The Impact of School Vouchers on College Enrollment," *Education Next* 13 no. 3 (2013): 59–64. This study has been widely misinterpreted as mostly positive even though it found no average effect. Rather, the initial version of the study and the reporting focused on the positive effects for just one subgroup, African Americans. While this is an important subgroup, reporting the results in this way masks possibly large *negative* effects on other students. For the latest version of this study, see Matthew M. Chingos and Paul E. Peterson, "Experimentally Estimated Impacts of School Vouchers on College Enrollment and Degree Attainment," *Journal of Public Economics* 122 (February 2015): 1–12.

20. Matthew M. Chingos, Tomas Monarrez, and Daniel Kuehn, *The Effects of the Florida Tax Credit Scholarship Program on College Enrollment and Graduation: An Update* (Washington, DC: Urban Institute, 2019); Joshua M. Cowen et al., "School Vouchers and Student Attainment: Evidence from a State-Mandated Study of Milwaukee's Parental Choice Program," *Policy Studies Journal* 41, no. 1 (2013): 147–67; Patrick Wolf et al., *Evaluation of the DC Opportunity Scholarship Program: Final Report* (Washington, DC: National Center for Education Statistics, 2010).

21. Chingos, Monarrez, and Kuehn, *Florida Tax Credit Scholarship Program.*

22. Douglas N. Harris and Tim R. Sass, "Teacher Training, Teacher Quality, and Student Achievement," *Journal of Public Economics* 95, nos. 7–8 (August 2011): 798–812.

23. While metric alignment might explain the negative results in the statewide programs, it cannot explain the negative Washington, DC, results, which are based on a low-stakes, norm-referenced test that likely better aligns with private school curricula.

24. Jeff Spalding, *The School Voucher Audit: Do Publicly Funded Private School Choice Programs Save Money?* (Indianapolis: Ed Choice, 2014).

25. Several factors make the comparison of vouchers with traditional public school spending per pupil misleading. First, most students in most voucher schools pay tuition, which means that voucher students benefit from the financial resources and classmate effects provided by tuition-paying classmates. Second, many private schools receive considerable non-tuition revenue, especially from affiliated churches. Finally, private schools generally do not serve the most difficult-to-serve students, who require more resources. There is also a broad conceptual issue here in all the cost calculations. If we are only interested in the fiscal implications of a small-scale program, then vouchers look good because the voucher level is generally below the per-student state funding provided to traditional public schools. However, we are interested here in how schooling systems operate at scale, and for that we need to compare the total average resources in private versus other schools to assess their efficiency.

26. The authors measured school quality using the online reviews of schools from Great

Schools. See Yujie Sude, Corey A. DeAngelis and Patrick J. Wolf, "Supplying Choice: An Analysis of School Participation Decisions in Voucher Programs in Washington, DC, Indiana, and Louisiana," *Journal of School Choice* 12, no. 1 (2018): 8–33.

27. Brian Kisida, Patrick J. Wolf, and Evan Rhinesmith, *Views from Private Schools: Attitudes about School Choice Programs in Three States* (Washington, DC: American Enterprise Institute, 2015).

28. Corey A. DeAngelis, Lindsey Burke, and Patrick J. Wolf, "The Effects of Regulations on Private School Choice Program Participation: Experimental Evidence from Florida," EDRE Working Paper 2018-08 (Fayetteville: Department of Education Reform, University of Arkansas, 2018).

29. Sude, DeAngelis, and Wolf, in "Supplying Choice," also considered tuition levels as an indication of quality, but this discussion makes clear why this is inadequate. If the elite (high-tuition) schools are least likely to participate because they benefit from exclusivity, then the fact that participating voucher schools charge lower tuition than nonparticipating schools is not informative about whether regulation reduces the quality of participating schools.

30. One recent study, in particular, showed that a national sample of charter schools receiving email inquiries from fictitious families were less likely to respond when the emails suggested potential students had disabilities. There was also some evidence of selection with traditional public schools, but it was more pronounced with charter schools. Peter Bergman and Isaac McFarlin, "Education for All? A Nationwide Audit Study of Schools of Choice," unpublished manuscript (2018).

31. The issue here with charter schools is a bit different than for private schools, which can exist without participating in voucher programs, whereas charter schools, by definition, depend almost completely on public funds. However, it is possible that some potential charter schools never open because of the regulations that would apply to them, yielding a similar type of selection.

32. Julian Betts, "The Competitive Effects of Charter Schools on Traditional Public Schools," in *Handbook of Research on School Choice*, ed. Mark Berends, Matthew Springer, Dale Ballou, and Herbert Walberg (New York: Routledge, 2009): 195–208; Figlio and Karbownik, *Ohio's EdChoice Scholarship Program*.

33. The Kickboard software mentioned earlier is a good example. Unlike almost every other aspect of schooling, software is intellectual property. Moreover, we were able to carry out a quasi-experiment among the schools that used it. The software did seem to generate positive results. Nathan Barrett and Douglas N. Harris, *A Different Approach to Student Behavior: Addressing School Discipline and Socio-Emotional Learning through Positive Behavior Intervention Systems* (New Orleans: Education Research Alliance for New Orleans, Tulane University, 2018).

34. Walter Isaacson, interviewed by author, August 29, 2018.

35. William Reese. *America's Public Schools: From the Common School to "No Child Left Behind"* (Baltimore: Johns Hopkins University Press, 2005).

36. Robin J. Lake, *In the Eye of the Beholder: Charter Schools and Innovation* (Bothell: University of Washington, Center for Reinventing Public Education, April 2008); Bryan C. Hassel, Gillian Locke, Juli Kim, Elaine Hargrave, and Nita Losoponkul and the Mind Trust, *Raising the Bar: Why Public Charter Schools Must Become Even More Innovative* (Indianapolis: Mind Trust and Public Impact, 2015).

37. Luis Benveniste, Martin Carnoy, and Richard Rothstein, *Can Public Schools Learn from Private Schools?* (Washington, DC: Economic Policy Institute, 1999).

38. Angrist, Pathak, and Walters, "Explaining Charter School Effectiveness."

39. Roland G. Fryer Jr., "Injecting Charter School Best Practices into Traditional Public Schools: Evidence from Field Experiments," *Quarterly Journal of Economics* 129, no. 3 (2014): 1355–1407.

40. Wilbur B. Brookover and Lawrence W. Lezotte, *Changes in School Characteristics Coincident with Changes in Student Achievement* (Washington, DC: National Institute of Education, Michigan State University, 1977). Also, note that the urban school effects may be conflated with the choice of no-excuses approach, a point made in Chabrier, Cohodes, and Oreopoulos, "What Can We Learn from Charter School Lotteries?" 57–84.

41. Jean Stockard et al., "The Effectiveness of Direct Instruction Curricula: A Meta-Analysis of a Half Century of Research," *Review of Educational Research* 88, no. 4 (August 2018): 479–507.

42. Geoffrey D. Borman et al., "Comprehensive School Reform and Achievement: A Meta-Analysis," *Review of Educational Research* 73, no. 2 (Summer 2003): 125–230.

43. Ludger Wöbmann et al., *School Accountability, Autonomy, Choice, and the Level of Student Achievement: International evidence from PISA 2003* (OECD Working Paper 13, OECD Publishing, 2007), 4.

44. Wöbmann et al., *School Accountability*, 4.

45. This is based on Sean Reardon, *Educational Opportunity in Early and Middle Childhood: Variation by Place and Age* (Palo Alto, CA: Stanford University, Center for Education Policy Analysis, 2018). While he does not report urban districts per se, his figures 8 and 10 show that achievement growth is lower in districts with higher percentages of low-income and racial minority students, which are disproportionately urban.

46. Joshua D. Angrist, Parag A. Pathak, and Christopher R. Walters, "Explaining Charter School Effectiveness," *American Economic Journal: Applied Economics* 5, no. 4 (October 2013): 1–27.

47. Julia Chabrier, Sarah Cohodes, and Philip Oreopoulos, "What Can We Learn from Charter School Lotteries?" *Journal of Economic Perspectives* 30, no. 3 (2016): 57–84.

48. Joshua D. Angrist, Sarah R. Cohodes, Susan M. Dynarski, Parag A. Pathak, and Christopher R. Walters, "Stand and Deliver: Effects of Boston's Charter High Schools on College Preparation, Entry, and Choice," *Journal of Labor Economics* 34, no. 2 (2016): 275–318.

49. Philip M. Gleason, Christina Clark Tuttle, Brian Gill, Ira Nichols-Barrer, and Bing-ru Teh, "Do KIPP Schools Boost Student Achievement?" *Education Finance and Policy* 9, no. 1 (2014): 36–58.

50. While the analysis is not detailed, a reference to the urban/suburban comparison can be found in CREDO, *National Charter School Study*.

51. Susan Dynarski, Daniel Hubbard, Brian Jacob, and Silvia Robles, "Estimating the Effects of a Large For-Profit Charter School Operator," NBER Working Paper 24428 (Cambridge, MA: National Bureau of Economic Research, 2018).

52. The geographic pattern of results may also lead to reinterpretation of some of the most negative voucher results. The negative results in statewide voucher programs might partly reflect the fact that they include rural and suburban areas. The only rigorous study to my knowledge that has explicitly studied the effectiveness of private schools (without vouchers) by geographic location also found no effect on student outcomes outside of urban locations. On this last point, see Derek Neal, "The Effects of Catholic Secondary Schooling on Educational Achievement," *Journal of Labor Economics* 15, no. 1 (1997): 98–123.

53. John White, interviewed by author, May 10, 2018.

CHAPTER 11

1. Henry M. Levin, "A Comprehensive Framework for Evaluating Educational Vouchers." *Educational Evaluation and Policy Analysis* 24, no. 3 (September 2002): 159–74.

2. Philosophers call this "negative liberty." Isaiah Berlin, *Four Essays on Liberty* (Oxford: Oxford University Press, 1969).

3. Berlin, in *Four Essays on Liberty*, calls this "positive liberty." Note that in this context "positive" and "negative" are not meant to signal that one is better or more important than the other.

4. I am using the economic definition of efficiency here, as opposed to social efficiency as defined by sociologists.

5. Similarly, our research team had trouble gaining the participation of schools in city-wide education projects, even those that had official endorsement from within the reform family.

6. Robert D. Putnam, *Bowling Alone: The Collapse and Revival of American Community* (New York: Simon & Schuster, 2000).

7. Milton Friedman, *Capitalism and Freedom* (Chicago: University of Chicago Press, 1962), 89.

8. For research on the effectiveness of federal special education policy, see, for example, Eric A. Hanushek, John F. Kain, and Steven G. Rivkin, "Inferring Program Effects for Special Populations: Does Special Education Raise Achievement for Students with Disabilities?" *Review of Economics and Statistics* 84, no. 4 (2002): 584–99.

9. Patrick Dobard, interviewed by author, July 19, 2018.

10. Taisha Payne, "The Role of Communities in Schools," panel discussion, "The Urban Education Future? Lessons from New Orleans 10 Years after Hurricane Katrina" conference, New Orleans, June 19, 2015.

11. The National Council of Nonprofits, for example, lists many duties of nonprofit board members. Duty to the public is not among them.

12. "About," Black Education for New Orleans (BE NOLA). http://blackedunola.org.

13. Even in the case of school vouchers, with their limited role for government, there is evidence that they might increase students' future political participation and altruistic behavior. See, for example, a review by David Figlio, "Voucher Outcomes," in *Handbook of Research on School Choice*, ed. Mark Berends, Matthew Springer, Dale Ballou, and Herbert Walberg, 321–27 (New York: Routledge, 2009). For more recent research, see Deven Carlson, Matthew M. Chingos, and David E. Campbell, "The Effect of Private School Vouchers on Political Participation," *Journal of Research on Educational Effectiveness* 10, no. 1 (2016): 1–25.

14. Robert Dahl, *On Democracy*, 2nd ed. (New Haven, CT: Yale University Press, 2008).

15. See chapter 9, as well as Kevin Lawrence Henry and Adrienne D. Dixson, "'Locking the Door before We Got the Keys': Racial Realities of the Charter School Authorization Process in Post-Katrina New Orleans," *Educational Policy* 30, no. 1 (2016): 218–40.

16. The wording here echoes the title of a book by the same title: Michelle Alexander, *The New Jim Crow* (New York: New Press, 2012). Also, note that I have focused here on African Americans; however, the city also has a long history of Vietnamese immigrants, and a newer wave of Latinx came to the city in the wake of Katrina.

17. This section delves into matters of political philosophy, in which I confess not to be an expert. I have consulted with those more familiar with these topics and have kept this discussion somewhat brief.

18. Friedrich Hayek, for example, argues that centralized planners fail because they can-

not possibly know everything that individuals know. Friedrich Hayek, *The Road to Serfdom* (Chicago: University of Chicago Press, 1944).

19. Many writers could be cited here, but I will focus on the most widely cited father of conservative political philosophy: Edmund Burke, *Reflections on the Revolution in France* (London: J. Dodsley in Pall Mall, 1790), retrieved January 1, 2019, via Gallica.

20. To the first point about separation of church and state, the US Supreme Court has ruled that government funds from vouchers can be used to fund religious schooling. *Zelman v. Simmons-Harris*, 536 U.S. 639 (2002).

21. Stephanie Ewert, "The Decline in Private School Enrollment," SEHSD Working Paper Number FY12-117 (US Census Bureau, Social, Economic, and Housing Statistics Division, January 2013).

CHAPTER 12

1. The New Orleans evidence was discussed above: Cowen Institute, *K–12 Education through the Public Eye: Parents' Perceptions of School Choice* (New Orleans: Cowen Institute, Tulane University, 2011). For the national evidence, see Madeline Will, "Parents Prefer Good Neighborhood Schools over More Choice, Poll Finds," *Education Week*, September 12, 2017.

2. See, for example, Douglas N. Harris, Michael Handel, and Lawrence Mishel, "Education and the Economy Revisited: How Schools Matter," *Peabody Journal of Education* 79, no. 1 (2004): 36–63.

3. Leslie Jacobs, interviewed by author, March 27, 2018.

4. La. Acts no. 91.

APPENDIX A

1. The US Census Bureau could only provide these data for the three parishes/districts with more than a hundred thousand residents (Calcasieu, Jefferson, and St. Tammany). These three also happen to be among the hurricane-affected districts, reinforcing the usefulness of this comparison.

2. Jacob Vigdor, "The Economic Aftermath of Hurricane Katrina," *Journal of Economic Perspectives* 22, no. 4 (2008): 145.

3. Bruce Baker, "What Should We Really Learn from New Orleans after the Storm," National Education Policy Center, 2018, 15.

APPENDIX B

1. Susan M. Dynarski, Steven W. Hemelt, and Joshua M. Hyman, "The Missing Manual: Using National Student Clearinghouse Data to Track Postsecondary Outcomes," NBER Working Paper 19552 (Cambridge, MA: National Bureau of Economic Research, 2013).

2. These student covariates include race, free/reduced-price lunch status, special education status, limited English proficiency, and grade repetition. In addition, we include bin indicators for each stratum in the matching process discussed later.

INDEX